JOYFUL
NOISE

JOYFUL NOISE

A GUIDE TO MUSIC IN THE CHURCH
FOR PASTORS AND MUSICIANS

WILLIAM S. SMITH

Providence House Publishers
WWW.PROVIDENCEHOUSE.COM
FRANKLIN, TENNESSEE

Printed in the United States of America

11   10   09   08   07   1   2   3   4   5

Library of Congress Control Number: 2007939053

ISBN: 978-1-57736-397-2

Cover photograph: Briarwood Presbyterian Church
Jackson, Mississippi, 2007
by Howard Barron.

Cover and page design by LeAnna Massingille

PROVIDENCE HOUSE PUBLISHERS
238 Seaboard Lane • Franklin, Tennessee 37067
www.providencehouse.com
800-321-5692

CONTENTS

~

INTRODUCTION

~

Before the church, before the synagogue, before temple and tabernacle, there was music. Music—a great primeval stream, ever changing, ever coursing through time and filling space, created and creating, fragile and evanescent, powerful and raging, calming and soothing, dominating and serving. Competing with commerce, culture, court, and circus, the church has appropriated from a boundless store of things musical what it wanted, claiming it as its own, adapting and using it to serve its purposes. The church has, over the centuries, directed the flow of its music, projecting its use even into eternity. The church has restricted the what and who and how of its music, fought over it, even abolished it. The church has dedicated lives to it and pronounced it to be superior to all other arts, second only to theology among God's gifts.

My intended circle of readers includes all ministers of the Word and Sacraments and all church musicians, as well as those preparing for these professions. Today's church is well acquainted with sharp differences of opinion about music in the church, as was yesterday's. Clergy who know or care little about music must be thought delinquent. Regrettably, their number is legion. Only in the rarest of cases do the bulging curricula of theological seminaries offer, even as an elective, anything dealing with music and its conspicuous role in worship. I hope this volume may help in some measure to fill the lacuna in this vital area, serving also to stimulate further investigation, reflection, and conversation.

It was perceived ignorance and lack of awareness on the part of pastors that initially led me to write this book. I soon realized, however, that I was writing not only for pastors, but also for musicians. No more than it is my intention to make musicians out of pastors do I aim to equip musicians to be pastors. But music in the church is a topic about which even many otherwise highly qualified musicians understand all too little. Just as a graduate of the theological seminary may not be able to distinguish a Sacred Harp tune from Anglican chant, so the university- or music school-trained musician may not be qualified to lead the singing of either one. In today's climate, moreover, musicians, just as much as clergy, are likely to feel threatened by some of the trends in the church's worship. This book began as one aimed at clergy; it has become one that has within its purview both clergy and church musician.

A little time spent perusing issues of *The American Organist* will expose the reader to something of the pain and suffering that church musicians claim to have experienced at the hands of clergy. I am convinced that many of the problems in this area come about not as the result of thinking, but rather of not thinking. Many clergypersons' awareness of a collegiality that includes the musicians participating in the service of worship is limited to just that, their participation in the execution of the service, not in whatever planning may take place.

I hope that this book may help improve the relationship between clergy and musician. My concern is that clergypersons not only know more about music, but also about musicians. I have included material from the musicians' world that, I believe, will help pastors walk in the musicians' shoes.

A second relationship often under stress is that between the church's professional staff and the congregation. Most often the flash point here is the worship service. That it should be in the area of worship that controversy most often surfaces is understandable, considering the centrality of worship in the life of the church—corporately and individually. That it should be related specifically to the subject of music in the service of worship is also understandable, and for the same reasons. In no other area of religious life do people bring with them such strong, long-standing, and emotional associations. Our congregations are made up mostly of people who likely know less than most clergy and musicians about music in the church—but who cherish feelings about the subject that are just as strong as those of the professionals. People seem to understand that, of all parts of the service, the congregation's song, more than any other, belongs to them. And in a very real sense it does. So we should not be surprised when they feel threatened in this area.

In this matter, too, the writer hopes to give help by preparing both clergy and musician to deal in helpful, pastoral ways with questions and criticisms that arise on the part of the congregation with respect to the church's music. Rather than merely dealing reactively with such situations as they arise, clergy and musician can patiently nurture the congregation in a growing understanding and deepening appreciation of the most wholesome musical diet available.

Yes, the book is about God and divine worship, specifically about the role of music in that worship. But as much as anything else, the book is about people, about people getting along. It is a book about the first commandment: to love God with all that we are and have. It is a book about the other commandment, too, one that is inseparable from the first: to love (look out for) our neighbor just as spontaneously and as intensely as we do ourselves. May we never think that we have to choose between these two commandments!

Some things in the book are quite simple, straightforward, and matter-of-fact. Thinking about music in the church, however, inevitably confronts us with questions for which there surely seem to be no easy, universally applicable answers—even to such basic questions as "What is going on when the congregation sings?" How can we quantify and evaluate that? And then there are seemingly simpler, more practical questions: "Where is a choir best situated: to the rear of the congregation or to the front?" In struggling with the more difficult theoretical questions and the more debatable matters of practice, I have not felt compelled to offer a solution in every case. I have tried to cover all the aspects that need to be considered, leaving it to the reader to analyze them in the context of his or her particular situation. The treatment of the subject moves from the theoretical to the practical, from the past to the present.

The source list near the end of the book lists all the sources to which references are made in the text (in parentheses). A list of Useful Resources is given at the end of each chapter.

ACKNOWLEDGMENTS

~

I am most grateful to my clergy friends who furnished the impetus for writing this book, including J. Knox Chamblin, Joseph M. Martin, and Richard K. Swayze; to those who read a first draft, including Ervie Chris Curvin (the "Contemporary Christian Music" chapter), Larry Frazier, Glenn A. Gentry, Michael Herrin, Billy Trotter, and R. Milton Winter; to those who read a chapter or two of a more advanced draft, including Emily R. Brink, Andrew Donaldson, Harry Eskew, Sue Mitchell-Wallace, David W. Music, David Partington, Iteke Prins, Paul Richardson, Morgan Simmons, Carol Tate, Larry Wolz, and Karl Zinsmeister; to those experts in the field who were kind enough to read the galley proofs and supply comments for the cover; to my editor, Nancy Wise, and other members of the staff at Providence House Publishers for their expertise, wisdom, and patience; to all those church musicians with whom I have been privileged to serve; and to all whose books and articles I have used as resources.

I would also like to express deepest thanks to my son, Matthew S. Smith, for the many hours given and patience shown in the word processing department; and to my wife and church musician Rosanne Jorgenson Smith, for sharing wisdom gleaned from many years of experience in the field.

~

The author wishes to express his gratitude to the following for permission granted to quote from the copyrighted works named.

ABINGDON PRESS:
Carol Doran & Thomas H. Troeger, *Trouble at the Table: Gathering the Tribes for Worship* (1992)
N. Lee Orr, *The Church Music Handbook: For Pastors and Musicians* (1991)
Erik Routley, *Music Leadership in the Church: A Conversation Chiefly with My American Friends* (1967)
James F. White, *Introduction to Christian Worship*, 2nd ed. (1990)

ALBAN INSTITUTE:
Linda J. Clark, *Music in Churches: Nourishing Your Congregation's Musical Life* (1994)

THE AMERICAN GUILD OF ORGANISTS:
Various citations from *The American Organist*

AUGSBURG FORTRESS PRESS:
Evangelical Lutheran Church in America, *Principles for Worship* (2001)
Robert Buckley Farlee, ed., *Leading the Church's Song* (1998)
Marilyn Kay Stulken, *Hymnal Companion to the Lutheran Book of Worship* (1981)
Paul Westermeyer, *Te Deum: The Church and Music* (1998)

BAKER BOOK HOUSE:
John D. Witvliet, *Worship Seeking Understanding: Windows into Christian Practice* (2003)

THE CHRISTIAN CENTURY:
Subscriptions: $49/yr. from P. O. Box 378, Mt. Morris, IL 61054. 1-888-208-4097
Patrick Henry, "Singing the Faith Together," from the May 21–28, 1997 issue
Carl Schalk, "Resounding Praise," from the March 23–30, 1983 issue

WILLIAM B. EERDMANS PUBLISHING COMPANY:
Marva J. Dawn, *Reaching Out Without Dumbing Down* (1995)
Cornelius Plantinga Jr. & Sue A. Rozeboom, eds., *Discerning the Spirits: A Guide to Thinking about Christian Worship Today* (2003)

Richard J. Mouw & Mark A Noll, eds., *Wonderful Words of Life: Hymns in American Protestant History & Theology* (2004)
Erik Routley, ed., *Rejoice in the Lord* (1985)
Hughes Oliphant Old, *Leading in Prayer: A Workbook for Worship* (1995)

GIA PUBLICATIONS:
John Bell, *The Singing Thing: A Case for Congregational Song* (2000)
Paul Westermeyer, *The Heart of the Matter: Church Music as Praise, Prayer, Proclamation, Story and Gift* (2001)
Paul Westermeyer, *Let the People Sing: Hymn Tunes in Perspective* (2005)

Michael S. Hamilton, "Triumph of the Praise Songs," in *Christianity Today*, July 12, 1999

HARVARD UNIVERSITY PRESS:
Don Michael Randel, ed., *The Harvard Dictionary of Music*, 4th ed. (1986), "Acoustics," p. 12

HERALD PRESS:
Marlene Kropf & Kenneth Nafziger, *Singing: A Mennonite Voice* (2001)

HOPE PUBLISHING COMPANY:
Erik Routley, *A Short History of English Church Music* (1997)
Carlton R. Young, ed., *Duty and Delight: Routley Remembered* (1985)

THE HYMN SOCIETY IN THE UNITED STATES AND CANADA:
Various citations from *The Hymn: A Journal of Congregational Song*

THE LITURGICAL PRESS:
Charlotte Kroeker, ed., *Music in Christian Worship: At the Service of the Liturgy* (2005)

Alice Parker, *Melodious Accord: Good Singing in Church,* published by Liturgy Training Publications (1991)

REFORMED CHURCH IN AMERICA:
"The Theology and Place of Music in Worship." 2005 All other rights reserved. ©Reformed Church Press

Neil Thompson Shade, *Acoustical Planning Concepts for Worship House Sanctuaries*, published by Acoustical Design Collaborative (2001)

UNITED METHODIST CHURCH, GENERAL BOARD OF DISCIPLESHIP WEB SITE:
Anne Burnette Hook, "To Project or Not to Project: Hymn Lyrics and Worship" http://www.gbod.org/worship/default.asp?act=reader& item_id=1790&loc_id=929,932,933

THE UNIVERSITY OF CHICAGO PRESS:
Celia Applegate & Pamela Potter, eds., *Music & German National Identity* (2002)

Paul Westermeyer, *The Church Musician*, published by Harper Collins (1988)

WESTMINSTER JOHN KNOX PRESS:
Ronald P. Byars, *The Future of Protestant Worship: Beyond the Worship Wars* (2002)
Brian Wren, *Praying Twice: The Music and Words of Congregational Song* (2000)

CHAPTER
ONE

THE ROLE OF MUSIC IN
THE CHURCH'S WORSHIP

~

Sidestepping the question, "What is worship?" I shall begin by asking an equally difficult one: "What is music?" Already we seem to be in trouble; the very rubric "music" is to be found in neither *The Concise Oxford Dictionary of Music* (1989) nor the much heftier fourth edition of *The Harvard Dictionary of Music* (2003)—and not even in the multivolume *New Grove Dictionary of Music and Musicians* (1980)! Perseverance brings us to paydirt, however. The second edition of *The New Grove* (2001) does contain the rubric "music," along with a twelve-page article! But not so fast. Imposing a single definition, it seems, is simply out of the question (17:425). Falling back on a household dictionary of our language, I find three definitions of music that are relevant to our study. The one indispensable element common to all three is the phenomenon of sound. Turning some pages, I find that sound is: a) vibrations in any medium that stimulate the auditory nerves and produce the sensation of hearing; and b) the auditory sensation produced by such vibrations. Thus we might title this chapter, "The Role of Vibrations in Worship." But of course none of us considers all vibrations that stimulate our auditory nerves to be music. Nor do we agree among ourselves as to which vibrations can be called music. Welcome to the world of music! May this

1

introduction serve to humble us at the outset, for this same opaqueness, this same inability to get a sure handle on the subject, characterizes so very much that concerns music.

To avoid at least some misunderstanding, we need to remember that the kind of music we are talking about in this book is not sacred music in general—music such as Verdi's *Manzoni Requiem*, or one of Handel's oratorios, or John Rutter's *Gloria*. (It does happen, of course, that parts of some sacred works not written specifically for the church's worship service are used as anthems or solos in the service.) Our consideration is restricted to music that is used in the church gathered for worship, "worship music." It should also be borne in mind that we are focusing on the worship music of only a part of the church, the Western church as it exists in today's North America.

VARIED VIEWS OF MUSIC IN WORSHIP

~

Music In Worship Is a Given

We may not be able to give a definition that will cover all the bases, but we know what music is when we hear it. It may also seem self-evident to most churchgoers that music not only has a place, but that it has an integral role in the church's worship, and that this is the way it should be. (In point of fact, music may be heard during a third or more of the duration of the average service of Christian worship in North America.) References to musical worship abound in both Old and New Testaments; from Genesis to Revelation, music is never far from the mighty acts of God. The same pairing may be seen down through the centuries of the church's history. Augustine, Luther, Calvin, and a number of popes wrote in glowing terms of God's surpassing gift of music. Both Luther and Calvin took pains to provide their disciples with music deemed fit for the worship service. Pivotal movements in the church—the sixteenth-century Reformation,[1] the rise of pietism in seventeenth-century Europe and Great Britain, the Great Awakening of the eighteenth century in Wales, the Great Awakenings on the eighteenth- and nineteenth-century American frontier, the worldwide missionary thrust and the urban revivals of the nineteenth century—all these great stirrings produced and were themselves energized by fresh outpourings of music.

Concerns Among Ancient Jews and Early Christians

The past also, however, provides us with examples of questions raised concerning the place of music in worship. A prophet of the eighth century BC lashes out at the folly of those who sing and play their harps in the assembly, all the while unconcerned about the injustice that pervades their society (Amos 5:23). No problem here with music as such, but there must be coherence between worship and life (Ps. 50:23). The Old Testament does not represent the ornate musical service of the early Israelite monarchy as instituted at the direct command of God.[2] It may well be that the elaboration of the musical part of Israel's worship was largely due to Israel's imitation of her neighbors.

Both Jewish and pagan thought developed the notion of a kind of internal sacrifice that is "spiritual" or "reasonable" (see Rom. 12:1; 1 Pet. 2:5), in contrast to the inferior, external sacrifice that involved blood. For whatever reason, some of the church fathers do speak of "silent song." Was there a principle involved here that ever led to the exclusion in worship not only of instrumental music, but of vocal as well? Not necessarily. It was not necessary to choose between the audible and the inaudible. It is clear, in fact, that Philo recommended both.[3]

Clement of Alexandria (c. 150–c. 215) distinguished carefully between music that is fitting for the church's worship and that which is not (*Paed.* 2, 4). Augustine (354–430) was torn between his appreciation of the powerful spiritual benefit of song and his realization that mere gratification of the senses might get the upper hand (*Confessions* 10.33, 49–50). Songs, moreover, were produced by heretics as well as the faithful; this realization contributed to a gradual increase in ecclesiastical regulation as to who could sing and what they could sing in the worship service.

Concerns of Two Sixteenth-century Reformers

Following a centuries-old drought, the reformers of the sixteenth century opened the floodgates to congregational song. But there were conditions. Though John Calvin permitted no instruments in the worship service and no choir, and though he restricted the repertory to Scripture (mainly metrical versions of the psalms of the Old Testament), he believed strongly in the rightness of congregational song—in unison octaves. The children were taught the songs beforehand so they could help the parent generation learn the music. Calvin echoes the cordial sentiments of Augustine (and even Plato) as to the efficacy of song in moving the heart. But, again like his predecessors, the Genevan reformer was sensitive to the siren dangers of music. It is not enough to delimit the text repertory: the church must see to it that the music is not "light and vulgar," but "moderate, in the manner that we have set it, to bear a gravity and majesty fitting to the subject" ("Letter to the Reader," in the "Preface to the Psalter" of 1543). Calvin distinguished between "music one makes to entertain men at table and in their homes, and the psalms which are sung in the church in the presence of God and his angels" (ibid.). Also, ". . . we should be very careful that our ears be not more attentive to the melody than our minds to the spiritual meaning of the words. . . ." (*Institutes*, III. 20.32).

The convictions of one of the most musical among the Reformers, Ulrich Zwingli, led him to exclude all music from worship. Zwingli under-stood the apostle (in Ephesians 5:19 and Colossians 3:16) to counsel singing in the heart—and only the heart, not like "the Jews," with the voice. For about three generations, no singing or any other kind of music was heard in the churches of Zurich.[4]

Contemporary Concerns

Ancient concerns persist. Calvin's criteria find an echo in the 2003 chiro-graph of Pope John Paul II, citing earlier authoritative pronouncements of the twentieth century: "Music used for sacred rites must have sanctity as its point of reference. . . ," and, "not all musical forms are appropriate for liturgical celebrations." There must be no "concessions to frivolity or superficiality."

From another contemporary quarter comes a possible reason for wari-ness about music in the worship service. Edward T. Cone maintains that in the marriage of a text to music, the music will tend to have the upper hand. Whereas in a poem it is the poet who speaks, in a song it is the composer, in part through the words of the poet. " . . . in most encounters between poetry and music, poetry can become the more powerful of the two only by the intentional acquiescence or the unintentional incompetence of the composer" (in Hull 2002, 15). Likewise Joseph Gelineau: In the singing of a hymn, the music carries the heavier burden, and the text is less important than the music (1991, 64). What Cone and Gelineau maintain is not an exclusively modern claim; it is in line with concerns expressed by many others, including Augustine, Calvin, and John Wesley—and, I have to confess, my own assessment. Perhaps it is an academic confirmation of the saying, "People would sing the phone book if it were set to a catchy tune." It is indeed the tune that most often determines the attraction a hymn has for people—at least initially. It is the tune that is most likely to come to mind in the hours and days following the worship service. Those of us who have long maintained that the words of the hymn have the primacy are hardly comforted by being told that it is the music that is in first place.[5]

What we may call "the troublesome tyranny of the tune over the text" may appear in yet another way. A crucial factor in the assembly's song is the matter of tempo: the rate of speed at which a congregation of a particular size sings a particular song within a particular worship space. Tempo must not be too fast or too slow. But who will tell us what is too fast or too slow? This is where the tune may find another opportunity to tyrannize. Just looking at the tune SOUTHWELL, for instance, as it is printed on the page, we can sing or play all the notes in the tune's two lines very quickly. A thoughtful reading of the sober text, "Lord Jesus, Think on Me," that is set to SOUTHWELL, however, will take more time. In such a case, it is very easy for the keyboardist's[6] tempo (and perhaps the tempo of some singers, as well) to be determined by the music in itself, without regard for the plaintive text. Measured against the sound of the organ or piano, the assembly may appear to be "dragging" the song. Perhaps this is indeed all there is in such cases. But is it just possible that the assembly's slower tempo, at least sometimes, is an intuitively-based resistance to the tendency of the music to tyrannize, to force the singers to surrender a thoughtful reading of the text?

Concerns of an altogether different sort might occur to anyone reading these descriptions by two twentieth-century Mennonites, one of them a woman, of what they experience when engaged in congregational singing:

"strands of sensual experience," "a very sensuous thing," "mesmerizing," "attractive," "a lot like sexual attraction between men and women" (Kropf and Nafziger 2001, 51). "Singing undresses us," "our souls are undressed," "real things start to happen" (ibid., 66).

Contemporary Restrictions

Even in the twenty-first century, we may, if we travel far enough, engage in Christian worship in which music is restricted to unaccompanied metrical psalms sung by the congregation (Free Church of Scotland and Reformed Presbyterian Church of North America), unaccompanied congregational hymns (Churches of Christ), or music produced only by a choir and instrumentalists (Episcopal Choral Evensong). It is even possible to find Christians worshiping corporately without any music whatsoever (the Quaker meeting, the Episcopal Morning and Evening Prayer Services).

BUT WORSHIP WITHOUT MUSIC? THE CONGRUITY OF MUSICAL PRAISE

~

Bedrock in the Bible is that human beings in general (Acts 17:24–31; Rom. 1:18–23) and God's covenant people in particular (Exod. 20:1–17; Rom. 12:1) are to respond to God's gracious initiative in appropriate ways. Because the Creator God is the Lord who has redeemed us, because God has in Christ shown us great mercy, we are a grateful people; the prime mover in our lives is gratitude. Will gratitude—that same dynamic that moves us to love God and to keep God's commandments in the service we render to our neighbor—let our tongues remain still and silent? When we have received bread from heaven and blood shed for the forgiveness of our sins, shall we not sing a hymn before we go out? If forgiven sinners are cheerful, if besieged believers are distraught, will they not sing? "Where there is life, there is praise" (Westermann 1981, 159).

That the response on the part of God's people can be expected to include worship in song is driven home by both precept and precedent in both Testaments. Given that the covenant-keeping God deals righteously with us, it is good, fitting, seemly, and appropriate that God's righteous, covenant-keeping people sing God's praises (Pss. 33:1–3; 147:1). To such a God, praise is due (Ps. 65:1. The Septuagint reads: "A hymn is due to thee, O God."). A favorite Mennonite hymn begins: "I owe the Lord a morning song." God's faithfulness, the divine steadfast love (*hesed*), comes "down," and our song goes "up" in response. There is a rationale, a congruity in the church's musical praise. It is not logic, of course, that moves us to pour out our hearts in song, but gratitude. It was gratitude for grace received that moved Moses and Miriam (Exod. 15:1–21), the psalmist (Pss. 28:6; 30, for instance), Mary (Luke 1:46–55), Zechariah (Luke 1:67–79), and Simeon (Luke 2:29–32) to sing.

> O enter then His gates with praise;
> Approach with joy His courts unto;
> Praise, laud, and bless His name always,
> For it is seemly so to do.
> (Wm. Kethe, Ps. 100, 3rd st., 1560)

Karl Barth may have gone too far when he claimed that "the community that does not sing is not the community" (*Church Dogmatics* IV.3.16.72.4). Barth did have Martin Luther for precedent: "For God has cheered our hearts and minds through his dear Son, whom he gave for us to redeem us from sin, death, and the devil. He who believes this earnestly cannot be quiet about it. But he must gladly and willingly sing. . . ." ("Preface to the Babst Hymnal"). Contemporary writers make claims like these: 1) If people do not sing in the worship service, they have a spiritual problem; 2) For believers, singing is "irrepressible"; 3) The church at worship has always "found itself breaking out into music, especially into song"; 4) ". . . congregational song is an indispensable part of Christian public worship." If we construe the two passages as I do, the apostle does indeed link being "filled with [under the control of] the Spirit" (Eph. 5:18–20) and being indwelt by "the word of Christ" (Col. 3:16) with singing praise to God, apparently in a causal relation. The Christian assembly that is vital can be charged with SUI: "Singing under the influence." The very experience of receiving divine grace is tantamount to receiving a song to sing; both the grace that delivers the psalmist and the song that witnesses to it together constitute one gift from God (Pss. 30:11–12; 40:1–10). No more than the psalmist can Mary, Zechariah, the angel choir,

Simeon, and Anna (Luke 2:36–38) hide the good news of deliverance in their hearts.

> I've sung the Psalms of David for nearly eighty years,
>   They've been my staff and comfort and calmed life's many fears;
> I'm sorry I disturb the choir, perhaps I'm doing wrong,
>   But when my heart is filled with praise I can't keep back a song.
>   (Thomas Chalmers Harbaugh, 1849–1924,
>   "Trouble in the 'Amen' Corner," stanza 15)

Notwithstanding these enthusiastic testimonies as to the nigh-indispensability of music in the church gathered for worship, I must at this point make a caveat: There are some people (I would guess relatively few) who take the Christian faith quite seriously, and yet fail to find music (at least congregational song) to be a means of grace for themselves. The late C. S. Lewis is a renowned instance. Rather than say that such people have a spiritual problem, I would rather leave it at considering them to be relatively rare exceptions to the norm. There certainly are dimensions of this wonderfully varied, created, evolving world that I have not yet felt drawn to, and countless aspects I have simply not gotten around to. Perhaps in the new creation, the new humanity will enjoy an ever-widening appreciation of all that is good and true and beautiful. It is hard to imagine that anyone will opt out of singing the new song of Moses and the Lamb (Rev. 15: 3–4). In the meantime, it is a safe bet that for anyone reading this book, music, including song, is an indispensable part of the congregation's worship—maybe even the most appealing part. But what is music's specific contribution to worship? (I refer here to musical sound in itself, not the text wedded to it.)

MUSIC IN WORSHIP IS WORSHIP

~

Before we move on to think about music's specific role in worship, we need to be clear about one thing: the relation of music to worship. My denomination for years has conducted very enthusiastically received summer conferences under the banner, "Worship and Music Conference." Worship *and* music? Citrus fruit *and* oranges? Granted, not all worship is music (though all of the service could have or be given a musical component). But is the kind of music we are talking about here not itself worship? A younger colleague, settling into a new pastorate, thought it well to substitute for the traditional rubric "Prelude" in the service bulletin, "Music for Worship." Music *for* worship? Is music to be understood, then, merely as facilitating worship? Something that goes on at the same time as worship? In both "traditional" and "contemporary" worship, at least a part of the music is often conceived of as having a preparatory role, music to prepare the people for worship. Is not the music in view itself worship? The Roman Catholic Edward Foley, citing the 1963 *Constitution on Sacred Liturgy*, enunciates this very clearly: "Liturgical music is not only music in worship, it is worship. Music, variously wed to text or ritual action, is one of the languages of the liturgy" (Foley 2001, 98). The music of the church's service is itself worship. Now, what is the specific role of music in worship?

THE ROLE OF MUSIC IN WORSHIP

~

Can Music Convey Truth?

There is no truer truth obtainable
By man than comes of music.
(Robert Browning, "Parleyings with
Certain People . . . With Charles Avison," VI)

Music tells no truths.
(Philip James Bailey,
"Festus. Scene xi. A Village Feast")

"Music: the universal language." Is it really? Is it true that music, unaccompanied by words, is capable of conveying meaning?

Communicating? Are the vibrations produced by the violin intelligible? The apostle was unwilling that the ecstatic utterances of those graced with the gift of tongues be exercised without accompanying interpretation; without such, those vibrations are unintelligible and therefore unedifying (1 Cor. 14:1–25). Is not this true also of wordless music? In the nineteenth century, some argued that "program" music, such as Beethoven's Sixth (*Pastoral*) Symphony, was indeed capable of conveying ideas. In contrast to program music was "absolute," or abstract, music, such as the symphonies of Haydn; absolute music was incapable of conveying ideas—other than purely musical ones. The truth, however, is that we would not understand Beethoven's *Pastoral* Symphony to be all about peasants frolicking in the countryside before and after a storm if the great musician had not told us that was the case. And who would guess that the liturgical compositions of Olivier Messiaen (1908–1992) of France relate to specific biblical themes had the composer not given them such explanatory titles? Contemporary musical theorists have pretty well dismissed the claim that music in itself is capable of expressing spiritual or moral meaning in any universally understood way. Many would argue that the only ideas that music can express are musical ideas (loud and soft, for instance); anything else that we hear in the music is due not to anything intrinsic to the music itself, but only to associations that we bring to the music. Music is, of all the arts, the most abstract; it says nothing outside of itself. By the same token, music is the art form that most readily absorbs meaning from without by association.

Thus there is no music that we may call intrinsically religious or intrinsically secular—certainly no music that we may label intrinsically Christian. There are no sacred sound waves, no holy vibrations; there are not any sanctified guidelines for the composer. For music to fulfill its function in the Christian worship service, however, especially if it be unaccompanied with words, it must be perceived by the worshipers as religious music, "the church's music." For this to happen, the church depends on the power of association—words or rites associated in the worshiper's mind with that music, or perhaps even the fact that the music comes from an organ. Music has not within itself the ability to communicate truth.[7]

Is What Matters That Music Be Beautiful?

If music in the worship service is not employed to communicate ideas and truth, is its raison d'être to be sought in the aesthetic realm? Both Hebrew and Christian Scriptures seem to have no place for the idea that music is ever beautiful (Smith 1962, 13). Music is never understood and valued in itself; the operative principle is never "art for art's sake." The psalmist's "joyful noise" may have been as apt then as it seems now to us quaint.

Whether it be God addressing humans, or humans addressing God, about the only quality of the voice that is noted is its loudness. The noise of worship carried far beyond the post-exilic assembly (Ezra 3:13; Neh. 12:43). The Jews praised at least one cantor because his voice could be heard all the way from Jerusalem to Jericho! Gabriel's could be heard from one end of the earth to the other. And of course the Lord God, whose voice is like thunder (Ps. 29), sings with a loud voice (Zeph. 3:17). Rock musicians were not the first to like their music loud! The ultimate criterion for evaluating music in ancient Israel was never the aesthetic.

It is not hard, nevertheless, to find some liturgical scholars today making a case for understanding the liturgy as an art form, one that employs several of the fine arts in its service. I join with such scholars in their challenge to contemporary artists to give of their very best in the service of the church. I would insist, however, that such artists understand that what is the best in this case is not to be judged ultimately by aesthetic considerations on the part of the artist or art critic. "Aestheticism is a corruption of worship" (Senn 1987, 29). This is not to say that no aesthetic considerations of any kind ever have any place in evaluating worship.

The Role of Music in Worship Is That of Servant

That aesthetic considerations have, at best, only the most humble of places in evaluating the worship of the church is easily referenced by any number of writers; it is also very much in line with ancient Hebrew thought about the arts in general. Music was viewed in quite frankly functional terms. Did the music fulfill its purpose, did it serve its intended end? Nicholas Wolterstorff points out that virtually all music ever created was intended to serve something (2005, 4). And music used in the service of the many and varied movements in the history of the church never worked alone; it was always music with words, or if without words, then at least accompanied by associations brought to it by the hearers, associations that are potentially expressible in words. This brings us to what must be the fundamental axiom of music in the church: The role of music in the church is that of servant; its task is functional, diaconal, and pastoral. "God has preached the gospel *through music*" (Martin Luther, *Works* 54:129–30, italics mine).

> We have put this music to the living and holy Word of God in order to sing, praise and honor it. We want the beautiful art of music to be properly used to serve her dear Creator and his Christians. He is thereby praised and honored and we are made better and stronger in faith when his holy word is impressed on our hearts by sweet music. (Luther, "Preface to the Burial Hymns")

If the music that is made be beautiful and sweet—at least in the worshiper's mind—so much the better. From a pair of twentieth-century witnesses, Erik Routley and Robin A. Leaver, we hear the same thing: Music is "essentially functional" (Leaver, in Young 1985, 47).

What matters ultimately is not that music in the worship service be beautiful, but that it work, that it attain its intended end, that it serve as the language of worship.[8] Here we stand, not without a measure of trepidation, before what is surely the ultimate challenge for many church musicians and not a few pastors. It is the challenge put before the church by both Jesus (Matt. 16:24–26) and the apostle (Phil. 2:1–11): the denial of self. Edward Foley challenges all who lead worship to have an "open hand." With a closed hand it is impossible to enter paradise, to make music, or to pray. We see in Jesus that no one can die on the cross with a closed hand. What is demanded is that we open our hand and be prepared to let go of all that we hold dear. This may lead to change, to growth "in a new understanding of liturgy, leadership, and, finally, *culture*" (2001, 99, italics mine).

Taking his point of departure from recent Roman Catholic pronouncements on that church's liturgy, Foley understands the congregation itself to be one of the prime actors in the liturgy and its music. What this understanding implies for the church musician may be a very bitter pill to swallow, that is, the acknowledgement that "the musical styles, tastes, and even language of [the congregation] are proper vehicles for shaping and expressing the faith of the church." For the classically trained musician there is a huge challenge implied in this admission—the challenge to enter willingly "the musical-cultural world of another as an experience of holy ground" (2001, 100). Shades of what the Lord said to Abraham (Gen. 12:1–4)? Or of what Jesus said to those who would follow him (Matt. 10:37–39; 13:44–46)? Key words for both clergy and church musician: deny self, facilitate, enable, serve.

The Role of Music In Worship: Servant of the Liturgy

But if the role of the church musician be that of servant, it is a splendid calling: To serve God by serving God's people by means of music, music that is distinguished by the function it fulfills, music that, like Mary, is the bearer of the word of life, "the handmaid of the words of the rite" (Leaver, on p. 55 in Young 1985, cites Gelineau. Martin Luther had said pretty much the same thing). By "word," I here understand not only the word read and preached, but also the word made visible in baptism and the Lord's Supper, the word as fleshed out in all the rites of the worship service; as Wolterstorff puts it, music in the worship service is servant of "the liturgy" (2005, 4). This is true whether that liturgy be "fixed" or "free."[9] And the liturgy is not a monologue, but a dialogue—God's initiating word to us, our responding word to God. Music serves both sides of a conversation that can run in both directions at the same time!

Music in the church is not first of all a matter of taste—God's or ours—but of service. No kind of music is barred from the church's worship as long as it is useful to the congregation. Understanding this can free us from divisive debates about taste, and can open us to the never-ending diversity of creativity. I may quibble about the music in my neighbor's church, but if it moves her to be concerned about my welfare and to seek justice and peace in our town and beyond, it has the main thing going for it. That means we've taken care of the second commandment. And what about the first? How much unhelpful verbiage, and how much cultural arrogance and idolatry have been served up in attempting to answer the wrong questions, "What kind of music is pleasing to God?" or "What is worthy music for the worship of God?" It is instructive to understand and remember that what God wanted on Mt. Moriah was not Isaac, the offering, but Abraham, the offerer (Gen. 22). The Lord rejoices "not with the gift of the lover as much as the love of the giver" (Adhikari 1989, 18). The main thought in Ephesians 5:18–20, a key passage for congregational song, is summed up in Paul's closing words about praising God with the heart. The apostle's concern is not the literary or musical merit of the Christian singing; the only thing that matters is the believer's sincere devotion that expresses itself in song.[10] So it is the case that what God wants is not our music per se, but *us*. That takes care of the other commandment. It can also take care of a lot of vainglory.

Theology has at times been so strongly influenced by Greek philosophy that the picture of God it presented was an abstraction, a God who is a one-sidedly transcendent and self-contained being. (Hymnwriters knew better!) The God we read about in the Bible, however, is a God who wants us, who yearns for communion with us. This God is "the Holy One," altogether sovereign and free—but who also condescends to be "the Holy One *of Israel*," to assume flesh and live among us as one of us in the person of Jesus of Nazareth. This God wants us as givers of praise, the kind of audible praise that only those creatures made in God's image can render, praise that involves our whole being—including our tongues, lungs, and diaphragms.

In the psalmist's mind, with respect to the dead, it is not just their intent to praise that God would miss, but also their audible praise (Pss. 6:5; 9:13–14; 30:9, 12; 94:17; 115:17). God made us corporeal, our bodies are very much a part of us, God redeems our bodies; they, too, belong to God. Therefore we must not think that the only thing that matters is our intention—unembodied. We may not claim, as did Zwingli, that what matters is that we sing inwardly "in our hearts." The communal worship not only of ancient Israel (Zwingli's "the Jews") but also that of the early church was not of the Quaker meeting variety, but audible. The costliest external worship is no substitute for the devotion of the heart (Isa. 29:13). But to speak of devotion without its externalization—without vibrations—is akin to a claim to faith that is unaccompanied by works (Eph. 2:8–10; Jas. 2:14–26).

Another reason why it is important that our worship be audible is that, though offered to God, our worship benefits all who are assembled with us, as we will discuss in chapter 2. This it can do only if it is heard by them.

> I have told the glad news of deliverance
> in the great congregation;
> see, I have not restrained my lips, as you know, O Lord.
> I have not hidden your saving help within my heart,
> I have spoken of your faithfulness and your salvation;
> I have not concealed your steadfast love and your faithfulness
> from the great congregation.
>
> (Ps. 40:9–10 NRSV)

Music Serves the Liturgy in Two Ways

Music Interprets the Liturgy

The church has something to say in its song, a word to be sung, a word to be acted out in its rites. Moreover, as the rabbis realized long ago, music does not bear the word set to it in some neutral, mechanical way. Rather, music bears the word hermeneutically. Music interprets the word. This insight was also shared by Martin Luther: "Music and notes, which are wonderful gifts and creations of God, do help gain a better understanding of the text, especially when sung by a congregation and sung earnestly" ("Commentary" on 2 Sam. 23:1–2). Similarly, the popes at the beginning and the end of the twentieth century, Pius X and John Paul II, respectively agree:

> Since it [music] interprets and expresses the deep meaning of the sacred text to which it is intimately linked, it must be able to add greater efficacy to the text, in order that through it the faithful may be . . . better disposed for the reception of the fruits of grace belonging to the celebration of the most holy mysteries. (John Paul II)

This function of music with relation to a text has been compared to the "illumination" with which medieval artists supplied biblical manuscripts. A clear illustration of the interpretive function of music with respect to the text set to it may be seen in connection with Psalm 2. The "Why?" at the beginning of this psalm may suggest that this psalm is one of the many psalms of lament. (See also Acts 4:23–31.) In this case, we might want to sing it with the plaintive tune HOLLINGSIDE. If, however, we understand (correctly, I think) the psalm to express mocking amazement that human rulers should rebel against the Lord, then the striding, confident tune SALZBURG may be seen as a very good match.

The musical character of a hymn "acts like a lens or filter through which the text is experienced, amplifying certain words and phrases, muting the effects of others" (Hull 2002, 21). "A hymn, then, is neither text nor tune alone, but the product of the reciprocal interaction of text and tune on one another" (ibid., 25).

Hymnological mathematics: 1 text + 1 tune = 1 hymn.

You may verify this for yourself by listening, for instance, to Handel's *Messiah*, not the way we usually hear it—the whole elephant all at once—but just one bite at a time. Find and examine thoughtfully a Bible passage that Handel has set to music. Then, using your compact disc player, listen carefully to just that music. If you are able, more or less, to read music and have access to the musical score for *Messiah*, examine that also. Note, too, that the hermeneutical function of the music extends beyond any one particular Bible text, serving to place every text within the movement of the whole, relating it to what went before and to what comes after. (Pastors might themselves profit and also score points with musicians if they asked them to assist with this exercise. An alternative would be to study the relationship between the music and the lyrics in a Bach cantata.) For musicians, this means, among other things, that before they play a hymn they should look first not at the musical notes, but at the words of the text; only in this way will it be possible for the music to live up to its potential for interpreting the text. There is a second lesson here for those who plan worship: The choice of music involves liturgical considerations; how does the music proposed for this spot relate to the rite it accompanies? How does it relate to what comes before and after?

Music Lends Power to the Liturgy

Music also serves the liturgy dynamically, investing it with power. We must be careful here not to identify "dynamic" with the level of the music's volume, though it may include that. The power we are speaking of here is the power to affect, the power to move. Even very soft music may possess this kind of power. It is at this point that aesthetic considerations may play a role, especially if the music in view is that offered by only a part of the assembly, to which the others present only listen. The only aesthetic evaluations relevant in this regard, however, are those made by the gathered worshipers, and such evaluations are probably most often formed unconsciously. Again, art is not the served, but the servant.

Music is capable of stirring and expressing deep emotions. About this there seems to be general agreement. On the most unsophisticated level, loud blasts on the shofar made the Hebrew people tremble in fear (Exod. 19:16–25). In the Near East, the eliciting and expressing of a particular mood, and even a specific ethos, has long been associated with each melody-type, or mode. One of John Calvin's goals in getting the Geneva Psalter together was to provide for every psalm a tune that matched the mood of that particular psalm—a rather tricky task, since many psalms express more than one mood! We face the same challenge today when we set about finding the most fitting tune for a particular hymn, not just for one stanza, but for all the stanzas of that hymn.

Music directs emotions and charges them with power. Music lends power to the truths of a text (Col. 3:16). A creed sung packs more weight than one merely recited. "Music is one of the best arts; the notes bring the text to life" (Martin Luther, "Table Talk," No. 796). Perhaps it is this same dynamic at work in the human utterance to God to which Augustine referred when he reportedly said, "Who sings well prays twice." Music can energize worship as the instrument of the life-giving Spirit of God (Eph. 5:18–20).

All their music, both vocal and instrumental, is adapted to imitate and express the passions and is so happily suited to every occasion that whether the subject of the hymn be cheerful or formed to soothe or trouble the mind, or to express grief or remorse, the music takes the impression of whatever is represented, affects and kindles the passions, and works the sentiments deep into the hearts of the hearers. (Thomas More, *Utopia*)

For us today, the song of the assembly has the wonderful capability of moving us from mere compliance ("Please open your hymnals to number 376.") to whole-hearted, full-throated devotion—being "lost in wonder, love, and praise."

The extent to which any one specific example of music is capable of arousing and giving expression to the same emotions universally may be debated. That there is a linkage between music and the emotive, however, seems undeniable. This linkage is at the heart of another, that between music and religion. Religion is not only about emotions, but it is inseparable from them, from affection, from the "heart." That music can serve as a powerful means to unite and inspire people to give themselves to some larger purpose has been appreciated and put to use down through the centuries, not just by religionists, but by social reformers, revolutionaries, ultranationalists, politicians, and the most maniacal, demoniacal tyrants.

Great communal song, in fact, can come only out of movements that stir people, movements that give people a passion. We noted above how major movements in the church's history have invariably been accompanied by the prolific production and enthusiastic singing of new music. In the worship service, song organizes and directs the emotions of the assembly into edifying channels—emotions that otherwise would result in no more than disorderly excitement (1 Cor. 14:26). Song-generated emotions reinforce the Word proclaimed in the assembly.

$\sim$

What musicians can help bring about through the music they make in the worship service is no small matter. It is far more than the mere frills it is so unfortunately sometimes thought to be. It is terribly important that both pastor and musician understand and do not forget this. In our next chapter we shall examine some of the things that may happen when music serves the liturgy.

– Useful Resources –

John L. Bell, *The Singing Thing: A Case for Congregational Song* (Chicago: GIA Publications, 2000), 29–35 on the hermeneutical function of music.

James McKinnon, *The Church Fathers and Musical Instruments* (New York: Cambridge, 1987).

James McKinnon, *The Temple, the Church Fathers and Early Western Chant* (Brookfield, VT: Ashgate, 1998). An anthology of previously published articles by the author.

James McKinnon, ed., *Music in Early Christian Literature* (1965 Columbia University doctoral dissertation, also published as a book in 1978).

David W. Music, *Hymnology: A Collection of Source Readings* (Lanham, MD: Scarecrow Press, 1996).

[W.] Oliver Strunk, *Source Readings in Music History* (New York: W. W. Norton, 1950).

N. B.:

Other recent Roman Catholic pronouncements that refer to music in the liturgy are:

Constitution on the Sacred Liturgy (1963), or *Sacrosanctum Concilium*, over the name of Pope Paul VI, following Vatican II. Its weakest section may be that dealing with music.

Instruction on Music in the Liturgy (1967), or *Musicam Sacram*, from the Sacred Congregation of Rites.

General Instruction of the Roman Missal, latest edition (2003), from the United States Conference of Catholic Bishops. The fruit of the liturgical reforms of Vatican II. Thoroughly indexed, 131 pages give details as to how Mass is to be celebrated.

These three instructive documents and the above named chirograph of John Paul II are all available on the Web. See also *Papal Legislation on Sacred Music: 95 A.D. to 1977 A.D.* (Collegeville, MN: The Liturgical Press, 1979).

CHAPTER TWO

WHAT CAN HAPPEN WHEN THE CHURCH SINGS?

~

If the length of this chapter is any indication, a very great deal can happen when we sing. The *Boston Globe* of March 13, 2001, carried a story by Maria Jo Fischer of the Knight Ridder news service concerning research publicized by the University of California, Irvine: "Researchers found increased levels of disease-fighting proteins in the mouths of choir members after they sang Beethoven's choral masterwork, 'Missa Solemnis.'" Could this evidence be the recruiting tool choir directors have been looking for?

SOME THINGS ARE NOT SUPPOSED TO HAPPEN

~

If you are a pastor or a church musician, please imagine that you have Sunday off and are worshiping with the congregation. What happens when you and I and the rest of the congregation sing? We know what sometimes goes through our minds: "Did I turn off the range after breakfast?" "The label on the blouse of the woman standing in front of me is sticking out, and it reads, 'Neiman Marcus, extra large.'" "I wish that man behind me would not attempt to sing the tenor part; it really throws me off." "Why does the organist have to play so loud?" These and countless other distractions can all too easily prevent our singing from pleasing God and being the means of grace for which it has the potential. Even the attempt to get the music right and to keep with the rest of the congregation can require so much of us that, when we have finished the song, we are unable to tell anyone what it was all about.

We noted earlier Augustine's dilemma—being torn between true piety and mere sensual gratification when listening to psalms "sung with a sweet and trained voice" (*Confessions* X. 33:49). We find an echo of this church father in one of the "Directions for Singing" given by a co-founder of Methodism:

> Above all, sing spiritually. Have an eye to God in every word you sing. Aim at pleasing him more than yourself, or any other creature. In order to do this attend strictly to the sense of what you sing, and see that your heart is not carried away with the sound, but offered to God continually; so shall your singing be such as the Lord will approve here, and reward you when he cometh in the clouds of heaven. (John Wesley, *Select Hymns*, 1761)

In all circumstances, it is possible that the merely aesthetic, if we may apply the term to the humble song of the congregation, outweighs all else. While worship need not exclude aesthetic experience, how can we distinguish between what is no more than that, and God-directed worship? In the preceding chapter we noted the testimony of two twentieth-century Mennonites as to what sometimes happens when they sing, a feeling that might be judged to be fraught with far more peril than mere aesthetic preoccupation.

Yes, all kinds of things can and do happen when we sing. We should, as John Wesley acknowledged, be aware of the possibility of missing the target, and sing vigilantly, for wonderful things can also happen. Apart from anything singing has in itself to commend it, singing has great potential for making happen the most important things in all the world. What begins in the course of singing, moreover, is not tied to those moments, but may bear fruit long after the last strains have died away. Let us consider what can happen when we, who claim to be the people of God gathered for worship, sing.

WHEN WE SING, WE WORSHIP GOD

~

At the Center Is God

Those of us who are Protestants, reflecting on the potential of music for teaching faith and morals, may need to be reminded of our tendency to conceive of worship so largely in utilitarian terms—a means for changing people (White 1997, 3, 105). (We do not have to choose between the worship of God and the edification of God's people.) In corporate worship we sing and make melody to God, to the Lord (Eph. 5:18–20; Col. 3:16); God is praised, blessed, and given thanks (1 Cor. 14:13–33; Heb. 13:15; Jas. 5:13). In response to God's revelation to us and in response to divine deliverance, we sing God's praise and express our gratitude: "Then my tongue shall tell . . ." (Ps. 35:28). This is what the core of the church's song is all about. It is what the classic hymn type, the "devotional hymn," is all about. Augustine said: "Hymns are praises of God with singing" ("Commentary" on Ps. 72:1). Our definition of what constitutes a hymn probably has to be much broader than Augustine's. Nevertheless, the core repertory of church music is indeed devoted to addressing God in thanksgiving and praise, lament and petition—or at least to speaking *about* God: "Holy, Holy, Holy," "I'll Praise My Maker While I've Breath," "Now Thank We All Our God." Or we may exult in God's good gifts: "How I Love Thy Law, O Lord!" (from Ps. 119). The recurring, fixed musical components (the ordinary) of the service in the worship of much of Protestantism and the Roman Catholic Mass are, in large part, ascriptions of praise to God.

The words and music of the church's song are responses to God's self-revelation to Israel and in Jesus Christ—known to us in Scripture. Like the psalmist in Psalm 19, the authors of our songs have also perceived God's self-revelation in nature: "How Great Thou Art," "This Is My Father's World," "I Sing the Mighty Power of God." Notwithstanding the denial of natural revelation by the late Karl Barth, modern hymnwriters continue to find the wonders of the natural world irresistible displays of the Almighty's handiwork. The divine providential care of the created world has also elicited praise and thanksgiving: "Great Is Thy Faithfulness," "Let Us with a Gladsome Mind," "We Gather Together to Ask the Lord's Blessing."

Singing Is Worship

We made the point in chapter 1 that music in the church is worship. The church sings not just to prepare itself for worship, certainly not just to prepare itself for the sermon; the church's song is worship. It is part of the "spiritual"—in contrast to a material—sacrifice offered to God:

> Through him [Jesus Christ], then, let us continually offer
> a sacrifice of praise to God, that is,
> the fruit of lips that confess his name.
>
> (Heb. 13:15 NRSV)

The same idea is to be found often in the Old Testament, the Apocrypha, and other Jewish writings, including those from Qumran. Judging by the glimpses given in The Revelation to John, the song of praise is the most heavenly part, the one everlastingly enduring part of the worship of God's people.

> Amen! Blessing and glory and wisdom
> and thanksgiving and honor and power and might
> be to our God forever and ever! Amen.
>
> (Rev. 7:12)

To sing God's praises is to worship God. To join the congregation in the worship of God is, to mix metaphors, both the wellspring and the capstone of our fulfilling the first commandment, the *Shema* (Deut. 6:4–5)—to love God with our whole being, to obey the commandments—as Clement of Alexandria (c. 150–c. 215 AD) observed. And with respect to song specifically, the church is under orders to use it as a means of worship (Eph. 5:18–20). Grace precedes law, of course, and it is gratitude that moves us to worship (Col. 3:16–17). In all of our lives of grateful obedience we are to worship God (Rom. 12:1–2). It is not a sense of duty, but the Word of Christ dwelling richly in us that moves us to sing. The reality, however, may well be otherwise; we sing because it is eleven o'clock on Sunday morning, and that is what we are supposed to do at that hour. Happily, singing has the capacity to stoke the fires of gratitude and prime the pump of praise. It is not "in vain we tune our formal songs" (Isaac Watts, "Come Holy Spirit, Heavenly Dove"). Sometimes it is the tongue's turn to lead, and the mind's and heart's to follow.

In the worship of the gathered people of God, the body of Christ, we present ourselves to the God who judges us and who shows us mercy. Our song and all else that constitutes the service of worship are like Jacob's ladder, a two-way trajectory established by God. As stated before, God's blessings come "down"; our thanks, praise, laments, and petitions go "up." Our song is a part of that process, it too being a means of our giving and receiving. The congregation's song is, in fact, the means par excellence by which all the people actively participate in worship. Singing helps to internalize the worship of the assembly, to make it our own. Investing ourselves in the congregation's song is an important guard against the deadening effects of mere ceremonialism.

When We Sing We Worship God with Our Whole Being

God wants all of us

"I believe that the best medium of conversation with God may be congregational singing, because it encourages the whole person—body, intellect, and emotions—to respond to the truth of Holy Scripture in the context of Christ's body—the Church" (Donald Hustad, in Wallace 2006, 14). How much of our whole person participates in worship? The apostle wrote to the Corinthian Christians: "I will sing praise with the spirit [in this context, the charismatically endowed self, resulting in ecstatic utterance], but I will sing praise [separately] with the mind [the understanding] also" (1 Cor. 14:15 NRSV. See also the mental engagement enjoined in Col. 3:16.) God wants us to love our Maker and Redeemer with "all our heart, and all our soul, and all our might/mind" (Deut. 6:5; Matt. 22:37; Eph. 5:18–20). In worshiping God in song, we worship not only with our brain, but also with our abdominal muscles, diaphragm, lungs, trachea, larynx, lips, and tongue. Earnest singers sometimes find themselves "leaning into the music."

James F. White tells us that "we need to take seriously the importance of the whole body, and all the senses in worship." Music is "a body art" (1997, 72). I like to think of Jesus' three lost parables in Luke 15 as paradigms for worship, not least of all for the part we sing. In all three parables, the finding of what was lost is cause for communal and celebrative rejoicing. When the prodigal returns, his father does not say to him, "You can have your room back." The order of the day, rather, is getting dressed up—a gown, a ring, shoes—and celebrating with dining, music, and dancing. What's all the fuss about? It's about joy in heaven and joy on earth, joy that cannot be contained, but spills over into physical expression that involves all five senses. All the stops are out, nothing is held in reserve.[1]

Doing what comes naturally

In the film *Rob Roy*, one of the characters makes a snide remark something like this about some rustic worshipers and their leaders engaged in singing: "They won't let the people stand up; they're afraid they'll start dancing." Indeed, it can be hard *not* to get physical when we are singing certain songs. Though the worshipers in Rob Roy's Scotland were probably not impelled to dance by the rather grave psalm tunes they sang, who can keep the knees from bending while singing Fred Kaan's communion hymn, "Let Us Talents and Tongues Employ" to its Jamaican folk tune? It is easy to find ourselves swaying ever so slightly when the congregation sings "Come, Thou Fount of Every Blessing." Its tune is in waltz rhythm! What movement seems natural when you sing "Infant Holy, Infant Lowly, for His Bed a Cattle Stall," or "A Little Child in the Earth Hath Been Born"—both lullabies? I had a Scottish professor in seminary who, in the worship service, sang only unaccompanied psalms. In the chapel service, though, those standing behind him could sometimes detect a discreet sway when a mere "hymn of human composure" being sung worked its influence. Surely, at least part of the popularity enjoyed by "Onward, Christian Soldiers" and "The Battle Hymn of the Republic" is due to the insistent march rhythm of their tunes. It is a challenge to sing these songs and remain still!

Advocates of movement—yesterday and today

David and all Israel were dancing before God with all their might,
with song and lyres and harps and tambourines
and cymbals and trumpets.
(1 Chron. 13:8 NRSV; cp. 2 Sam. 6:5)

Vigorous, elemental, and physical expressions were common in ancient Israel and still are in some societies today. Following an initial period characterized by spontaneous reaction to perceived events, societies tend to move to a ritualized, contemplative, formal, and symbolic worship. We can trace this spiritualizing tendency in the history of Israel; there is a movement from music's power to possess, in informal, spontaneous worship, to its ability to express, to symbolize, in more formal worship. It is not easy for the church to hold on to both the ecstatic and the disciplined. Unfortunately, the church today is divided between those who stress one of these and those who stress the other (Wilson-Dickson 1992, 23). Referring to Augustine's ambivalence with regard to the song of the worship service, John D. Thornburg writes:

> . . . hymnody is one of the places in which we stand at this extraordinary intersection between the raw power of music to elicit our deepest and most uncontrollable emotions, on the one hand, and the enterprise of channeling, interpreting, and, in some measure, controlling those emotions purposefully, on the other. (1992, 9)

In the contemporary church in some cultures, bodily movement is an essential part of worship. Many black congregations are quite free of inhibitions with regard to bodily movement in worship. Surely the modern charismatic movement in non-Pentecostal churches in North America, and the subsequent evolution of the praise and worship movement came into being, at least in part, as protests against the rather minimal physicality of worship in so much of the church. Like the revivalists of an earlier age

(White 1997, 137), charismatics seem to understand that if we want to move people spiritually, it will probably help to move them physically. Some twenty-first century descendants of Luther have gone on record as declaring, "We worship God with our bodies, through singing, movement, dance, and gesture" (Evangelical Lutheran Church 2001, 31. See also Plantinga and Rozeboom 2003, 144–49). Do they indeed? Do you?

Are we missing something?

The best-known tune we have received from Calvin's Geneva Psalter is the one we call OLD HUNDREDTH, and to whose very sedate and majestic strains we sing—as sedately and majestically as we are able:

> Him serve with mirth, His praise forth tell,
> Come ye before him and rejoice.
> (Wm. Kethe, Ps. 100, 1st st., 1560)

I have experienced that mirth and joy deep down inside, and I am very grateful for that. It is the real thing, even though no one else may detect what is going on inside me. But what about letting that mirth and joy out, and letting it move us back and forth, from side to side, or up and down— even if only sedately? Ronald Byars, a former professor of worship in one of my denomination's seminaries, has expressed the same longing: "I long for movement!" (2002, 35). What inhibits us? Timidity? Fear of what others might think? Fear that we might lose control, or get "lost in wonder, love, and praise"? Many would say that it is high time that the church got over its suspicion of rhythm and its fear that people might start to dance. Perhaps the influx of significant numbers of people from other cultures into our North American society in recent years will nudge us to enlarge our worship tents.

There is no denying that the particular form our worship takes is in large measure culturally determined; Christians in different cultures will not worship in just the same way. And that is as it should be; that is the "vernacular principle," according to which we all worship in our own language—like the Jews and proselytes at Pentecost. Just because other Christians clap their hands when they sing does not mean that *we* should—not, at least, until it has become for us a natural response, *our* language. Our worship must be our own, employing the forms that come naturally to us.[2]

Expanding How We Conceive of God

There is more than cultural diversity involved here, however. The style of music we use in directing our songs to God has everything to do with how we conceive of God. If our worship is to have any integrity at all, there must be congruence between our conception of God and the way in which we address God. If our conception of God is overwhelmingly solemn and majestic, then Isaac Watts's "Before Jehovah's Awful Throne" (Ps. 100) may seem to be the key to entering into the divine presence.

Struck by the amazing love of the Father's gift of his Son, on the other hand, we may find our song in the more energetic "To God Be the Glory" of Fanny Crosby. It seems appropriate to address a transcendent God by Walter Chalmers Smith's "Immortal, Invisible, God Only Wise," one who is immanent by "Jesus, Thou Joy of Loving Hearts" attributed to Bernard of Clairvaux. If you are like me, you have plenty of room for all of these rather different songs. God is always so much more than even the whole church, in every place in all the ages, can imagine. It is always just possible, however, that songs—both text and tune—different from those we have been singing may alert us to our need to expand or modify our conception of God. In this way, the church's song may serve as a corrective to our worship.

Singing Makes Us Want to Worship God Even More

Weak is the effort of my heart, And cold my warmest thought;
But when I see thee as thou art, I'll praise thee as I ought.
(John Newton, *Olney Hymns*, 1779)

My utmost powers can never quite,
Declare the wonders of God's might.
(Johann Mentzer,
"O That I Had A Thousand Voices," 1704)

Singing is not only something we do; singing does something to us. In singing God's praises, we are both subject and object, both giver and receiver. Singing God's praises turns up the temperature of our praise and moves us to praise God yet more and with more fervor. Music serves the liturgy by lending it power. Though there are reasons for believing that the apostle intended the being "filled with the Spirit" in Ephesians 5:18–20 to be understood as preceding singing, we may also believe that the other order may take place. Similarly, feeling cheerful is cause for singing (Jas. 5:13), but singing can also contribute to our cheer.

Some voices from the past

Augustine observed that some of the churches in North Africa neglected "the singing of hymns and psalms . . . that is so useful for moving the soul to devotion and igniting divine love in the emotions. . . ." (Letter no. 55, chap. 18). A millennium later, John Calvin wrote: ". . . it will be good to introduce ecclesiastical songs, the better to incite the people to prayer and to praise God" (*Draft Ecclesiastical Ordinances*, 1541). I believe that I know well what the reformer had in mind; when I get to the end of singing Charles Wesley's "Love Divine, All Loves Excelling," there is a very good chance that I shall indeed be "lost in wonder, love, and praise." In 1542, Calvin wrote: ". . . singing has great power and vigor to move and inflame men's hearts to call upon and praise God with a more vehement and burning zeal" ("Letter to the Reader," in "Preface to the Psalter," 1542). What Calvin refers to in these passages involved both text and tune. He does not distinguish between the contributions of the two to the heightening of the singers' praise. It is clear, however, that Calvin attributed a potential power to a sung text that the same text unsung does not possess, as Augustine (attributed) put it, "One who sings well prays twice." In any worship that tends toward being intellectualistic—that relies heavily on rationality, the cognitive, and the didactic—the stoking of affection, passion, and imagination should not only be welcomed, but sought. As Fred Pratt Green wrote in his praiseful hymn, in making music we find "a new dimension in the world of sound" ("When in Our Music God Is Glorified," 1972).

Three centuries after Calvin, Dwight L. Moody understood full well the power of song to move people. His musician, Ira D. Sankey, was to lead the

crowds in song until they were ready for the evangelist's message. Countless
other evangelists and revivalists followed suit. (We should bear in mind
that the goal of such services was not primarily worship, but evangelism,
conversion, or revival.)

Does any of what we have been saying smack of working the crowds?
Of manipulation? Of playing with people's emotions? As in connection
with other means of grace, as in fact in all our dealings with people,
abuses and distortions can happen. Here, too, is another possible pitfall to
guard against.

> It is . . . important that the emotional power of music in worship be evoca-
> tive rather than manipulative, honest rather than manufactured, and that the
> congregation's singing allow for the full range of emotions in worship.
> (Reformed Church in America 2005, No. 7)

This church position paper distinguishes between fleeting emotional states
and the persevering feeling, for instance, of gratitude; it is this ongoing
state that we seek to elicit and nourish. Isaac Watts gives us an example of
this linkage in his "Alas! And Did My Saviour Bleed":

> Thus might I hide my blushing face
> While his dear cross appears;
> Dissolve my heart in thankfulness,
> And melt mine eyes to tears.

Any emotion altogether unrelated to responsibility is suspect.

The challenge today

Perhaps in much of the church today, however, any problem may seem
to be elsewhere. So many congregations have never experienced for themselves the power inherent in the singing assembly. And so many worship
leaders seem to be unaware of the potential of congregational song. They,
too, are inexperienced. Why don't congregations sing, and why don't they
sing better? Is the moribund congregational song that characterizes so
many North American churches simply due to the performer-spectator

orientation of our culture, in which only the professionals sing, while everyone else just listens? Or is it evidence of something more serious, because indeed, the people are unaware that they have anything to sing about? It is at least possible that people do not sing simply because they have never in all their lives experienced the joy of singing. Here is what may well be the major musical challenge confronting pastor and musician. Joining forces in meeting this challenge surely qualifies—next to the faith itself—as the principal tie that binds pastor and musician in one common task.

WHEN WE SING, WE PRAY, AND WE LEARN HOW TO PRAY

~

Singing Is Praying

The corporate worship of the assembly is all about prayer and praise. The topic of worship we have just considered includes the element of prayer; when the assembled congregation prays, it is engaged in worship. The fact that prayer has such a specific connotation for us, however, warrants a separate mention of it here. Many North American Protestants tend not to think of prayer as sung (unless perhaps it be "The Lord's Prayer" at weddings or funerals); hymns are sung, prayers are spoken. But prayer, including the Lord's Prayer, may be spoken *or* sung. See Psalm 42:8, for instance, in which prayer and song stand in apposition to one another. The whole book of Psalms, as a matter of fact, is a collection of sung prayers—prayers that are at the same time songs. As noted above, one who sings well prays twice. John Calvin referred to congregational song—which, in his case, referred to the Scripture his followers sang—as "the prayers of the people." It is likely that many of the earliest references to the church praying refer to sung prayer; it is impossible for us to ascertain with certainty whether the utterance in view was what we would call song or spoken word.

I attended a service recently in which, just after we concluded the singing of a hymn, the pastor said, "Let us now come before the Lord in prayer." But we had just been in prayer before the Lord, having prayed the words of the hymn, "Just as I Am"! If we would close our eyes when we sing, as indeed we may at times—especially when singing a familiar or repetitive chorus or refrain—perhaps we would more readily understand that what we are singing is indeed a prayer. The church's service bulletin reinforces the common failure to understand the relationship between prayer and song, referring as it normally does to "prayer" and "hymn" as two different categories of worship. The Episcopalian is confronted in worship by two books in the racks: a hymnal and a prayer book.

Spending a little time reflecting on the texts of some of our hymns may lead us to being amazed at how much praying we have been doing when all the while we thought we were only singing! The simple, repetitive refrains of gospel songs, our contemporary Scripture choruses, and the Taizé choruses—all these can help us grow in our appreciation of sung prayer (Hawn 1997, 26–27). Being aware, while we are singing, that we are engaged in prayer is a strengthening—and sobering—realization. Helping their people understand this is one of the most valuable contributions clergy and musicians can make. One of the treasures of the church is the Episcopal prayer book (The Book of Common Prayer). But every church that has a hymnal has a prayer book. (Admittedly, of course, even defining prayer very broadly, it would be stretching the language too much to label *all* the songs in our hymnals as prayers.)

Congregational song is corporate prayer. "As Luke puts it in his report of an early Christian prayer meeting, 'they lifted their voices together to God' (Acts 4:24). . . . Uniting our voices together is just what we do when we sing" (Old 1995, 321). The psalmist exhorts the assembly, "Come into his presence with singing" (Ps. 100:2). God's people are to come into God's presence not as so many individuals, but all together, as one people gathered in worship, their many voices made one in singing. The fact that our sung prayers are corporate lends them a structure and a discipline that are often lacking in our private prayers.

Singing Can Improve Our Prayers

Not only may we pray when we sing psalms and hymns; song has the potential for improving our prayers: facilitating prayer, expanding prayer's horizons, making our prayers more fervent. Related to its ability to expand the way we conceive of God is singing's potential for enlarging our prayer vocabulary, giving us concepts, images, and words to express ourselves. Singing "In Christ There Is No East or West" enlarges our prayer to include the whole body of Christ. Even though I would not identify "church" and "kingdom" as did Timothy Dwight, his "I Love Thy Kingdom, Lord" helps me to pray more positively for a church that all too often depresses me. Surrendering myself in the ancient Irish "Be Thou My Vision" centers my prayer on the One who alone is worthy of my heart. For a church that may be inclined to forget that "here have we no lasting city" (Heb. 13:14 NRSV), a few of the many stanzas of the very old "Jerusalem, My Happy Home" can lend a joyful strand of yearning to our prayer life, freshening it with images that might never occur to us. My own prayers tend to begin with the word "Father," or a rather indiscriminate "Lord." A fair number of hymns remind me that I may also pray to Jesus and to the Holy Spirit.

The image-filled prayer that is Thomas H. Troeger's 1987 hymn, "Wind Who Makes All Winds That Blow," is capable of renewing and energizing our concern for the church's task of getting out the message. Carl P. Daw's 1982 "O Day of Peace" can help guide our prayers for peace, and Walter Russell Bowie's 1909 "O Holy City, Seen of John," our prayers for a more just world. All of this improvement of our prayer life presupposes, of course, more than a nodding acquaintance with the church's store of song. (On the value of repeated exposure to the psalms for learning the language of prayer, see Old 1995, 58.)

In our personal prayers, it may well be that most often it is petition that sooner or later gets the most attention. We find the same thing in the prayers recorded in the Bible: No matter what else may be their content, they nearly always get around to asking. This is all right, for asking God for something is also a way of honoring God. Moreover, is this not what we should expect of finite, fallen creatures? But what do we ask for? The prayers we sing from the hymnal can help us get our asking agenda more nearly right, help steer us into asking for those things that matter most—for ourselves and for our neighbors.

How many people have any idea at all why they are asked to sing in church? How many have even wondered why? If you asked the question of your people, how do you suppose they might reply? Of all the reasons for singing mentioned in this chapter, it may well be that the one we have just examined has the potential for being the most readily helpful for your people: the understanding that when we sing, we pray. When we sing, we all pray one and the same prayer together—with all our being.

> Come, my soul, thy suit prepare: Jesus loves to answer prayer;
> He Himself has bid thee pray, Therefore will not say thee nay.
> Thou art coming to a King, Large petitions with thee bring;
> For His grace and power are such, None can ever ask too much.
> (John Newton, *Olney Hymns*, 1779)

SINGING BUILDS US UP IN THE FAITH

~

Potential and Limits

[Music,] being an integral part of the solemn Liturgy, participates in the general purpose of the Liturgy, which is the glory of God and the sanctification and edification of the faithful. (Pope Pius X, 1903)

Contemporary Roman Catholic Edward Foley writes of the ancient tradition on which the three major branches of the church today agree: "The act of worship is the church's first theology and a prized faith expression." Worship not only "expresses the church's faith," but also "creates it" (2001, 97. See also Hawn 1997, 27–28). Another Catholic, Michael S. Driscoll, urges us "to take seriously the power of the rites to convey deep meaning and truth" (2005, 32). We learn by engaging in the liturgy, we learn through the *experience* of worship. This is precisely what I want to tell some pastors who feel they must explain in words the rationale for every act that takes place in worship, instead of letting the liturgy itself do the work of teaching.

We understand and give thanks for the fact that we are built up in the faith while we worship. This, however, must not cause us to emphasize instruction at the expense of doxology. In the summer of 2003, I participated in a Lutheran Vesper Service in London's Southwark Cathedral which included congregation, choir (from the U.S.), organ, and orchestra. Nice! One of our hymns—all eight stanzas—was about baptism. Certainly, by today's standards at least, it was much too compendious, erring on the didactic side. There are limits as to how much theology the church should try to teach through hymnody; the church's song is not the church's only educational tool. Moreover, what has been understood to be true of the psalms holds in equal measure with regard to the church's store of hymns: Their purpose is not primarily didactic, but doxological.[3]

The Creedal Function of Singing

One of the blessings built into hymns, however, is their capacity to carry theological freight. For the people in the pews, ". . . hymns may be the most important carriers of the Christian faith, especially so in a time of biblical and theological illiteracy" (Fackre 1999, 32. Gregory the Great and John Chrysostom shared the same enthusiasm in their day). We may call this the creedal function of hymns. The Credo (Nicene Creed) has for centuries been a part of the Latin Mass. Creeds and parts of the church's confessional statements have also been set to music for singing by the congregation. By singing "spiritual songs and psalms from their hearts to the Lord," Luther wrote, "God's word and Christian doctrine may be instilled and practiced on a regular basis." God "is thereby praised and honored and we are made better and stronger in faith when his holy word is impressed on our hearts by sweet music" ("Preface to the Burial Hymns"). The reformer made available four-part songs so that youth might sing Christ in place of "love tunes and carnal songs" ("Preface to the Wittenberg Hymnal").[4]

The seventeenth-century hymn of Tobias Clausnitzer, "We All Believe in One True God," is distinctly creedal. In the nineteenth century, Cecil Frances Alexander wrote hymns for children that are based on the articles of the Apostles' Creed; from "I believe in God the Father Almighty, Maker of heaven and earth," she developed the simple words for "All Things Bright and Beautiful" (1848). A Dakota melody has been used as a setting for the resurrection confession found in 1 Corinthians 15:1–8, titled "This Is the Good News." A brief, contemporary hymn presenting the theology of baptism is Michael A. Saward's "Baptized in Water" (1981)—only three stanzas in my denomination's hymnal. Some hymns owe their origin and their contents to doctrinal controversy; for instance, the ancient "Of the Father's Love Begotten," and the nineteenth-century "The Church's One Foundation." Paul Gerhardt, Isaac Watts, Charles Wesley, and countless others have helped shape, deepen, enliven, and expand the faith of many generations of those who have sung their hymns.

> Through the songs sung in worship, God's people, including children and those new to the faith, learn their language about God and the story of salvation. These songs remain with people through life, persist when memory fades, give meaning in later life, and are a comfort in death. (Evangelical Lutheran Church 2001, 30)

S. Paul Schilling claims that the effectiveness of hymns as teaching instruments derives not only from the fact that they embody basic beliefs, but also from the form or manner of that embodiment, involving: 1) the cumulative power of repetition; 2) the link with emotions; 3) poetic imagery, especially metaphors that enable hymns to deepen insight and enrich understanding in ways not readily accessible through literal prose alone; and 4) new hymns can show contemporary significance and relevance of the faith (1981, 136–37). More than a half-century earlier, Louis F. Benson had written:

> What poetry can do for doctrine is to humanize it, to set it in the light of imagination and to clothe it with feeling. And it is this handling of doctrine that has made the church hymn book the actual creed of countless thousands of Christians who have never so much as had the historic church confessions in their hands. (1956 [1927], 147–48)

Songs Can Compensate for What Is Missing

In certain periods, even over the long haul, elements of the faith that were neglected or underemphasized in some areas of the church's life have been kept alive within the church through song and other expressions of devotion. The former is true even in connection with nothing less than the central and overwhelming fact of God's great love. The Western church's long history of confessing and teaching the faith has only rarely given the topic of divine love its rightful place. In contrast, "In almost all evangelical hymns the love of God in Christ for ordinary women and men was central, which is why so many of the hymns of Isaac Watts were so popular for so long" (Noll, in Mouw and Noll 2004, 8). We can appreciate this fact even more when we bear in mind that hymnwriters have at their disposal very few English words that rhyme with the word "love." The late Swedish theologian, Gustav Aulén, pointed out (in 1931) that though the classical view of the atonement that pictures Christ as the victor in the struggle against Satan was not then in favor among theologians, it remained alive in the church's Easter hymns.[5] In the church, as in all other human endeavors, fads come and go. Faith expressions preserved in hymns from other periods can help save the church from fads today. They are like ballast that keeps the ship on an even keel, and listing neither to port nor to starboard.

Songs Can Test the Authenticity of Our Theology

Authentic theology begets singing. If we cannot sing what we say we believe about God—indeed, are not compelled to sing about it—we need to examine what we believe. Does what we say we believe really matter? Good preachers are rightly concerned with whether this or that idea "will preach." We can give a lecture on just about anything, but we cannot preach a sermon on just about anything. We can lecture an audience, for instance, on the subject of infralapsarianism (the divine decree of election followed, rather than preceded, the fall of the first humans). We can lecture on traducianism (every soul, just as every body, is procreated by the parents, rather than being freshly created by God at conception). But God forbid that we should attempt to *preach* on these topics! (Although it has been done.) If such matters are not grist for a sermon, even less are they material for a song. We may find such topics treated at length in some old texts on theology, but we should not expect to find songs about them, for such topics never moved anyone to sing.[6]

In a review of a work by the late Dutch theologian G. C. Berkouwer, the reviewer likened the writer to someone who would exhaustively present all sides to a theological question, and then stand on the fence and sing the Doxology. Is that a shortcoming in a theologian? We may remember and perhaps sympathize with President Harry Truman in his exasperated plea for a one-armed economist, an expert in the science who is not given to saying, "On the one hand, this, and on the other hand, that." But can anyone talk about the One whose judgments are inscrutable, whose thoughts are not our thoughts, and use only one hand? Like the apostle (Rom. 11:33–36), when we have thought and said all we can think and say about God, we are not finished. Authentic theology begets song. If the theology we have been believing is authentic, relevant, we *have* to sing about it.

> Immortal, invisible, God only wise,
> In light inaccessible hid from our eyes,
> Most blessed, most glorious, the Ancient of Days,
> Almighty, victorious, Thy great name we praise.
> **(Walter Chalmers Smith, 1867)**

SINGING BUILDS US UP IN DUTY: SONGS AND THE SECOND COMMANDMENT

~

The church's song presents to us not only what we are to believe, but what we are to *do*, not only the true faith, but also the commandment to love our neighbors, and how that commandment may be fleshed out. In a hymn from the church in beleaguered twentieth-century China, "O Christ, the Great Foundation," we are challenged to stand up in the face of tyranny and be counted. Karen Lafferty's "Seek Ye First" (Matt. 6:33; 7:7) is one praise chorus that has made it into mainline hymnals, setting before us, in its first stanza, one of Jesus' sayings about our social responsibility. Jeffery W. Rowthorn's "Lord, You Give the Great Commission" (1978) confronts us with the church's full-menu mission to the world: healing, preaching, living with integrity, service, teaching, peace-making, intercessory prayer, sharing, and concern for social justice.

To descend to a more mundane level, not long ago I was driving myself to a meeting at a church, driving myself in more than one sense, for my heart was really not in it. It was 100 percent sense of obligation. Though I consider myself to be rather sober-minded, I must say that en route, there came to me as a strengthening means of grace, out of the blue, a phrase from a hymn I learned as a youth growing up in what had been part of the Confederacy: "Where duty calls or danger, be never wanting there"—a line from the abolitionist hymn by George Duffield: "Stand Up, Stand Up for Jesus."

What is going on in the church's singing is not merely didactic—words to learn and remember—but something dynamic and motivational. We have already noted the words of Calvin: ". . . singing has great power and vigor to move and inflame men's hearts" ("Letter to the Reader" in the "Preface to the Psalter" of 1542). In 1543 he added these words to the 1542 letter:

> . . . for there is scarcely anything in this world more capable of turning or bending hither and thither the customs of men [than music], as Plato has wisely remarked (*Rep.* 3.12, 401B; *Laws* 2.8,664B). And actually we know by experience that it has a secret power, almost unbelievable, to move morals in one way or another.

The melody-borne message has the power to influence our conduct long after we have stopped singing.

WHEN WE SING, WE EXPERIENCE OUR ONENESS IN CHRIST

~

If we confined our singing in worship, as Zwingli thought we should, to making melody in our hearts and not with our mouths, much that we have talked about thus far in this chapter might happen. But none of what follows could take place.

Singing and Community

> Young men and women alike,
> old and young together!
> Let them praise the name of the Lord . . .
> **(Ps. 148:12–13a NRSV)**

The ideal of the oneness of the assembly manifesting itself in song is encountered in the New Testament (Acts 4:24; Rom. 15:6; see also 2 Chron. 5:13), in the rabbis, and in the early church fathers. "There is one body of Christ (1 Cor. 10:17), and one Spirit, whose presence and activity manifest the unity of the body (Eph. 4:3–4), and issue forth in praise (Eph. 5:18–19)" (Smith 1962, 28). The gathered community is by definition a fellowship of all sharing together in that which everyone brings to the gathering, including songs (1 Cor. 14:26). John Calvin wrote of the church's vocal manifestation of its essential oneness:

> . . . the chief use of the tongue is in public prayers, which are offered in the assembly of the believers, by which it comes about that with one common voice and, as it were, with the same mouth, we all glorify God together, worshiping him with one spirit and the same faith. (*Institutes*, III, 20, 31)

Who, reading this book, has not joined hands with other believers and sung the first stanza of this hymn?

> Blest be the tie that binds our hearts in Christian love:
> The fellowship of kindred minds is like to that above.
> **(John Fawcett, 1782)**

In this particular hymn the theme itself is all about our being bound together. But all congregational song carries the potential for promoting our experience of all-togetherness, of our together being a local manifestation of the one body of Christ. "The singers give up ego, selfhood, and control to enter that world of 'vibration'. . . ." (Parker 1991, 117). Singing is an event, one that draws people into it, connecting them to one another (Clark 1994, 23). In a society in which musical preferences tend to divide along generational lines, is there any activity that is more intergenerational than congregational singing?[7]

Vital congregational song is a protest and a protective barrier against that form of spirituality that is described by Princeton University sociologist Robert Wuthnow as exclusively a "spirituality of seeking" (2003). In this radically individualistic form of spirituality, congregational song is likely to be in very short supply, for participation in the life of any congregation is likely to be only occasional.

"Singing actually constitutes us as a worshiping community" (Driscoll 2005, 30). As members of the one singing assembly we breathe together, taking in a fresh supply of air at the comma or the end of the phrase. Together we enunciate the words, together we go up, and together we come down. In the words once again of John Wesley:

> Sing modestly. Do not bawl, so as to be heard above or distinct from the rest of the congregation, that you may not destroy the harmony; but strive to unite your voices together, so as to make one clear melodious sound. (*Directions for Singing*, 1761)

This direction is particularly hard to follow when we are strongly moved to sing, and the congregation's singing is anemic!

It is not only the physical activity in which we are mutually involved, and our opening ourselves to all the others present when we are singing, that draw us together. Something like this can happen when almost any group sings. But we are talking here about a very particular body of people, a people who were "no people, but who now are God's people." How they got to be who they are is their story; it is this that they sing about. This is the burden of a good number of the Old Testament psalms. By singing such songs we remember, and our children learn, who we are. That is one reason why singing our story is so terribly important. When we sing in church, it is the one story that we are singing—the story of who we are and how that came to be. One reason it all came to be is so that we might tell the story (1 Pet. 2:9–10).

What we sing not only relates us to the one people of God, the one body of Christ; the particular collection itself from which we sing, if it be the hymnal of our denomination, may well serve to establish and strengthen our particular denominational identity. Encountering the familiar denominational hymnal in an unfamiliar setting—a church we are visiting while on vacation, for instance—is like meeting an old, well-known friend. "This church uses the same blue hymnal we use at home!"

Singing hymns, one of the few things people actively do together anymore, is among the last vestiges in our culture of communal activity that has kept societies intact since the dawn of the human race. One reason people keep gathering to sing is instinctual: we have to sing together to be who we are. (Henry 1997, 500)

The power of the church's song to unite is not restricted to the worship service; indeed, it may be experienced even more palpably in other contexts. All too often, in meetings of the church's governing bodies and committees, heated debate, fueled by sharp differences of opinion, threatens to divide the participants into warring factions. In precisely this situation, a thoughtfully chosen prayer sung by all present can save the assembled from the centrifugal forces of evil, returning them together to the shared center of the church's faith. Singing together not only can "inflame men's hearts" (Calvin); it also has the power to *calm* them. Possible candidates include "I Greet Thee, Who My Sure Redeemer Art," "Gracious Spirit, Dwell with Me," and "Love Divine, All Loves Excelling."

In Every Age and Place

Singing not only unites us with the other members of the one body who are present; it also enables us to share the songs, thus the faith and life, of generations of the church in other ages and in other places.

When I look at the saints, especially in the New Testament, the story is the same. I can hear voices of rejoicing in their tabernacles, joyous songs and hymns of salvation and victory, with the help of God. And we sing along and join in the praise and thanks, just as we are one in our faith and trust in God and also share in suffering. (Martin Luther, "Commentary" on Ps. 118)

When these words [of the Psalter] please a man and fit his case, he becomes sure that he is in the communion of the saints, and that it has gone with all the saints as it goes with him, since they all sing with him one song. (Martin Luther, "Preface to the Psalter")

. . . congregational song handed on across time and place links the memory of individuals and particular communities to the longer corporate memory of the church. (Evangelical Lutheran Church 2001, 30)

The psalms we sing were sung by Israel more than two millennia ago, and have been sung by the church since its beginning. Most of our hymnody is a gift from those who have gone before us, some from long before. From Prudentius (348–413) of Spain comes the lovely Christ-hymn, "Of the Father's Love Begotten." We could sing our way from there on into the present century. Some hymns, like Bishop How's "For All the Saints," put us in mind of our spiritual predecessors quite explicitly. In singing hymns, not only do "we come before our fathers' God," but before One who was just as much "our mothers' God." "Hymns were . . . one of the few means open to women for the public expressions of their faith" (Noll, in Mouw and Noll 2004, 12).[8]

"The Day Thou Gavest, Lord, Is Ended," situates us in a church on which the sun never sets. In "Lord, You Have Come to the Lakeshore," a Spanish writer and a Mexican composer from the late twentieth century invite us to meditate on Jesus' call to his disciples. "Music is an ecumenical bridge—and served as such long before there was an ecumenical movement" (Henry 1997, 500). We learn, in singing hymns, "that the household whose stories we sing includes the glorious company of the apostles, the goodly fellowship of the prophets, the noble army of martyrs, the whole cloud of witnesses, all things visible and invisible" (Henry 1997, 501). The oneness and universality of the church is symbolized by the very hymnal from which we sing, it being a gift to us from the church in every time and place. Paging through our hymnal we come across Ambrose, Louis Bourgeois, Philipp Nicolai, Isaac Watts, John Bunyan, Paul Gerhardt, the Wesley brothers, Robert Lowry, Fanny Crosby, Fred Pratt Green, Hae Jong Kim, Gracia Grindal, Pablo Sosa, and scores of others.

You and I, years ago, were also a part of the church that may have been in a different place, and that for sure existed in a different time. Our singing here and now helps connect us with life in the church there and then. Our personal song repertory both affords continuity with our past and reflects the growth that took place along the way.

Congregational Consciousness

It is not hard to understand that the life-giving, life-directing things that may take place when the church sings have a better chance of happening if we, while singing, are not simply believers in the communion of the saints, but are existentially aware of others around us, conscious of our "congregationalness" (see Pss. 22:22, 25; 35:18; 40:3, 9–10; 42:4; 109:30; 111:1; Rom. 15:9–11; Heb. 2:12). We should be aware not just of others' presence, but also of their facial expressions, their body language, and the sounds they are making—all those things that foster communication.

> . . . the very presence of sound makes us present to one another at worship in a way our physical presence does not. We have to disclose ourselves to one another when we sing. . . . We express ourselves and become vulnerable to God and to one another in a unique way. (Westermeyer 2001a, 49–50)

Do you remember the words of a contemporary Mennonite cited in the first chapter? "Singing undresses us." Is it any wonder that many people experience congregational singing as intimidating? Where we sit and stand in relation to our fellow worshipers within the worship space is not immaterial. Optimally, we should be facing one another, and no one should be farther than four feet from the nearest neighbor. We shall talk more about this in chapter 8.

Demons to Be Exorcised

Two demonic assumptions need to be exorcised from the church. The first is that the corporate worship service is primarily just another opportunity, albeit a very special one, for people to practice their private devotions—"just me and the Lord." On occasion after occasion, the psalmist expresses his awareness that he is part of a multitude, "the great congregation," that he is among his sisters and brothers. One of the so-called benefits of lots of carpet and cushions is that they help muffle the intrusive sounds of other people. Being seated as most congregations are—face to back—also contributes to the sense of privacy.

The second is that the congregation is an audience, merely spectators watching and listening to the actors up front. As is the case so often with demons, probably most congregants are not even aware of the existence of these two. But exist they do.

Short of major alterations to the worship space, three of the most effective means of decommissioning these miscreants are 1) leaving our seats to go forward to give our gifts or to receive the Lord's Supper; 2) greeting others/"passing the peace"; and 3) engaging in congregational song and reciting a creed.

WHEN WE SING WE PROCLAIM A MESSAGE TO OTHERS

~

We Build Up One Another

All congregational singing is done in the company of other singers. Many of what are commonly called hymns are indeed addressed not to God, but to one another. Through our singing we confess God before others (Ps. 40:1–10; Rom. 14:11; Heb. 13:15); we recite, acknowledge, and proclaim the mighty acts of God (1 Pet. 2:9). The same Spirit who enables us to confess "Jesus is Lord" (1 Cor. 12:3) moves us to sing. Being moved by the Spirit of God (Eph. 5:19–20) and indwelt by the Word of Christ (Col. 3:16), the church has something to say. Paul, in 1 Corinthians 14:13–25, includes song as an exercise of the church's prophetic ministry within an assembly— one that may include unbelievers susceptible to the message they hear. The song of God's people serves the word entrusted to the church, a word for the church, a word for the world. "Faith comes from what is heard" (Rom. 10:17), whether that word is spoken or sung. Our response of faith to God in song is at the same time a witness of that faith to others. The congregation's song witnesses both to the objective body of truth confessed by the church, and the congregation's personal, subjective appropriation of that truth. That the song of the worshiping community has a double reference, to God *and* to humanity, is seen throughout the Bible. The psalmist,[9] the angelic host in the Gloria (Luke 2:14), the aged Anna (Luke 2:36–38), the Jerusalem welcoming committee in their Palm/Passion Sunday anthem (Luke 19:38)—all are, in their singing, engaged in multitasking.

The two parallel passages in Ephesians and Colossians are the classic New Testament utterances having to do with the church's song. It is clear from both that the song of the congregation was highly valued by the apostle. But something in Colossians 3:16 that is important for what we are discussing just now is not clear: What is the relation between singing and the teaching and admonishing? Questions of syntax and how to punctuate the Greek text make it impossible to be sure. I opt for the translation given in the King James Version (punctuation modernized):

> Let the word of Christ dwell in you richly in all wisdom,
> teaching and admonishing one another
> in psalms and hymns and spiritual songs,
> singing with grace in your hearts to God.

This translation in no way strains any grammatical rules. The only problem is a felt one, and a modern one. We (in contemporary North American society, at least) do not think of teaching and admonishing one another by means of singing. But 1 Corinthians 14 gives us a larger understanding of the connection between edification and song. The point of 1 Corinthians 14:1–33 is that in and through the congregation's worship, the church must be built up, edified, and instructed. It is for this reason that in the church's praying-singing, intelligible communication must take place. Prayer and singing in the form of unintelligible utterances may, without further measures, be profitable to the individual who utters them. But in public worship, such utterances are to be limited in number and never without accompanying interpretation; those present must be able to understand the prophetic message. There is no shortage of references in both Jewish and early Christian writings that make it plain that the notion of instruction being given through singing was not at all strange in the ancient world. The church father Tertullian (c. 150–155–after 222) lends a homey touch to this kind of pedagogy in his reference to believing spouses mutually edifying, exhorting, and encouraging one another in song (*Ad uxor.* 2:8). As a matter of fact, we ourselves as a matter of course engage in just this practice when we sing, for instance, "Onward, Christian Soldiers," or what has in some quarters become its slightly more modern counterpart, "Lift High the Cross." Whom are we addressing in these hymns? Surely it is not God, but others—and ourselves. In countless hymns we instruct, admonish, and encourage one another as we sing. (By our example we do this even when we sing songs addressed to God.) Both Ephesians 5:19–20 and Colossians 3:16 appear in contexts rich in materials for building up the life of the Christian community.

The Congregation's Song as Pastoral Care

The church's song not only may direct us to care for our neighbor; as we have just noted, it is itself a means of caring for those neighbors present in the congregation. One whose preaching elicited no little acclaim, Henry Sloane Coffin, points out that a hymn can sometimes speak to a need untouched by a particular sermon (1946, 115). We may say, then, that congregational song has a potentially pastoral function.

> Worship is thus through its "moral" working protected from slipping into a mere aesthetic or ecstatic self-blessedness; it binds the members of the congregation together in obligatory service, the one to the other. (Delling 1952, 159; trans. mine)

Is the congregation aware that, when singing, it may be engaged in pastoral care? This is a stimulating and encouraging realization for everyone in worship.

Evangelize Through Singing?

Do any of the songs we address to others ever serve the purpose of evangelism? Certainly the summons to believe is the thrust of numberless gospel songs—"Jesus Is Calling," "Only Trust Him," "Softly and Tenderly." In some of the gospel songs, there is not only admonition and encouragement, but a certain amount of instruction in the faith. Gospel songs may well not be used in the normal Sunday morning worship service of the church you serve. But we can hear the Gospel in many standard hymns of the church as well; God's unconditional love is proclaimed in one hymn after another, whether they are addressed to God or to others.

No, the purpose of the church's worship service is not to evangelize, but to worship. Nevertheless, the evangelistic potential of worship, including not least of all its musical parts, does not have to be denied, any more than does music's potential for edification. Worship at its best "embodies the gospel so *whole*-somely that one who participates in it will learn to see what the gospel is and what it is not" (Byars 2002, 29).[10] On a grander scale than our normal worship service, the psalmist exhorts us:

> O sing to the Lord. . . . sing. . . . tell. . . .
>   declare his glory among the nations,
> his marvelous works among all the peoples.
>
> **(Ps. 96:1–3)**

The psalmist apparently views the congregation's songs of praise as a means of grace whereby all the ends of the earth remember the Lord's delivery and turn to Israel's God (Pss. 22:3, 25–31; see also 9:11; 18:49; 40:3; 105:1–2). Strikingly, the ministry of Jesus himself is figuratively cast as a musical proclamation before the Jews (Matt. 11:16–17; Heb. 2:12) and before the Gentiles (Rom. 15:9–12). When the incarcerated Paul and Silas prayed and sang, "the prisoners were listening to them" (Acts 16:25. This translation is preferable to the more casual "and the prisoners heard them" of the King James Version).

In extraordinary circumstances, the church's song (even when borrowed by "the world") may have extraordinary power to impress those who hear it. We see this at gatherings like those held in Washington's National Cathedral in connection with the horrors of September 11, 2001. Informal, spontaneous outbursts of song may have the same potential: Witness the singing of "Amazing Grace" by a grieving family gathered on the coast of Nova Scotia after Swissair Flight 111 plunged into the sea on September 2, 1998. It is as though God, in the midst of however horrible the tragedy, gives human beings, however weak and helpless, the last word.

Even if none of the above considerations were taken into account, we would still have strong and clear evidence from the New Testament for the potential for evangelism through the medium of the church's song. Through hearing the church's prophetic message, whether it be delivered through speech or song, unbelievers who are present in the assembly may be brought to acknowledge that the church's claims are true (1 Cor. 14:24–25). Singing the faith is as near as many believers come to telling the story "of Jesus and

His love," affording them some justification for singing "I Love to Tell the Story" with a straight face.

Pre-evangelism?

One of Sinclair Lewis's favorite targets for satire was the Rotary Club. He even managed to work the Rotarians into his acceptance speech when receiving the Nobel Prize. One of his barbs is in the form of poking fun at members of the club who raise their voice in song during their weekly meetings—and this at high noon and when all present are dead sober! Similarly, the singing congregation may well draw attention to itself; for sober, grown men and women to sing together, not self-consciously, in broad daylight is, in contemporary North American society, counter-cultural. This is especially the case when the congregation is made up of people who have enjoyed more advantages in life, and they sing enthusiastically. That relatively sophisticated people should find so much pleasure in the simpler things of life that are accessible to everyone! (Illustration: the British upper class at royal weddings and funerals.) For those who simply enjoy group singing, an assembly that sings with enthusiasm can itself be an attraction, affording for would-be singers one of the rare opportunities to be found in contemporary North American life. The congregation sings its songs in a larger context of a gathering that is itself a manifestation and a reminder of the distinctiveness of the church in the world (1 Cor. 14:25). The singing congregation is a visible, audible, and dynamic manifestation of that unity that witnesses to the reality and the life of the Triune God (John 17:20–23).

> Some to church repair,
> Not for the doctrine, but the music there.
> **(Alexander Pope, *Essays on Criticism* II.53)**

Certainly the music of the church can exert a very strong appeal. I remember a "tall steeple" pastor in a large Northeastern city who came to the conclusion that some of those in the Sunday morning service had come not because of his preaching, but because the high quality of music they heard there appealed to their aesthetic sensibilities. The pastor's reaction was to drastically scale down the church's musical program. Whatever their reason for visiting that church, was there any possibility that some of the music lovers might have been evangelized? The contemporary English novelist Susan Howatch has testified as to the important role of the Anglican service of Evensong in her mid-life conversion. Against those of their own number who are critical of the Mormon Tabernacle Choir's going so very public, its defenders cite the breaking down of prejudice that results from the choir's efforts; people who have been impressed by the choir are more likely to admit Mormon missionaries into their homes to explain the faith (Marini 2003, 213–38). Music thus conceived serves as a kind of pre-evangelism, part of the larger Mormon strategy to mainstream what was for so long an ultraseparatist sect. The ever-more glitzy television productions of the Mormon Tabernacle Choir, of course, are not services of worship. It is at least possible that, in the rationale given by some churches for their public offerings in the fine arts, a kind of pre-evangelism motive is lurking. Churches are among the prime places where North Americans encounter the arts, especially music. The Princeton University sociologist Robert Wuthnow, having argued for a correlation between contemporary North American spirituality and the role of the arts in religious life, believes churches that want to attract people should be more intentional in their use of the arts (2003).

WHAT HAPPENS WHEN THE CHURCH SINGS? LOOKING AT IT FROM ANOTHER ANGLE

~

Singing as a Means of Grace

Realizing that such store is to be set by the song of the congregation, it hardly comes as a surprise that some are prepared to speak of the church's music, and specifically the church's song, as mediating God's grace, as being a means of grace, even a sacrament, or something akin to it. The Roman Catholic Edward Foley writes: "Broadly speaking, liturgical music can be considered a sacramental act" (2001, 98). It surely would be hard to find a higher view of music, and congregational song in particular, than that expressed in the recent Mennonite publication noted previously. Seminary professors, preachers, and members alike testified to the supremacy of song in their corporate worship experience. By singing together, the congregation can accomplish almost everything in the worship service that needs to be done. Singing, the primary act of their worship, functions for Mennonites "as sacraments do in liturgical churches." In singing, worshipers "encounter God most directly. We taste God, we touch God when we sing" (Kropf and Nafziger 2001, 27).

Singing as the Work of the Holy Spirit

In sum, the Spirit makes possible each broad movement in worship—both the human-Godward movement of praise and prayer; and the God-human-ward movement of proclamation and spiritual nourishment. In the drama of worship, the Spirit has the leading role. Worship is charged with divine activity. (Witvliet 2003, 274)

God gives the psalmist something to sing about. Divine deliverance carries with it the gift of song. The Lord's very act of delivering the psalmist is tantamount to putting a new song into the psalmist's mouth, a song about deliverance, a song sung for all within the great congregation to hear (Ps. 40:1–10). The church's song is more than human performance; it is also and ultimately a divine gift. What can happen when the church sings? Whatever good happens takes place because the church's song is more than the church singing. All worship is the work of the Holy Spirit. When the church speaks and sings its prayers, it is the Holy Spirit praying in our hearts (Rom. 8:15–16; Gal. 4:6). When the church praises Jesus as Lord, it is because the Holy Spirit is at work (1 Cor. 12:3). The same Spirit who moved David to speak the psalm moves the church to worship boldly (Acts 4:24–31). As wine is to drunkenness, so is the Spirit to the church's song (Eph. 5:18–20). The church sings spiritual songs—Spirit-derived songs (Eph. 5:19; Col. 3:16). Liturgy is the work of the people, and liturgy is the work of God.[11] Those gathered pray for the Spirit's illumination as the Word is read and proclaimed, for the Spirit's activity at baptism, and for the Lord's Supper. (See Pss. 51:15; 119:8; Acts 2:1–4; 4:24–31; 10:44; 1 Cor. 3:7; 6:11; 12:3; Eph. 5:18.)

Let's Be Honest!

Why do I sing? Because I love to sing! Because I delight in it! And the pleasure singing gives is in inverse proportion to what it costs me. What happens when the church sings? This part of the church experiences an emotional high. John Calvin, who himself was not excessively musical, put it in these terms:

> Now among the other things which are proper for recreating man and giving him pleasure, music is either the first, or one of the principal; and it is necessary for us to think that it is a gift of God deputed for that use. ("Letter to the Reader" in the "Preface to the Psalter" of 1543)

Though the pleasure is never greater than within the community gathered for worship, it is not restricted to that, but "may extend yet farther . . . even into the homes and the fields. . . . " (ibid.). For Charles Wesley, too, music and song were a "holy pleasure." In singing, I am, among other things, ministering to myself, to my own needs—both immediate and long-term— giving wholesome expression to my own joy and gratitude, my own fears and uncertainties. " . . . congregations and choirs who sing know penetrating health in a profound way, even if they seldom articulate it or may not even know how to articulate it . . . they know a deep wholeness and shalom that comes in their singing" (Westermeyer 2001a, 50). In a world in which "in-your-face" is never in short supply, singing the songs of the faith is for me a Gilead in which I, year after year, have found a balm that also abounds. Just as many who stutter find singing to be beneficial, so I find emotional release. My native self-consciousness and reserve are suppressed, and I am in only an instant gifted with words and melody that would never naturally occur to me—but that in singing become my very own. To sing is to practice pastoral care—of ourselves. Yes, "*Soli Deo Gloria!*" But, as we see so clearly in the fourth Gospel, God's glory is not at war with our good. God's glory is our good, and our good is God's glory. (We can see the same connection in Ps. 29.) In the words of Erik Routley's hymn,

"For Musicians," in the praise of God both "duty and delight" meet. Having myself experienced so strongly the joy and so much else that may result from singing, I want to share the treasure with those who have not yet discovered it.

And there is more. Neither Luther nor Calvin believed that the pleasure of singing is restricted to the worship service. Indeed, I am thankful that I am able to sing in other places as well, and at other times. That happens mostly when I am alone, however, behind a steering wheel. Being in corporate worship, on the other hand, means that I can lift up my voice in song in public—unashamed and unafraid. Like most people, I do not have a solo-quality voice and, as I age, what I do have does not move me any closer to a Carnegie Hall performance. But like most people, I do have a congregational-quality voice. So I sing in the one place where I can every week sing in public. It is being a part of the singing congregation— the church's primary choir—that gives me that liberty. And by my singing I am one of the givers of that same gift to all the others assembled. In singing together, we blend all our voices and it comes out all right. Congregational singing is the original blended worship.

And After We Have Finished Singing? The Song Keeps On

~

Music, when soft voices die,
Vibrates in the memory.
(Percy Bysshe Shelley,
"To—: Music, When Soft Voices Die," st. 1)

Music has the potential not only for teaching about God and the Christian life and for experiencing life in community, but also for helping us remember what we have learned and experienced. The ancient rabbis understood this quite well. Perhaps you, like me, learned the books of the Bible by singing their names in biblical sequence. Though my mind has been subject to the shaping forces of theology from many sources for many years, the theology that comes most readily to my tongue is that embodied in the church's creeds, catechisms, and hymns that I have over the years committed to memory. The theological store I have accumulated from the hymns has a leg up on that derived from all other sources, because: 1) It is married inseparably to music that I sing—and sing not just one time, but in the course of a lifetime, again and again, both in and out of church; 2) As Louis Benson put it, poetry humanizes doctrine, sets it in the light of imagination, and clothes it with feeling. Our learned store of hymns is like a "time-release capsule. . . . Friends, hymnody, at its best, is the bottled energy of God waiting to be opened again and again" (Thornburg 1996, 9–10). Those of us who visit in nursing homes are sometimes amazed to find patients who, in spite of severe mental deterioration, are still able to open that bottle. When worshiping in a certain church, the seat I gravitate to is near the usual place where a woman of my age, but with a choir-quality voice, is to be found. The woman's dementia is betrayed by her invariably asking the same questions, time after time. But when it is the congregation's turn to sing . . . !

~

At this point we may once more indicate something of the essential role of music in the worship service of the church, music that serves the Word, the liturgy: Good church music is music that is, or that brings about, all the good things we have discussed in this chapter, things that give glory to God and life to the world. The only music that can make all this happen is the song of the congregation.

– Useful Resources –

John L. Bell, *The Singing Thing: A Case for Congregational Song* (Chicago: GIA Publications, 2000), 17–20 about song as a means of expressing our identity, 47–65 about the role of song in transmitting the story and shaping faith.

S. Paul Schilling, *The Faith We Sing: How the Message of Hymns Can Enhance Christian Belief* (Philadelphia: Westminster Press, 1983). An analysis of a large number of hymns for doctrinal content.

Frank C. Senn, *The Witness of the Worshiping Community: Liturgy and the Practice of Evangelism* (New York: Paulist Press, 1993). Expounds a contemporary Roman Catholic view of the evangelistic potential of the liturgy.

CHAPTER
THREE

So Who Sings?

~

I n the preceding chapter, we looked at some of the things that can happen when the congregation sings. But down though the centuries in the history of the church, has it been the congregation that sang in the worship service? Was it the whole congregation? Was it just the assembled males? Or was all song the exclusive province of a choir, or even of a single cantor?

As It Was in the Beginning

~

In trying to picture for ourselves what the musical part of early Christian worship was like, we are severely hindered by both the paucity of references and the uncertainties of interpreting the ones we do have. As noted in chapter 2, in some cases we cannot be sure whether a reference is to speaking or singing. Both are forms of utterance, sounds distinguished from one another only by varying degrees of shadings; the verbs used to refer to their production do not themselves in every case indicate precisely the nature of the utterance. In this area, therefore, we can do little more than make educated guesses.

During the first six or seven decades of the twentieth century, Christian liturgical scholars were virtually all of one mind about one thing: The pre-Eucharistic part of the early church's worship service derived, as to its formal structure, from the synagogue: Scripture readings (including, for the church, of course, writings not read in the synagogue), exposition of the Scriptures, prayers, and psalmody. What could seem more natural than such borrowing? More recently, however, this account of the origins of Christian worship has been subjected to very strenuous criticism.[1] How, then, may we gather some idea of what the very earliest Christian worship was like?

In distinction from the Hebrew Scriptures, the New Testament knows no holy men who worship on behalf of the common people. Every believer is a member of the priesthood with full access to God (Rom. 5:1–2; Heb. 4:16; 1 Pet. 2:9–10); every believer is a partaker of the one Spirit (Rom. 8:9; 1 Cor. 12:3). In Romans 12, 1 Corinthians 12, Ephesians 4, and other passages, the apostle names (even gives lists of) a variety of gifts and offices; it is significant that in these passages leading in prayer is never singled out as the prerogative of any one class within the congregations. To lead in prayer, spoken or sung, is the prerogative of *all* those gathered. That individual members of the church did in fact participate—were *expected* to participate— in the musical parts of the earliest Christian worship seems evident from passages such as Acts 4:24–30; 1 Corinthians 14:15–16, 26; Ephesians 5:19; and Colossians 3:16. It may be difficult for us to understand how they might have done it (unison participation would have required memorization of both words and music), but Acts 4:24 may point to the congregation singing together in a united voice. Is Romans 15:6 a reference to the unison song of the church? (The unity in view here may well be the unity of the inner disposition; all are to be of the same mind.) What about Revelation 5:13? Clement of Alexandria (c. 150–c. 215) gives us an early reference to unison singing by the congregation. Of course, it may not have sounded very musical by modern Western standards. There are reasons for believing, however, that solo singing, as is clearly in view in 1 Corinthians 14:15, 26, may have been more common; after one person sang, others present responded with an "amen," or some other word or words. There are also reasons for believing that not only individual males sang, but also females.[2]

As we would expect, there is no evidence that choirs were employed in the earliest church. Did the early church know the role of cantor? The call-response pattern of some of the psalms and other sung texts suggests interplay between a solo voice and the assembly. A person with more than average musical gifts would have proven very helpful in starting and maintaining the song. There are hints of the role of cantor in very early documents, but we have no direct evidence of such before the fourth century.

A handful of references to the church's song from the second through the fifth centuries have survived. Some have to do with the singing of the congregation—men and women together. Both antiphonal and responsorial chant are mentioned. Psalms, hymns, responses, and antiphons (a short refrain sung after a verse or part of a verse, as in Ps. 136) were sung. The precise import of these references is not always clear. We should probably also understand at least some early references to prayer as references to song (sung prayers).

One thing is clear: Singing in the early church was *everyone's* privilege. We should understand that this was not due to the fact that proper choral music had not yet been devised by the church, or that the church had simply not gotten around to organizing choirs. We understand that congregational song, whether the utterance of the whole assembly together, or of only one member soloing, is the principal and only indispensable form of the church's music. We accept congregational song as our benchmark, however, not simply because this is what we find in the New Testament and in the early church, but because it is the outworking of a fundamental principle: the universal priesthood of all believers. The liturgy is the responsibility and privilege of all the saints.

The Congregation Loses Its Voice

~

At the Council of Laodicea (about 364) it was resolved that only canonical (authorized, appointed) singers, having mounted the pulpit/lectern, would sing in the worship service. It is possible, however, that it is not that congregational song is here prohibited, but only that the leader's part is restricted to a recognized cantor; others in the assembly might well respond audibly. In any case, the purview of this council was only provincial. We know, moreover, that congregational participation in the music in worship did continue, at least in some places, after this date. As the structure of the church and of its liturgy developed, however, musical forms grew increasingly complicated; congregational participation, where it did not disappear altogether, tended in time to be limited to the singing of short responses at certain points in the Mass. Music in the medieval worship service tended to be the more or less exclusive province of trained choirs of monasteries, cathedrals, and school chapels. Any singing of vernacular hymns in the worship service was evidently quite exceptional.

That the church's music had been made so complicated, and thus so far removed from the capabilities of common people, was not without its critics, including John Wycliffe (d. 1304) and Erasmus (d. 1536). Things had gotten so out of hand that at the Council of Trent (1545–1563) it was even proposed that all music in the church be abolished!

If, however, the common people had at most only a minimal role in the church's song, they were free to sing outside the church. And sing they did, both secular and religious songs, including carols.

THE CONGREGATION REGAINS ITS VOICE— IN A PART OF THE CHURCH

~

The Congregation Is Given Songs to Sing

More than a century before the Protestant Reformation began, John Huss, professor at the University of Prague, supplied his followers with hymns in their own language; the waves of a restored congregational song were beginning to lap at the edges of the church. A certain amount of vernacular congregational song could, in fact, be heard in some churches in Germany. The beginnings of a flood would come with the sixteenth-century Reformation. Martin Luther and John Calvin both firmly believed that the duty and privilege of singing in the worship service belonged to all members of the body of Christ. To this end, Luther saw to the preparation of psalms and hymns and their musical settings. Demand for printed copies of Psalters and collections of hymns resulted in a bonanza for publishers. In Geneva, Calvin gave singing exclusively to the congregation. Calvin's rejection of the choir's independent role in the worship service would persist among his disciples for at least two centuries, and among a few of them even to this day.[3]

The Congregation Is Given Help to Sing

In both Lutheran and Reformed congregations, children were taught the new songs, which they, in turn, helped the other members of the assembly to learn. The gradual elimination of the musical role of the congregation had carried with it the demise of the cantor. After the reemergence of congregational song brought about by the Reformation, it is not surprising to find cantors employed in the Lutheran Church, one being no less than J. S. Bach. In Great Britain and North America, the Reformed Church's version of the cantor was the precentor (a song leader), who led the congregation by singing the song, line by line, for the people to imitate. It was the post-Vatican II (after 1965) recognition that active participation in worship is the duty and privilege of the whole people of God that led to the more general reemergence of the role of cantor in the Roman Catholic Church. In several branches of Protestantism, the renewal of worship in the same period introduced the weekly reading/singing of a psalm or psalm portion with its potential for the cantor-response pattern. The song leader found in many Protestant worship services is the nearest thing in them to a cantor.

THE CONGREGATION'S SONG AGAIN AT PERIL: THE CHOIR

~

In what follows I shall speak of several practices and conditions as imperiling or competing with congregational song. My intent is not to derogate all such practices and conditions; I even make a case, for instance, for the employment of a choir, and for the use of the vocal soloist. Some of the things mentioned are in themselves at least potentially beneficial for worship. I simply want to point out how various things, even some that may in themselves be helpful, can serve to diminish the most important music in the worship of the assembly: the song of the congregation.

The Proliferation of the Choir
in Protestant Churches

Luther sanctioned the continued use of the choir in worship, as did the Anglican Church—at least in cathedrals and some other settings and, beginning in the early eighteenth century, in parish churches. In both of these communions, in contrast to the Calvinist branch of the church—which did not sanction choirs in the worship service—great choral traditions developed, building on the extensive pre-Reformation heritage. In the latter part of the nineteenth century, as part of the Oxford (and Cambridge) Movement, Anglican choirs began leaving their traditional place in the rear gallery of the church to be given a place up front with the clergy. As congregations watched, clergy, choristers, and men or boys carrying appropriate paraphernalia processed in while singing the first hymn, setting a triumphal tone for the service. Likewise, they trooped out singing at the conclusion. All of this was especially grand and impressive in the great space of a cathedral.

Apart from the dictates of doctrine, choirs have been much more likely to be found in larger congregations in urban centers than in the country church. In nineteenth-century North America, the proliferation of church choirs in urban and rural areas alike was stimulated as much by practical need as by fondness for choral music; as variety and number of tunes and singing styles developed, many pastors, feeling their inadequacy to lead the singing of the congregation, looked to a choir, or at least a precentor/song leader, to assist the people. It was also the case that those who had taken part in the singing schools popular in the early nineteenth century came to be enthusiastic about the somewhat more sophisticated music to which the schools had exposed them, and, for whatever motive, were more than willing to share their new-found pleasure with the rest of the congregation.

Following the American Civil War, large and affluent Protestant congregations in the urban centers of the Northeast began to invest more in their music programs, seeking academically trained musicians to serve as musical director, organist, choir director, and paid singers in choir or quartet ("quartet choir"). Throughout the nation, congregations with fewer resources began to adopt this model to the extent they were able. Choirs that were unable to recruit a tenor could find anthems that called for no tenor—only soprano, alto, and bass. What passed for choir robes or vestments, minimizing distinctions among the choristers and distinguishing them from the congregation, could be cut and stitched together by women in the congregation.

Two major institutions established to meet the growing need for professional church musicians in this context were the Westminster Choir College in Princeton, New Jersey, founded in 1926 and now a part of Rider University; and the School of Sacred Music at Union Theological Seminary in New York City, founded in 1928. In the 1970s, the Institute of Sacred Music at Yale University was established to replace the latter. Another effort to upgrade the local church's music program took the form of conferences for church musicians, most often denominationally sponsored. And of course, choirs have to have music. Publishing firms issued music from English and North American composers. Denominations also promoted the graded choir program as a means of strengthening not only the choir, but the song of the congregation as well. Surely one reward for a denomination's maintenance of colleges has been the supply of graduates with choir experience.

The Rationale for a Choir

That a congregation should have a choir is virtually a given in most of the church in contemporary North America. Knowing how the choir has historically tended to infringe upon the song of the congregation, even usurping it altogether, what should we say in defense of the institution of the church choir?

Apostolic warrant: A sharing of the gifts of some for the edification of all

We must remember that a choir is also part of a congregation (to the extent that it is not made up of paid outsiders)—that part of the congregation trained and rehearsed for its specific task in the service of worship. It is well and good to oppose any tendency to reduce the larger congregation's role to that of passive spectator; but the notion of being edified through the gifts of others (choristers, for instance) is very much in line with the apostolic instructions given in 1 Corinthians 12 and 14. These chapters, and the precepts of Ephesians 5:18–20 and Colossians 3:16, should biblical warrant be sought, may be understood both as making room for choirs and as a hedge against granting to them a monopoly on song in the worship service. The universal priesthood of all believers does not mean a universal, equal giftedness. Believers shy of a particular gift may serve the gifted precisely by furnishing the latter with the opportunity to share their gifts (1 Cor. 12:22–27). Not all are sufficiently gifted vocally to qualify for a place in the choir. Enough gift to enable one to join the congregation in song, however—and happily—is an almost universal endowment. Let it be clear that the choir under discussion here is one that, whatever role it may have in supporting the singing of the congregation, may itself sing before a silent congregation.

> Just as there is a wide variety in styles and forms in the music of worship, so also there is variety in the levels and ways people participate in music. At times, all participate actively in the music-making event, as in congregational singing. At other times, the congregation participates by responding, as in call and response forms or responsive refrains. At still other times, most of the people may participate by actively listening, as in a choral anthem or organ voluntary. (Evangelical Lutheran Church 2001, 29)

Choir as caring community

Probably most of us think of a church choir chiefly, if not exclusively, in terms of its contribution to the worship service. N. Lee Orr sets forth a pastoral justification for the choir. In keeping with his central thesis that the church musician's focus must be on people, not products, and with Lyle Schaller's claim that the church's music program has the potential for being the best single means of assimilating new members of the church, Orr writes: "The mission of the choir has two broad goals: forming a caring community and preparing music for Sunday worship" (1991, 29). (By no means is every choir a caring community. Rehearsal time is always at a premium; there is much work to be done. Thus there is not always much time for members to get to know one another.) A choir has the potential not only for assimilating the church's new members, but, if it is competent, also for gaining and holding members—for the congregation and for the choir specifically.

Choir as means of grace for choristers

Beyond the potential for making a contribution to the worship service and for being the caring community Orr has so helpfully emphasized, a choir can be a means of grace to its own members, giving them an opportunity they find all too rare: to join their voices with others to sing deeply cherished choral music.

The Role of A Choir in the Worship Service

Varied opinions

On a communication from the committee of a church searching for a director of music, I read these words: "The centerpiece of music at [name of church] is the sanctuary choir." Is that so? At this juncture, it is time to enunciate another indisputable verity: Within the church there is no clearly stated, universal agreement as to the role of a choir in the service of worship. The imprecision in the language in some statements on the subject may reflect a lack of clarity of thinking, disagreement among committee members, or simply a desire to leave the matter open.[4]

A tentative definition

The role of all who are assembled for worship, including clergy and choir, is the worship of God and the edification of God's people. Thus the choir, like all others in the assembly, is involved in all those activities discussed earlier. Like the clergy, however, and in distinction from the rest of the congregation, the choir has allotted to it a certain place in the liturgy for fulfilling a part of this prophetic and priestly ministry. At such times, the congregation is silent; its participation, except for possible audible response, is limited to the internal and reactive.

The choir is also distinguished from all others in the assembly, both clergy and congregation, by the kind of whatever music that it alone sings. Choral music not being subject to the criterion of congregational accessibility, a capable choir (and instrumentalists) can give expression to a wide range of feeling that exceeds the capabilities of the congregation. What a choir has the best chance of communicating to a congregation is not so much intelligible, the meaning of a text, but something more in the realm of feeling or emotions, which the congregation may appropriate for its own. Thus may we understand, at least in part, the references often made to choral music "enriching" or "enhancing" worship.

Having said this much, let me now state my own conviction regarding the primary role of the choir—as choir—in worship: The primary role of a choir (and all other musicians in the service) is to help the congregation sing.[5] The choir may help the congregation sing by its vocal support of the song of the congregation, and by its modeling singing both in its choral and its congregational song. Such modeling is audible and, if the choir is in front of the congregation, visible.

A Choir in Every Church?

"They [choirs] do remove the best voices from the congregation, and there are choir members all over the country who have never been next to their families during the liturgy. Maybe some rethinking is in order." Thus does Alice Parker, that valiant crusader for congregational song, challenge us not to take the necessity of a choir to be a given (1991, 97). The employment of a choir as a regular feature of the congregation's worship service involves a subtle but ongoing risk for congregational singing. What are enthusiastic singers among the congregation likely to hear after the service from those standing close to them? "You should be in the choir." If we sing, we should not be out in the congregation; that's for people who can't sing, or who at least can't sing very well. Singers belong in the choir.

Not every church, moreover, even among those of medium size, has the resources to field a choir that sings passably. Any decision to hire outsiders to strengthen a choir must be evaluated by the requirements of integrity and good stewardship of the church's resources. Aesthetic criteria do come into play in connection with any singing not done by the entire congregation. Is it helpful to present a choir that sets musically sensitive members of the congregation on edge by the sound it produces, and that may also fail to model singing for the congregation? It is more helpful if the ungifted do not attempt to share gifts they do not have. Frank Brownstead asks what it is that distinguishes a choir from the rest of the congregation if what the choir offers is not truly beautiful. Unless the choir offers both leadership and beauty, we cannot justify its existence (1991, 88).

OTHER POTENTIAL THREATS TO THE CONGREGATION'S SONG

~

Competitors Within the Worship Service

In addition to the choir, other possible competitors for a place in the hour or so given to worship on Sunday morning include:

1) Other vocal ensembles—children's, men's, seniors', and youth. These types of choirs most often sing only occasionally in the worship service.

2) Praise team. Contemporary worship services heavily utilize these groups.

3) Vocal soloists. The same warrant found to justify the employment of a choir may serve also with regard to the use of vocal soloists. As noted above, this may have been the primary means of musical expression in the earliest church. (In that period, however, any member of the congregation might sing a solo.) Henry Sloane Coffin felt that soloists tend to draw too much attention to themselves. But this can happen to preachers, too! Both musicians and clergy should ever be mindful of John the Baptist's words: "He must increase, but I must decrease" (Jn. 3:30). Frank Stovall values the vocal solo for its function as the personal testimony of the soloist (1976, 4); so do I. The Wesleys used soloists as effective means of evangelizing large crowds in open-air meetings. William Booth, founder of the Salvation Army, was suspicious of choirs, and the Army's officers were instructed: "One voice alone is much to be preferred . . . because the words can be heard with so much greater

distinctiveness" (in Wilson-Dickson 1992, 138–39. See Huizinga
1990, and Halter and Schalk 1978a, 22). It is indisputable that the
text is less likely to be obscured in a vocal solo than it is in all
nonunison, multivoice music. In part-singing, intelligibility is
bound to suffer—especially when the parts move at different
times. If my experience is at all typical, the memory banks of
churchgoers are also much more likely to contain words they have
heard over the years in vocal solos than the texts of anthems. It is
unfortunate, indeed, if the employment of a vocal solo is disdained
because a choir is seen as more prestigious; a vocal solo in the
worship service is not a last resort! And when there is no anthem
in a service, choir members still have the opportunity to fulfill
their most important function—to help the congregation sing.
This they can do outside the choir loft. Many choristers and their
friends and family among the congregation would welcome this
opportunity to be together in worship (any exclusive role of the
choir with respect to service music must be taken into account).
Preparing for one less anthem at choir rehearsal would provide
time for working on other music, as well as giving extra attention
to the congregation's songs for the following Lord's Day. The vocal
soloist who is visible enjoys another huge advantage over a choir,
whether the choir is seen or unseen. Whereas choral singers ideally
focus their attention on their director, the soloist is free to engage
listeners face-to-face, communicating with them directly. The
vocal soloist standing before a congregation has at his or her
disposal facial expression, gesture, and body language. He or she can
respond to whatever signals the listening congregation is sending.

4) A variety of musical instruments. Historically, the voice was
   first on the scene, but once admitted, the tendency of instruments is to dominate.

> I think one of the most difficult things for organbuilders and other
> musicians to understand is that the primary musicians of any
> church are not the choir but the mass of people in the pews. And
> the organ has its primary function to support and lead that group
> of musicians. (Walter Holtkamp Jr., in Ferguson 2001, 56)

5) Overly long sermons, interminable announcements, pastors who, instead of just letting the liturgy do its work, feel obliged to preach an explanatory "sermonette" before each rite in the service. Edward Farley asks: "Is the essence of Protestantism the replacement of adoration with proclamation, where grace comes by listening, not adoring?" (1998, 276)

Factors Outside the Worship Service

There are also currents at work outside the worship service itself that contribute to the erosion of congregational song:

1) Many pastors lack both knowledge and enthusiasm. Education in music is inadequate or even nonexistent in the training of clergy. Many competent musicians have little or no training or interest in congregational song. It was not congregational song, or even church music in general, that led them to study music. Many children today receive very little musical education and experience in school.

2) The emphasis of church music conferences tends not to be on congregational song, but on choir, organ, handbells, and other instruments.

3) A very large number of North Americans today tend not to be producers of music, but consumers only. Music making is left to the professionals and young wannabes. In how many homes today do people gather around the piano to sing? Even the singing of the national anthem at civic events is most often the monopoly of a solo performer. (Is "Happy Birthday" the last holdout of communal singing in North America outside schools and religious assemblies? It seems that everyone is always ready to join in this one song—with no inhibitions whatever.)

4) The style of the performer-listener music that is accessible to us 24/7 conditions us to think in musical terms altogether different from those involved in congregational song.

5) The texts of hymns are poems, the content is theology, and poetry and theology are not thriving in North American society today.

6) Though North American society has, from the outset of European settlement, been characterized by large-scale migration, the trend has accelerated in recent years; also, more recent migration has become more individualistic. Many North Americans also migrate denominationally. This unsettledness is unfavorable to the development of a community with a shared store of song.

7) Throughout the world's history, a tradition of a shared folk music has united the generations in song. The young and the no-longer-young in North America, however, tend to live in different musical worlds.

8) The rising average age of congregations contributes to failing physical and mental faculties, making active participation in the congregation's song more difficult.

9) Upward social mobility and increased sophistication tend to lead to delegating singing in the worship service to trained professionals.[6]

THE RESTORATION OF CONGREGATIONAL SONG IN THE ROMAN CATHOLIC CHURCH

~

In the Roman Catholic Church, the great worship renewal movement that was initiated in the 1960s by Vatican II opened wide the doors to congregational song, much as had the Protestant Reformation more than four hundred years before. Catholic clergy and musicians and music publishers scrambled to supply songs for the congregation.

Not all Catholic musicians and liturgical scholars have been happy with the new directives, or at least not with common interpretations of them. Some have expressed concern about a loss of mystery and transcendence in

the Mass and about the Mass being overly didactic. Does the active participation mandated by the Vatican necessarily translate into a requirement that
the congregation sing? Can we not actively participate by giving ourselves
wholeheartedly to listening? It is argued that reactive participation is in
some ways more profound than active, freeing the listeners from the technical activities, both mental and physical, that are involved in singing, thus
enabling them to experience the totality of the event (Collins 1992. See also
Piunno 2004). A contemporary, nationally known organist, Haig
Mardirosian, agrees that a core definition of liturgy involves an active
congregation. Nevertheless he asks, "Yet how is the concept of collective
listening, active listening, any different from the more obvious overt demonstration of song, word or movement by all?" (1984, 211) The Anglican
musician Lionel Dakers expresses another concern: The idea "that everyone
should be doing something all the time is questionable, for it runs the risk
of necessarily reducing the music to the lowest common denominator" (in
Routley 1997, 122). That sounds like congregational song!

I concede that diligent, thoughtful listening may qualify as active
participation. But as was made clear in chapter 2, only physical, audible
participation can facilitate the happening of all of the good things we noted
in that chapter.

> One function of music, then, is the offering of something we consider to be
> beautiful [?], no matter how meager our own musical accomplishments may
> be. And this is why actually singing oneself involves more participation than
> listening to someone else singing, no matter how superior the other's musical
> attainments may be. (James F. White 1980, 99)

With respect to reactive listening to the music of a choir that is likely to
afford an experience of anything approaching transcendence or anything
truly moving, this presupposes a better choir than a great many churches
can field. As for the verbal message sung by any choir, how many in the
congregation really do understand enough to respond in edifying ways?

In spite of reservations on the part of many throughout the Catholic
Church, the Vatican-mandated active participation has revolutionized the
status of congregational song in that communion.

THE FUTURE OF THE CONGREGATION'S SONG?

~

It is heartening to read what the Evangelical Lutheran Church in America unambiguously and boldly declared in 2002: "The assembly is the primary musical ensemble, and its song is the core of all music in worship" (2001, 28). Standard-bearers for congregational song over the last quarter century have come from various traditions. We give thanks for them all. We are also grateful for The Hymn Society in the United States and Canada, North America's only organization devoted exclusively to the development and promotion of congregational song. The song of the congregation is threatened today from all sides. It always has been. At times the song of the assembly has been robust. But it has also been wretched. For centuries, it was nonexistent, or virtually so. One thing is sure: The church's worship, in particular, and the church's life, in general, have never been more vital than was the congregation's song. The title of David M. Cherwien's guide for keyboardists (1997) should be posted where pastors and musicians could not help but see it often: Let the People Sing![7]

– Useful Resources –

James McKinnon: See under Useful Resources for chapter 1.

William S. Smith, *Musical Aspects of the New Testament* (Amsterdam: Ten Have, 1962). References to musical practice in the early church.

John D. Witvliet, *So You've Been Asked to Sing a Solo* (Grand Rapids: CRC Publications, 1996). A practical, nineteen-page pamphlet that includes emphasis on the oft-neglected spiritual preparation.

Wayne Wold, *Preaching to the Choir: The Care and Nurture of the Church Choir* (Minneapolis: Augsburg Fortress, 2003).

Carlton R. Young, *My Great Redeemer's Praise: An Introduction to Christian Hymns* (Akron: OSL Publications, 1995), 1–13, 35–38.

Two works setting forth late twentieth-century Roman Catholic views about music in the church are: Donald Boccardi, *The History of American Catholic Hymnals Since Vatican II* (Chicago: GIA Publications, 2001), and Michael Joncas, *From Sacred Song to Ritual Music: Twentieth Century Understandings of Roman Catholic Worship Music* (Collegeville, MN: The Liturgical Press, 1997).

CHAPTER FOUR

GETTING IT RIGHT:
WORDS, TUNES, AND COLLECTIONS

~

Does it matter what people sing? Even if you did not buy into what I argued in chapter 2, you probably would say yes. What should people sing in church, and what can be done to ensure that they sing what we believe they should sing? These are questions for church authorities. Down through the centuries, those in authority have many times expressed concern about the texts and the tunes employed in worship by their constituencies. Decrees regulating congregational song were handed down. In the sixteenth century, the gifted musician Louis Bourgeois whiled away some hours in a Genevan jail for tampering with the music for the psalms. As recently as 1820, the question of what could be sung in the Anglican Church was clarified in a civil court. Even toward the end of the twentieth century, what committees preparing denominational hymnals were perceived to be doing with well-known hymns received no little attention in the secular press. People in the pews reportedly said, "They've stolen my hymns." For the purpose of our discussion, let us assume that in a society so largely driven by populist impulses as is ours today, there is still such a thing as ecclesiastical authority, however diminished and localized that authority may be. For the ecclesiastical authorities charged with the oversight of those committed to their care, what criteria need to be borne in mind when evaluating the songs they will ask the congregation to sing?

THE WORDS WE SING

~

Does It Matter? A Matter of Integrity

> The fineness which a hymn or psalm affords
> Is, when the soul unto the line accords.
> **(George Herbert, "A True Hymn," st. 2)**

We all know that much singing is rather mindless—even in church. How many in the congregation could tell us, if asked, what they had just finished singing? "Hymns are loved and sung with fervor chiefly because the tune is familiar, no matter how meaningless or archaic the text may be or how banal the tune. Too often they are sung with spirit but with little if any understanding" (Beach 1987, 28).

My concern here, however, is with something else: the fact that people often sing words that, for them at least, simply are not true. Remember, we are not talking here about singing by people gathered around a piano at home (if anyone still does that). Our subject, rather, is what we sing in the worship of our Maker. The congregation's songs are not "fun songs" any more than the congregation's spoken prayers are just "fun prayers." The congregation's songs are prayers. In worship, even those songs that are full of joy are dead serious, in that we mean what we sing. At home around the piano we may heartily sing "The Church in the Wildwood," even if we have never seen a "little brown church" anywhere. But we should not sing it in church. The concern is an ancient one. In the fourth century, the Fourth Council of Carthage put it like this: "Take heed that what you sing with your mouths, you believe in your hearts, and what you believe with your hearts, you show forth in your works."

I shall not soon forget the experience of hearing for the first time Charles Wesley's "And Can It Be That I Should Gain," set to the spine-tingling, over-the-top tune SAGINA. The singers were gathered for an InterVarsity Christian Fellowship conference a half day's drive north of London. That was singing! But was that my song? It is a wonderful recounting of what apparently did indeed happen to Charles Wesley. An untold number of Christians, moreover, have found Wesley's experience to have been theirs also. They can claim the hymn as their song. But, like many other believers, I did not come to the faith in this way, as recounted in the fourth of the six stanzas. Nor do I look for assurance, as Wesley did, to the "whispers" of a "small inward voice" (stanza five). There remain, of course, four great stanzas which I can sing wholeheartedly.

Another example: Many years ago, my then-young nephew and I would sing "Amazing Grace" while working on my wee tree farm in central Louisiana. Buoyed along by the irresistible folk tune, NEW BRITAIN (and recordings by Mahalia Jackson, Judy Collins, the Royal Scots Dragoon Guards, et al.), this song has since become my country's unofficial national hymn. But there is one stanza of this hymn that I really cannot sing with a straight face, the second—at least not in church. The hymn's author, ex-slaver captain John Newton, and countless others have apparently come to the faith in just this way, through having been brought to fear, and then being relieved of that fear. (It was 1 Chron. 17:16–17, however, that moved Newton to write this hymn.) To bring people to such a crisis and its relief has, in fact, been the method consciously used by many revivalists and people engaged in personal evangelism. For all who came to the faith in this way, this is their song. For those of us who cannot remember when we did not trust Christ as our Savior, however, the words simply do not ring true.

What we are talking about here are the fundamental requirements of integrity, sincerity, and truth. Surely no one would question the importance of these in worship. Singing words that are not true, words we cannot seriously mean, has no place in worship; what we sing in worship is well meant, not just from the mouth, but deeply felt "from the heart" (Ps. 40:6–8; Isa. 29:13; Matt. 15:8; Eph. 5:19; Col. 3:16; see Smith 1962, 172–73).

> The Church with psalms must shout,
> No doore can keep them out:
> But above all, the heart
> Must bear the longest part.
> (George Herbert, "Antiphon I")

> They chant their artless notes in simple guise;
> They tune their hearts, by far the noblest aim. . . .
> (Robert Burns, "The Cotter's Saturday Night")

And when we sing, and when we pray,
Help us to mean the words we say.
(Edith Florence Boyle Macalister, 1873–1950)

Having said this, we must admit that we sing some prayers, even as we speak some prayers, in which we ask for more than we earnestly, honestly, consistently want. We pray for the coming of God's perfect reign, but, like Augustine in his prayer for chastity, have some qualms about it coming just now; we have projects we would like to get done first, some unfinished business. The topical indexes of hymnals commonly include the rubric "Aspiration." Under it are included some hymns in which we give expression to a yearning for "a closer walk with God," or our firm readiness to "let goods and kindred go, this mortal life also." We solemnly declare:

Riches I heed not, nor man's empty praise,
Thou mine inheritance, now and always.

And, if you are Methodist, Baptist, or Presbyterian, you may get more specific:

Take my silver and my gold,
Not a mite would I withhold.

Episcopalians evidently found these last two lines a bit much, for though this communion includes the hymn in its current hymnal, this petition has been expurgated.[1]

Opinions will vary as to how much is too much in such prayers of resolution and aspiration, but our prayer life would be poor indeed if we prayed only for those things we are completely ready to receive now. Such overreaching prayers on our part can at least be understood to imply a willingness to be made totally willing to receive that for which we ask, and to yield that which we promise. They also serve as goads to our continued growth in consecration. Integrity demands that, whether we speak them or sing them, we do so not with our fingers crossed, but in all seriousness.

One last thing about the integrity of our song: If we are to sing with integrity, we must resist the temptation to make a joke or encourage the making and telling of a joke about any of the words of a song. When a joke involves language from a hymn, we may rest assured that any who heard the joke will for the rest of their lives pay a price for it every time they sing that hymn. Thou shalt not sacrifice hymnic spirituality on the altar of humor! (The same, it hardly needs to be said, applies to the words of Scripture.)

The Language of Hymns: Literary Quality

A Christian hymn must be not only spiritual—having to do with the things of the Kingdom—but must also be simple. It must be understandable by ordinary people, even at first sight, even by those who have to devote a part of their brain to the music they are endeavoring to sing. There is no time, when we are singing with the congregation, to pause to reflect on what the words might mean. Both the text and the tune of the hymn must pass under the bar called "congregational." This requirement does impose boundaries for the work of the poet, but it by no means rules out the possibility of hymns being poetic:

> All beautiful the march of days, as seasons come and go;
> The hand that shaped the rose hath wrought the crystal of the snow;
> Hath sent the hoary frost of heaven, the flowing waters sealed,
> And laid a silent loveliness on hill and wood and field.
>
> **Frances Whitmarsh Wile,**
> **("All Beautiful the March of Days," 1911)**

Traditionally, hymns and metrical psalms have employed rhyme, and have employed it in a variety of schemes. "Amazing Grace" yields the simple scheme ABAB. "My Song Is Love Unknown" incorporates the more complicated ABABCDDC. Some modern verse is less concerned with rhyme—even as rhyme is not a characteristic of the Hebrew psalms. Rhyme is one of the delights of poetry, however, and in addition, aids the memory.[2]

The Language of Hymns: Contemporary Issues

Apart from the strictly literary questions applied to hymns, several other concerns with respect to language have risen in the course of time. It is well to bear in mind that our concerns in this area extend not only to the songs we sing, but to the language used in all our worship life, both corporate and private. Changes in liturgical language that are unmet by corresponding revisions of the language of Scripture, for instance, result in a degree of disconnect within the language of the worship service. (How serious a problem is this for the average worshiper?)

Personal pronouns: Number

At least since the nineteenth century there have been some who insisted that there is no place in congregational song for "I" and "my," but only for "we" and "our." But no one makes such an alteration to Psalm 23 or Psalm 51. The psalms of the Old Testament furnish examples of songs that had their genesis in the life of an individual, but were subsequently adapted to be used by the assembly in worship. Hymns of Christian experience are always hymns deriving from the experience of an individual. Ray Palmer's "My Faith Looks Up to Thee" is also a good example. In congregational singing, it is possible for the individual to participate in both the personal and the congregational orientation. "A statement of deep devotion or commitment to God may require us all to say 'I' as we sing it together, because 'we' is less intense and commits the individual singer less strongly" (Wren 2000, 185). The oneness of the body of Christ does not erase the distinctions among the individual members.

Archaisms

Since a number of the hymns we sing are very old, it is to be expected that parts of the language may seem archaic to us in the twenty-first century. "If Thou but Suffer God to Guide Thee" can more readily be understood today if we change it to something like "If Thou but Trust in God to Guide Thee." Some problems may require a little more ingenuity: In William Kethe's sixteenth-century paraphrase of Psalm 100, "All People That on Earth Do Dwell," the last line reads: "His truth at all times firmly stood, And shall from age to age endure." The word "truth" is here used as it is in our King James Version of the Bible; for us today it would be more accurate to speak of God's "faithfulness." And what are we to do with the King Jamesian "thee," "thou," and "ye"? Modernizing these, if the need be felt, does not often seem to cause consternation in the pews, but adjustments may have to be made in the rhyme scheme of the hymn. A reasonable strategy is to leave unchanged the old forms of pronouns as they occur in older songs, but to use contemporary forms in new hymns.

Remote images

Images can also accumulate the dust of the ages, and mean less to us today than they did to our ancestors. Images having to do with ships, the sea, and pastoral life came naturally to British poets of earlier ages; they may not speak with the same force to nonseafaring North American urbanites today. Biblical imagery may present a problem for modern generations who border on biblical illiteracy. Consider the word "Ebenezer," for instance, in the hymn "Come, Thou Fount of Every Blessing." What are people likely to understand by this name from the Old Testament?[3] Many old hymns (some of Watts's, for instance) present no problem to the understanding; it is just that their language seems quaint.

Hierarchical/political images

A more recent and far more controversial concern to surface in some quarters (not only Christian, but also Jewish) has been with regard to images drawn from the political sphere, that of a hierarchical society: "king," "lord," and "master." For starters, there is the matter of gender: These images are all masculine. Also, "Lord" is an English translation of a proper name of God in the Old Testament, a title applied to Jesus Christ in the New Testament. Brian Wren is one who has called for a critical evaluation of this class of images. The subject is complex. For that reason I have assigned its treatment to my online resource. (See Online Resources.)

The battle over battle language

The *New York Times Magazine* for May 21, 2006, was "The Architecture Issue" of that newspaper. The lead caption on its cover read:

Building to a Fight
Why Architecture Is the Only Art Form We Still Battle Over

Had the editor never heard of the battles being fought over the language of hymns? Might the editor think that such battles are not significant enough to note? Or was it that he does not consider the hymn to be an art form? This issue also is rather complex (see Online Resources). Let me say here that I acknowledge the validity of concerns that have surfaced about the language of battle in Christian discourse. There is a kind of militancy that can endanger the very heart of Christian discipleship. In certain contexts, "Onward, Christian Soldiers," or even "A Mighty Fortress is Our God" may be the very last thing a particular congregation needs to sing. It is not enough that a song be thought biblical. It is also critical that all song choices be guided by broad, wise, pastoral concerns. The kind of tune used with such songs must also be taken into consideration. The tune ST. GERTRUDE, for instance, reinforces the militancy of "Onward, Christian Soldiers." The tune WYE VALLEY, on the other hand, would tone down the text a bit.

Gender language

This is the language concern that is the most sensitive and that has gotten the most attention, especially in North America. This concern operates on three levels: language used in addressing or speaking of God, language with reference to human beings, and language that attributes gender (usually feminine) to nongendered entities such as ships, cities, countries, and the church. Opponents of the alteration of gender in a song may regard the change of God-language as blasphemous, and that on the human level as nit-picking.

Israel's God, in contrast to human beings and to the gods of ancient Israel's neighbors, is revealed in neither exclusively male nor exclusively female terms. Both the Bible and longstanding Christian tradition, however, refer to God and humanity in overwhelmingly masculine terms. This usage is said not only to offend some women, and to denigrate even those who are not personally offended by it, but also to be theologically inadequate. Some believe that to think of God only as Father is to misunderstand the nature of God; it may also be idolatrous. The Bible itself has been combed for any descriptions of the divine or of divine activity that reflect qualities we are more likely to associate with the female—giving birth, nursing, nurturing. (See Gen. 1:2; Isa. 66:12–13; Luke 13:34. In Numbers 11:12 and Isaiah 49:23, we encounter the image of "nursing/foster father." Should we be more likely to associate "nurture" with females?) Christian tradition has also been enlisted to supply a corrective to an exclusively masculine terminology with reference to God. The fourteenth-century Julian of Norwich has been found to be helpful in this regard. Substitution of "God" or some other word for the personal pronoun "He" has often been done. Many find the use of the neologism "Godself," in place of "God Himself," to be acceptable, requiring no more than a slight getting used to.

The Trinitarian, relationally-based formula (Father-Son-Spirit) has been analyzed, and linguistic substitutions sought (the functionally-based Creator-Redeemer-Sustainer, for instance). James F. White, quite open generally to implementing helpful linguistic changes, insists that there are seven places in the liturgy that require that "Father" be used (1997, 205–7). Whether used within or without the liturgy, "Creator" cannot for me possibly substitute the Jesus-given, intimacy-laden "Father." Many of us must confess that to address God as "Mother" may continue in this life to be something we have to work on. To alternate between masculine and feminine images of God is certainly not easy for all of us, and may not be helpful.

Concern over gender discrimination on the human level has caused far less controversy than concern for God-language. Perhaps the negatives noticed in regard to the former have more to do with an awkwardness in the language occasioned by some revisions, and the occasional experience of being disconcerted upon discovering that the words we are singing to a familiar hymn are not the words printed in the hymnal. Terms that have been understood generically, like "men" and "brothers" have been broken down into "men and women" and "brothers and sisters." The substitution of "widowed" for "widow" is probably painless for most people, but "parentless" for "fatherless"?

Hymns written and hymnals published since 1988 tend to reflect a concern for language that is deity-neuter (if not feminine) and people-inclusive. Some adjustments to the language of already existent hymns have been facile and painless. Others have compromised the theology and sometimes the poetry of hymns. Some of the hymns of Brian Wren move further than any others I have seen in addressing and referring to God as Mother. Perhaps the furthest in reflecting contemporary linguistic concerns that any hymnal has gone is to be found in *The New Century Hymnal* (1995) of the United Church of Christ.[4]

As for gendering of nongendered entities, "The Church's One Foundation" is a good example. The church, as in Ephesians 5:22–33, is the "holy bride," sought and bought by "Jesus Christ her Lord." Another example is "I Love Thy Kingdom, Lord," inspired by Psalm 137, and borrowing language from Deuteronomy 32:10; Isaiah 49:16, and other passages. Here again the church is viewed as feminine.

Other sensitive linguistic areas

References to color or shading ("black," "dark," and "white") raise questions in a few songs. One of the best known is Fanny Crosby's "Though Your Sins Be as Scarlet" (Isa. 1:18 in King James Version; see also Ps. 51).

References to handicapping conditions constitute yet another concern. How are people who are unable to stand likely to react to "Stand Up, Stand Up for Jesus"? Perhaps no hymnic reference in this category has had so much attention focused on it as one of the seventeen stanzas of Charles Wesley's signature hymn, "O for a Thousand Tongues to Sing":

> Hear him, ye deaf, his praise, ye dumb,
> Your loosened tongues employ;
> Ye blind, behold your Savior come,
> And leap, ye lame, for joy.

One approach taken by hymnal preparation committees to such references is simply to omit them. If included in the hymnal and not omitted in the service, such a reference may be understood: a) as referring to the future completion of redemption, as in the underlying biblical passage, Isaiah 35:5–6; b) by charismatics as a reference to promised healing in the present; and c) spiritually, as in the "was blind, but now I see" of "Amazing Grace."

After twenty or more years of attempting to raise the consciousness level of society to linguistic discrimination, it is easy to understand that some advocates may be disappointed at the apparently meager results, even within the church.[5] Some might say that it is not in the real world, but only in the church and academia (and by no means everyone, not every woman, even in these two realms) that anyone gets exercised about linguistic gender discrimination. But then the church, at least, is just the institution that we might expect to bend over backward not to hurt anyone—even by words. Whatever side we come down on in the ongoing discussion, it is at least a good thing that our sensitivity level with regard to language has been raised. Time will tell which of these concerns and solutions have been judged to have merit. Meanwhile, most hymnwriters who hope to have their work published are exercising care, as are the committees charged with preparation of hymnals.

Dare We Alter What Others Have Written?

In many—perhaps most—hymnals published in the twentieth century, we can find on some pages the abbreviation "alt.," indicating that the original text of the hymn has been altered to give us the text on the page. That this should in some cases take place without the consent of the deceased author strikes many as downright dishonest. Let us note that we are talking here only about such hymns as are no longer under copyright. We have no word from heaven on this, but here are some considerations, if not proof of the rightness of altering hymns, at least reasons why they are altered:

1) There is a very long history of precedents, not only with respect to hymns, but also the psalms of the Old Testament, some of which appear to have undergone alteration (before they were gathered into our canon of the Old Testament) to make them appropriate for the worship of the assembly. Mary's Magnificat (Lk. 1:46–55) is in very large measure an adaptation of Hannah's song (1 Sam. 2:1–10). Likewise, the songs of Zechariah (Lk. 1:68–79) and Simeon (Lk. 2:29–32) are pastiches made from a far older coinage of worship. Likewise the songs found in Revelation. New Testament writers relate the people and events in their writing to types they find in the Old Testament; historical material (such as the exodus and the wilderness motif) is recycled. In the Middle

Ages, Trinitarian doxologies were added to the individual psalms
of the Old Testament.

2) Sooner or later, all intellectual property becomes community
   property. Hymns that survive will continue to be altered to
   express the faith of succeeding generations.

3) Every psalm, and every hymn that is a translation from another
   language, involves alteration.

4) Some alterations are made to undo previous alterations in order
   to recover the original.

5) In some cases we do not know what the original text was.

6) Many of our hymns did not start life as hymns, but as poems
   with lines that had to be omitted or rearranged if they were to
   serve as hymns.

7) Many older hymns are simply too long for today's congregations.

8) No language remains forever the same; changes can be made
   precisely out of respect for the intent of the author.

9) Some words of the original language may offend—"black,"
   "white," "dark," "deaf," and others.

10) Some hymns are altered for theological reasons. Faber's "Faith of
    Our Fathers" in the original includes a stanza expressing the
    conviction that Mary's prayers will result in England's being
    won again for Rome.

11) Sometimes singing the text to a certain tune makes alteration
    advisable. For instance, if we sing "Jesus Shall Reign" to DUKE
    STREET, the "pe" in "peculiar honors" receives an unfortunate
    stress, but not if we make the slight change in the text to

"honors peculiar." (And, while we are altering, what about "peculiar"?) Another example: Changing "Hail to the Lord's Anointed" to "All Hail to God's Anointed," when sung to the tune ROCKPORT, allows us to stress the word that should be stressed, not "to," but "hail."

12) A number of hymns whose texts may or may not have undergone alteration are in any case sung with tunes other than those for which the hymnists wrote. A good number of hymns have been altered by adding a refrain.

13) Not only texts, but tunes have also undergone alteration—by change of key or rhythm or by shortening or by lengthening, for instance.

Some hymns' shelf life has expired. Sometimes it is better not to attempt revision, but rather to replace. Martin Luther, speaking in the pre-copyright era, understood that, ultimately, the church's songs are the patrimony of the whole church:

> St. Ambrose composed many hymns of the church. They are called church hymns because the church accepted them and sings them just as though the church had written them and as though they were the church's songs. Therefore it is not customary to say, "Thus sings Ambrose, Gregory, Prudentius, Sedulius," but "Thus sings the Christian church." For these are now the songs of the church, which Ambrose, Sedulius, *et al.* sing with the church and the church with them. When they die, the church survives them and keeps on singing their songs. (*Works* 15.274)

The profound truth of these words informs the efforts of the church in every age to claim for itself the songs of the saints who have preceded us, even if this means making some adjustments to them. The process of revision of the church's songs is an aspect of the hymnological implementation of the church's belief in the communion of the saints.

The Rise and Fall of "Amen"

In hymnals published in the last two decades or so of the twentieth century, some have seen what they considered to be an unforgivable alteration: the omission of "amen" at the end of most hymns. Truth does not always triumph over prejudice, but here are the facts:

1) The only hymns that originally had "amen" associated with them were those relatively few that included it as part of the text of the hymn (not an appendage).

2) Hymns did not originally have the word "amen" appended. To attach the "amen" is relatively newfangled.

3) In the late nineteenth century, editors of hymnals in Great Britain began to append the word to hymns, being inspired by the "amen" that was part of the Trinitarian Doxology that had been added to psalms and hymns as early as the Middle Ages.

4) Subsequently, hymnal editors in North America followed suit. The first hymnal in my denomination to adopt the practice was published in 1927. Not all North American hymnal editors adopted the practice. Some who did used the "amen" selectively.

5) The appending of "amen" to all the hymns was done only in English-language hymnals and such others as had been influenced by English-speaking missionaries.

6) The effect of singing the usual (plagal) "amen" at the end of a hymn is in nearly all cases anticlimactic, often deadening. In many cases, it is contrary to the spirit of what has been sung. Try it at the end of "Joy to the World!"

The abolition of the obligatory "amen" at the end of every song is a distinct gain. If the hymnal you are using gives them, and it be resolved not to sing them, the congregation should be informed of this decision and the reasons for it.

THE TUNES WE SING

∽

Two Kinds: Folk and Composed

The kind of tune that people find easiest to sing is a folk tune—a tune that came into being without benefit of any composer known to us, and which has come down to us (to a certain point) through oral, rather than written, tradition.[6] People in North America instinctively feel comfortable on hearing a folk tune for the first time, even if it comes from seventeenth-century Scotland or Germany. Our folk tradition thus is quite large—relatively extensive as to both geographical and chronological origins.

Church authorities have at times disdained folk tunes. Happily, the twentieth century brought a renewed appreciation for this music of the people—first, in the English-speaking world, in Great Britain. In 1940, my denomination published a collection of just over three hundred songs that gave me my first-ever acquaintance with FOREST GREEN, SLANE, LLANGOFFAN, and other old tunes from the British Isles. Subsequently, the lovely and appealing tunes from our own Southern Uplands have made their way into the hymnals of most communions. Tunes such as BEACH SPRING, DOVE OF PEACE, and RESIGNATION have been welcomed by modern-day worshipers; composers have also arranged many of them for keyboard. And where would "Amazing Grace" be on the charts if it were not now married to the Appalachian tune NEW BRITAIN? In the same period, folk tunes of African Americans found their way into the collections of many communions. Many of the "global songs" now being imported into North America are of folk origin.

Normally, folk tunes to which hymn texts are set are tunes no longer in use with secular texts. The familiar LONDONDERRY AIR is one folk melody, however, that has been married to at least two different hymns. This practice is questioned by many, though, for hearing a well-known tune brings to mind the secular song for which the tune is used, in this case, "O Danny Boy."

The other kind of tune, looked at from the standpoint of origins, is the composed tune. We do not always know the name of the composer. In any case, the composed hymn tune is as easily identified by the untrained as is the folk hymn tune. "It *sounds* like a hymn." We sing "Holy, Holy, Holy! Lord God Almighty!" to the stately tune NICAEA. This tune was composed specifically for this text by the Englishman John B. Dykes. Only a few tunes were written by world-class composers to serve as psalm or hymn tunes. The tune SINE NOMINE, by Ralph Vaughan Williams, and matched, albeit imperfectly, with "For All the Saints" is one such. A few tunes now married to hymns were composed for other purposes, and were subsequently adapted for use in church; from Beethoven's Ninth Symphony comes the joyful tune to which we sing "Joyful, Joyful, We Adore Thee." (The tune *was* written for a hymn, though not one to be sung in church: Schiller's "Ode to Joy.") Though the twentieth century witnessed a large increase in the number of folk tunes employed in the church, current North American hymnals still contain far more composed tunes than folk.

Now, singing unfamiliar folk tunes is generally easier for us than singing unfamiliar composed songs. " . . . while all kinds of music can be used in worship by choirs or organists or other instrumentalists as long as it is broken to word and sacrament, at the central locus of the people's song a folk idiom is required or the people can't sing" (Westermeyer 2005, 302). It is, however, a very wonderful thing that our repertory need not be confined to folk and folk-like songs. We can and do learn composed songs. As just remarked, they make up the largest part of our repertory. And we can add to that stock all through life. The tunes we sing in church, thus, are both folk and composed. "This is the music we need in our churches: authentic folk music along with composed music that combines idea, craft, and communicative power, songs that capture our language, concerns, and 'accumulated emotion'" (Parker 1991, 25).

While folk and folk-like tunes sound "down home" to our ears, most of those we encounter in our hymnals are not, in fact, tunes we have heard outside the church. Thus we may recognize even the folk music we hear in church as different from music we hear outside the church. Should church music be different from secular? Music is music, as we noted in chapter 1, and there is no inherently religious music or any inherently secular music. By a process of association, however, some music in our culture will sound to us like church music, and some will not. Of course, church music does not all sound the same; some of it will not sound to us like our kind of church music; but at least a very large part of it still sounds to us like somebody's church music.[7]

Does the vernacular principle mean that we should, for the church's worship service, seek music that sounds the same as any other music common to our particular culture? Church authorities have not demonstrated complete agreement on this matter, but in general they have leaned toward favoring the proposition that there be at least a modicum of distinctiveness about the music used in church.[8] It is precisely here, however, that what is generally termed contemporary Christian music parts company with the musical tradition of the church. Except for the lyrics, the music of a pop-style duo in church sounds, intentionally, just like the music of a pop-style duo performing outside the church.

What Is a Good Tune?

By what criteria shall we judge the music we use in church? To take an aesthetic approach to answering this question is surely tempting for some of us: Is this music tasteful? One word used in this connection is "integrity." Does the music have integrity? Or we may read, "God does not need for the music to be good, but we do." Or "Only artistically sound music will be effective in the long run," and judgment "should be made by competent musicians" (*Music in Catholic Worship* [American bishops, 1972], 26, cited in Carvey 1999, 19). In a similar vein, Alice Parker writes:

> The situation in many churches where it is counted democratic to let anyone influence the music program is an absurdity. We don't let the church plumbing or counseling be handled by people with no experience in the field. Why should music be different? (1991, 34)

Competent musicians, especially, will employ some standards in their judging the fitness of music for worship. What standards will these be?[9]

I have already more than shown my hand in this: Good church music is music that accomplishes those good things mentioned in chapter 2. (Aesthetic criteria as ultimate are rejected.) Good church music is music

that *works*. This is an altogether pragmatic view of the subject. With respect
to congregational song, this view implies first and foremost that the music
be singable, not just by a choir, but by a congregation. We can break this
down a bit:

1) Melody should be memorable, involving a sequential development
   of a satisfying musical idea, thus not just catchy, but one that
   grows on us. "The listener must *want* to commit a tune to memory,
   and provoking that desire is a responsibility of the composer"
   (Calvin Hampton, cited by Schulz-Widmar 1985, 206);

2) Maximum range should not exceed an octave, more or less, from
   middle C to the C above it; if the tune does go above this range,
   it should not remain there very long;

3) Rhythm should not be overly complex;

4) Any leaps (big intervals) between notes should be within the
   chord;

5) Some North American worshipers are more likely to prefer
   music written in a major key over that written in a minor key or
   one of the ancient modes. Any atonality or excessive dissonance
   in music should be given to the choir, not the congregation;

6) The repetition of a musical phrase—once or even twice—makes
   a tune less demanding. Thus a four-line hymn might have
   identical first, second, and fourth lines, only the third being
   different. (A tune whose first and second lines are the same,
   followed by a third line that is different, is a tune in what is
   called bar form [from the German *Barform*, and having no
   relation whatever to a saloon!]. There are many such tunes.)

7) An ideal tune is one that, among other things, we feel when we
   first meet it that we have known all along. It seems natural to us.
   This is sometimes called "pre-hearing."

A good hymn tune is one that can be sung by ear after two or three hearings; it is one in which, without too much musical sophistication, the singer can "hear" the next note coming . . . . In 1946, C. S. Lewis wrote: "The door is low, and we must stoop to enter it." (Routley 1985, 9)

In an effort to make tunes simpler even than they originally were, many tunes were, in the course of time, "ironed out" (or "flattened out"), that is, notes that were of different value have been made the same. This procedure has also resulted in tunes that are less interesting. (See if you can find a copy of the tune for "A Mighty Fortress Is Our God," for instance, that gives the original rhythm, and compare it with the rhythm most often followed today. The tune OLD HUNDREDTH furnishes another example.)

Hymnals normally contain tunes of varying degrees of difficulty. A musician can help the pastor determine the relative difficulty of a given hymn. It is important to take such into account when selecting hymns for a service. Some hymns may be best left for a choir. A good hymnal will offer a variety of music, and every text will be matched with a suitable tune; this means that the meter, the accent, and the mood of the tune correspond with those of the text. Preferences within a congregation vary; the music should aim at the broad middle.[10]

Sing Just the Tune?

When singing a song with the congregation, do you like to sing one of the voice parts that are below the melody? The majority of hymnals and Psalters published in North America give us music that is written for all four voices for most of the songs. Perhaps you have had to listen to someone complain about the fact that your hymnal gave only the tune for a particular song, and the complainant likes to sing the bass part. Perhaps you, like me, enjoy singing one of the parts below the melody, and you also are at least a little bit unhappy that there is a trend just now for hymnals to present more songs that are to be sung not in parts, but in unison (or unison octaves, if both upper and lower voices are singing). Even though some of the proponents of unison-only singing would like for it to happen, I do not see—or hear—a revolution taking place in this regard. But perhaps congregational song in North America is evolving in that direction. The considerations given here may prepare you better to answer the next complainant. They might also even convert you into a revolutionary!

Sing all the parts (harmonize)

This would normally mean that one or more singers in the assembly would sing the tune (melody), and one or more singers would sing each of the other three parts below the tune, that is: alto, tenor, or bass.

1) This gives everyone a greater opportunity to sing in a comfortable range of pitch. Especially as we grow older, it becomes harder to hit the high notes, and it takes more energy. An older woman thus may find it easier to sing the alto part than the melody.

2) For the musically trained in the congregation, singing in harmony does add a wee bit of sophistication to congregational song.

3) Some argue that part-singing makes us more aware of others (some of whom are singing different parts) in the assembly than does unison singing.

4) Harmonizing is fun. (I totally agree.)

All sing only the tune (sing in unison)

1) Part-singing by the congregation is a relatively recent development. Throughout the history of the church, unison song has been far more prevalent, and in many parts of the church still is. The earliest song of the church was solo or unison. The church's ancient chant is unison. The reformers' congregations might harmonize all they pleased in their homes, but in church sang only in unison.

2) Singing a part, especially the tenor or alto, can easily confuse the less musical persons standing nearby.

3) Unison singing also means that the song of the congregation appears to outsiders as less of an in-group phenomenon.

4) By all singing the melody only, we can reinforce one another.

5) Focusing on the melody enables us better to give attention to the words of the song. Do you remember what was said in the first chapter about music's hermeneutical role in the service of the Word? Except in those of our songs in which the rhythmic component is very strong, it is the melody that most often does the hermeneutical heavy lifting. Remember that what we match with the text is, above all else, the melody, the tune. To paraphrase George Herbert: "But, above all, the tune must bear the longest part." Or, in the words of Alice Parker: "The first things are melody, melody, melody" (1991, 52). A century earlier, Ralph Vaughan Williams had affirmed the same (in the preface to the *English Hymnal* of 1906): "In any case the congregation must always sing the melody and the melody only" (perhaps so that organists might improvise?).

6) Some people do get some help in singing a tune that is not overly familiar by following the ups and downs of the music printed on the page. They find this easier to do if only the melody line is printed, or if it is separated out.

7) The hymnal will weigh less, use fewer resources, and be cheaper to produce if, in its pew editions, only the tunes are printed with the texts.

8) The composer, not being restricted by having to write three voice parts below the tune, can allow his or her creativity free range in creating the accompaniment for the melody.

9) It is the melody that we carry away from worship and that we store in our memory banks.

10) A number of persons have seen unison singing as emblematic of
    the church's oneness, and in other ways particularly appropriate
    for the Christian community. One such was the German martyr
    Dietrich Bonhoeffer (1906–1945), who wrote, in his *Life Together*:

> The purity of unison singing, the simplicity and frugality, the
> humanness and warmth of this way of singing is the essence of all
> congregational singing. . . . Unison singing, difficult as it is, is less of
> a musical than a spiritual matter. Only where each person in the
> group is disposed to an attitude of worship and discipline can unison
> singing give us the joy which is peculiar to it alone.

COLLECTIONS

~

Finding Our Way Around in a Hymnal

A collection or anthology of songs for the congregation to sing is
called a hymnal or hymnbook. Hymnals currently used in North America
include about six hundred songs, more or less, but a few give more—even
up to a thousand or so. A hymnal supplement will contain a far smaller
number of songs, as will collections aimed at a particular population—
youth, for instance. Hymnals are published by denominations,
parachurch organizations, commercial publishers, and individuals.

No one getting a hymnal together today will simply put the songs in
willy-nilly, but always in a certain order, according to the topics or emphases
of the respective hymns. No two hymnals are alike in this regard. There is
one feature, however, that tends to put a hymnal in one camp or another with
respect to order—the church year. Hymnals published for fixed-liturgy
churches will have a good number of hymns placed together in the order of
the church year. This particular arrangement is absent from hymnals
published for free-liturgy churches. (Many of the same hymns, however, may
be found in the same sequence in these latter hymnals in a section devoted
to the life of Christ.)

In any case, all hymnals follow a logical sequence in their ordering of the songs they include. The order varies considerably from one hymnal to another. What matters is that you familiarize yourself with the rationale followed in the hymnal you use. You can see the organizational chart for your hymnal in the table of contents near the front of the book. From it you can move directly to that portion of the hymnal that gives songs dealing with any particular topic you have in mind.

If you have the name of a particular hymn in mind, it is easy to look in the indexes in the hymnal (now usually in the rear) and find the appropriate number. What we may have in mind, however, is not one particular hymn, but a certain topic—suffering, for example—and we want to look at all the songs that a hymnal contains that deal with that topic. Turning to the topical index in the rear of the hymnal, we can find an entry for "suffering" (or for some word with similar meaning); there we shall find numbers for such hymns. The topical index is more detailed than the table of contents, listing many rubrics that are not found in the table of contents.

Indexes commonly found in North American hymnals today include those of:

- First Lines and Common Titles: This is the index you will most often use.

- Topical: Consult to find songs dealing with this topic or that.

- Scriptural Allusions: When you want a song especially appropriate in connection with a specific passage of Scripture.

- Metrical: Useful for matching texts with tunes other than those to which they are set in your hymnal.

- Tunes/Tune Names: You cannot remember the name of the hymn, but you can remember the name of the tune to which the text is set. So look in the tune or tune names index to find where that tune occurs, and voilà! You will see all the numbers where that tune may be found.

- Composers, Arrangers, and Sources: Tells you who composed and/or arranged every song, or in what collection it is to be found. Both this and the following kind of index may serve in the same way as does the tune names index: to help you find a hymn whose title you have forgotten but whose composer or author you remember.

- Authors, Translators, and Sources: Information relative to the texts of the songs.

Most hymnals contain some service music. Hymnals prepared for fixed-liturgy churches often contain not only more service music, but also liturgical forms—materials for worship. A few denominational hymnals include doctrinal standards. Some give selections of Scripture, usually arranged to be read responsively. Currently, only a very few hymnals in North America have a section for psalms distinct from the body of hymns.

How Many Hymnals?

C. J. McNaspy calls our attention to people's surprising degree of dependence on the use of only one familiar collection; people feel more secure if they are asked to sing from the one hymnal to which they are accustomed (1991, 76). How many collections of hymns should a church use in its principal worship space? From the standpoint of simplicity, space limitations, avoiding a cluttered look, economy, and the goal of developing a core repertory of congregational song, there is much to be said for using only one hymnal in the congregation's primary worship space. Several denominations have published supplements for their own hymnals. There is indeed a steady flow of new texts and tunes available—long before the likely publication of a new hymnal that might include any of them. A supplement is one way to deal with this period between hymnals. Gordon Truitt advises, however, apparently sharing my own concerns, that a church should add a supplement to its basic collection only when absolutely necessary (1991, 95). Having a supplement available for occasional use, however, need not lead to supplanting our standard repertory.

Some of the same criteria used in selecting a hymnal apply to the choice of a supplement, though obviously not all.

Included in all good hymnals are many standard hymns that are appropriate for children and youth—from the standpoints both of appeal and accessibility—perhaps indicated to be such. Children who learn these hymns can immediately join with their parents and others in singing them in the worship service. As discussed previously, children have long assisted the adults in learning new music. They also acquire a treasure from which they can draw all their life long. (Would that I had learned lifelong hymns like "Now Thank We All Our God," instead of "Follow the Gleam" and "Ivory Palaces"! These latter two were in our denominational hymnal for youth.) Worthy collections of songs for children and for youth are available. (See "Choristers Guild," in chapter 11, under Useful Resources.) Literature used in Sunday school and in vacation Bible school often comes with songs. All such should be evaluated by the clergy and musician. There is a place, of course, for the occasional throwaway song or chorus, in which not too much time need be invested.

In many churches, it seems to be the case that there are two areas in which the leadership of the church exercises no responsibility in the choice of hymnals: adult Sunday school classes, and gatherings of the congregation on Sunday evenings and midweek, often in venues outside the primary worship space. Sometimes the most recent former hymnal is used in these settings. This may help smooth the transition to a new hymnal. In many other cases, a hymnal rather different from the congregation's primary hymnal is used. "Let the people sing what *they* want to sing." Such gatherings are sometimes thought of as times of "Informal Worship." Does it matter what people sing on such occasions? Is it all right for people to sing at such times words that for them are not true? In my youth our congregation would, on Sunday and Wednesday evenings, sing songs like "Love Lifted Me," whose lyrics certainly did not correspond with the spiritual journey of many present, if of any at all. This might seem to be a moot question for many congregations, since they do not gather on Sunday and Wednesday evenings. The question is not moot, however, for not being able to sing such songs in informal, evening gatherings, some old-timers urge their inclusion in Sunday morning fare.

In many churches, while the choice of the hymnal for the worship service is determined by the pastor and governing board, in consultation with the musicians, the choice of hymnals for use in other settings is very often left to other parties. Here too, those charged with leading the congregation surely have a responsibility.

Choosing the Best Hymnal for Your Church

Perhaps switching hymnals is the furthest thing from your mind. In no case is consideration of such a change to be taken lightly; people very often have a great deal invested in a particular hymnal—more than they may realize. Switching to a different collection may have negative effects on your efforts to develop within your congregation a core repertory of song that people are over the course of time making their very own. It may be that what would benefit your congregation's song far more than a new hymnal is harder work of pastor and musician with your present collection. On the other hand, it may be that a new hymnal would be of great benefit to the song of your congregation. If the hymnal you currently use has been in service for twenty or more years, or if it was a poor choice at the outset, then you should at least consider whether the time has not come for a change. Pastors and musicians should think and pray about it, and talk it over among themselves. Keep the discussion confidential unless and until you plan to proceed and the plan has been approved by your governing body. If after due consideration, you resolve to go forward, by all means consult "Choosing the Best Hymnal for Your Church," listed in Online Resources, which also deals with the crucial matter of how a new hymnal is best introduced.

– Useful Resources –

Louis F. Benson, *The Hymnody of the Christian Church* (Richmond: John Knox Press, 1956). A reprint of 1927 edition. See pages 122, 152–55, 195–220 on revision.

Donald G. Bloesch, *The Battle of the Trinity: The Debate over Inclusive God Language* (Ann Arbor: Servant Books, 1985).

Horace C. Boyer, *The Golden Age of Gospel* (Urbana and Chicago: University of Illinois Press, 2000).

Harry Eskew and Hugh T. McElrath, *Sing With Understanding: An Introduction to Christian Hymnody,* 2nd ed. (Nashville: Church Street Press, 1995).

David Jasper and R. C. D. Jasper, eds., *Language and the Worship of the Church* (New York: St. Martin's Press, 1990).

Austin C. Lovelace, *The Anatomy of Hymnody* (Chicago: G. I. A. Publications, 1982). A unique aid to better understanding the relation of a specific poetic meter to the ethos of the songs in which it is found. Reprint of the 1965 edition.

Erik Routley, *The Music of Christian Hymns* (Chicago: G. I. A. Publications, 1981).

Erik Routley, *A Panorama of Christian Hymnody* (Chicago: GIA Publications, 2005). An edited and expanded version by Paul A. Richardson of the original 1979 work.

Erik Routley, *An English Speaking Hymnal Guide* (Chicago: GIA Publications, 2005). An updated version by Peter W. Cutts of the original work published in 1979 and republished in 1984.

S. Paul Schilling, *The Faith We Sing: How the Message of Hymns Can Enhance Our Faith* (Philadelphia: Westminster Press, 1983). Pages 213–28 deal with the subject of inclusive language.

Jon Michael Spencer, *Protest and Praise: Sacred Music of Black Religion* (Minneapolis: Augsburg Fortress, 1997).

James R. Sydnor, *Hymns and Their Uses* (Carol Stream, IL: AGAPE, 1982), 23–45.

James R. Sydnor, *Hymns: A Congregational Study* (Carol Stream, IL: AGAPE, 1983).

Robin Knowles Wallace, *Moving Toward Emancipatory Language: A Study of Recent Hymns* (Lanham, MD: Scarecrow Press, 1999).

J. R. Watson, *The English Hymn: A Critical and Historical Study* (Oxford: Clarendon Press, 1997).

Paul Westermeyer, *Let the People Sing: Hymn Tunes in Perspective* (Chicago: GIA Publications, 2005).

John Wilson, "Looking at Hymn-Tunes: The Objective Factors," in Young, ed. (1985), 123–52. Also issued as "Occasional Paper" of The Hymn Society of Great Britain and Ireland, Second Series No. 1, June 1991.

Brian Wren, *What Language Shall I Borrow? God-Talk in Worship: A Male Response to Feminist Theology* (New York: Crossroad Publishing Company, 1989).

Carlton R. Young, *My Great Redeemer's Praise* (Akron, OH: OSL Publications, 1995), 129–36.

CHAPTER
FIVE

WHAT IS THERE TO SING?
THE CHURCH'S VAST REPERTORY OF SONG

~

Our focus in this chapter will be on the song of the church's "first choir," the song of the congregation. That repertory is as varied as it is large. The apostle's "psalms, hymns, and spiritual songs," while not a guide for dividing within the church's song according to genres—then, or now—can at least be seen as a hint as to the scope and variety of the church's repertory of song in every age.

THE CHURCH SINGS SCRIPTURE

~

The Psalms: From the Reformation to Today

John Calvin's years-long efforts to provide his converts songs for the worship service culminated in the Geneva Psalter[1] of 1562. This landmark collection of texts and tunes gave the metered (for the meaning of "meter," see appendix), rhymed versions of the complete texts of the 150 psalms, the Song of Simeon, and the Ten Commandments—in the French language. There is no evidence that Calvin or his early successors ever made a law of the principle of singing only Scripture in the worship service. The reformer did maintain, however, that when it was Scripture that was sung, we could be certain that God had "put the words in our mouths" ("Letter to the Reader," in the "Preface to the Psalter" of 1543).

The reformation of the English-speaking church, just as that of the church on the continent of Europe, returned to the congregation (in that part of the church that had become Protestant) the duty and privilege of song in the worship service. The reformed church in the British Isles might have followed Luther, and begun singing not only psalms, but hymns as well. It was the view of John Calvin, however, that was adopted: Anglican and Presbyterian congregations alike would sing not fresh hymns, but ancient Scripture. They would thus continue the ancient tradition of the Benedictine monks—pretty much restricting their singing in the worship service to only the psalms of the Old Testament and the Gospel canticles. Unlike the Benedictines, however, who chanted Latin versions of the texts of the psalms themselves, English-speaking Protestants would sing the psalms in restructured, metered, rhymed, vernacular versions. (In what follows, I shall mainly use the word "psalms," for it was the psalms that constituted the bulk of what was sung.)

The production of metered, rhymed English translations of the Hebrew psalms became the next thing to a cottage industry. In contrast to the enduring quality of Calvin's Geneva psalms in the French language, no single English-language Psalter ever took the field for long—excepting the Scottish Psalter of 1650, which continued in service into modern times. Between 1414 and 1890, more than 350 partial or complete Psalters saw the light of day in England, Scotland, and North America. The two most influential in England were what came to be called the "Old Version," the work of Thomas Sternhold and John Hopkins and others (1562); and the "New Version," published by Nahum Tate and Nicholas Brady in 1696. The first book of any kind printed in British North America was the *Bay Psalm Book*, at Cambridge, Massachusetts in 1640.

It was the polymath English Dissenter Isaac Watts (1674–1748) who radically changed this course of congregational song in the English-speaking world. Watts put forth his principles thus: 1) The church is not under obligation to sing only the Bible. On the contrary, Christian praise must go beyond the Bible to include the church's own expressions of devotion and thanksgiving; 2) If the church is to use the psalms in Christian worship, they must be "Christianized."[2] The first of these principles led to the publication of Watts's own hymns in 1705 and 1707. Implementation of the second resulted in an updating of the Psalter for Christians of eighteenth-century England and North America, *The Psalms of David Imitated in the Language of the New Testament* (1719).[3] Thus did Watts begin to steer the English-speaking Protestant church back to the original, inclusive repertory of song, the position taken also by Martin Luther almost two centuries earlier.

Watts's *The Psalms of David Imitated* was first reprinted in North America by Benjamin Franklin in 1729, at Philadelphia. Whether to use Watts or some other version of the psalms came to be a source of great controversy in some denominations. A metrical, rhyming, English version of the psalms that is faithful to the original Hebrew text was and is impossible to achieve. Whatever degree of faithfulness to the text they did manage to achieve, versifiers of the psalms often made rather rare use of the English language. Watts's versions of the psalms were, of course, quite free; the distinction between metrical psalms and psalm paraphrases became blurred. Watts believed, correctly I think, that some of the psalms (137, for instance) are better read as God's Word to us rather than sung as our praise to God. (A well-chosen tune, however, can sometimes lessen the difficulties felt in singing a problematic text.) Congregations were offered the option of singing the longer psalms piecemeal.

One of the blessings of exclusive psalmody was that it gave the congregation a fixed repertory of relatively short compass; nothing was to be added, nothing subtracted. The scope of the collection was small enough that, by singing nothing else in the worship service, people could, in a lifetime, make the texts and tunes their own. I have heard Dutch farm women singing the psalms from memory as they went about their domestic chores. I have seen how citations of the psalms abound in the writings of those theologians brought up on a diet of psalm singing. Psalm singing gave its practitioners a deep well from which they might draw great strength all their life long. The enduring nature of metrical psalmody was demonstrated in the interfaith service of prayer and remembrance at the National Cathedral in Washington, D.C., on September 14, 2001. That service included the singing of Watts's paraphrases of Psalms 23 ("My Shepherd Will Supply My Need") and 90 ("Our God, Our Help in Ages

Past"), and Luther's adaptation of Psalm 46—"A Mighty Fortress" (minus the second stanza). Watts's Psalm 90 was also sung by a choir at the service for the late Gerald R. Ford in the same venue.

But exclusive psalmody represents a deformation of the church's song, a departure from what seems to have been the original repertory that included Christian response to God's work in Christ. We know the early church (at least parts of it) not only sang the psalms of the Old Testament, but also produced hymns. Themes or occasions for the use of such new songs might have included the work of Christ, baptism, the Lord's Supper, and martyrdom. The New Testament itself incorporates, in whole or in part, what may have been some of the earliest such creations.[4] Our "O Gladsome Light" is a translation of a surviving hymn from the third century. To Ambrose (c. 340–397) are attributed a number of extant hymns, including our morning hymn, "O Splendor of God's Glory Bright." Moreover, the theology and ethics of some of the psalms raise questions that, however they may be answered in the classroom, cannot be addressed while the congregation is singing.

Most North American churches in the eighteenth and early nineteenth centuries gradually forsook exclusive psalmody for a congregational song that also included hymns. The titles of collections morphed from *Psalms and Hymns* to just *Hymns*. The number of psalms included in hymnals decreased. Those that remained gradually came to be treated as all other items in the collections, that is, as hymns.

The second half of the twentieth century ushered in a renewed interest in the psalms of the Old Testament, including their use in corporate worship. Lutheran and Episcopal churches had had available all along the psalms set for chanting (as had the Roman Catholic Church, though not for the congregation). The spread of the use of a lectionary to other denominations meant that a psalm or psalm portion was to be included in every Lord's Day service. A renewed interest in singing Scripture in general (not just the psalms) included churches and Christian groups that did not use a lectionary. Thus, once again, the congregation's repertory tends—in some denominations, but by no means in all—to include a portion of its most ancient song, the Psalms of the Old Testament. The texts of the psalms included in current collections manifest varying degrees of faithfulness to the original.[5] Worship planners who want to expose their congregations to the message of a particular psalm, and who wish to accomplish that through the singing of a metrical setting of that psalm, will want to examine the latter for its faithfulness and completeness.

To What Music May the Church Sing the Psalms?

Some form of chant

Chant, in its various forms, enables us to sing the words of psalms and other passages just as they are found in one of our translations of the Bible. Plainsong chant (referring most often to the repertory of Gregorian chant) is still the officially favored form of tune in the Roman Catholic Church. Though this ancient chant form is historically sung by unaccompanied, unison, male voices, a few plainsong tunes have been employed as congregational settings for hymns, for instance, "O Come, O Come, Emmanuel," and "Of the Father's Love Begotten." In such cases, all present sing the melody, while a keyboardist plays harmony.

Congregations today may chant the psalms in several ways:

1) "Psalm tone": The congregation sings a psalm that has been pointed (marked to indicate a change in the melody where so pointed), using one of a number of simple melodies (psalm tones) provided.

2) Responsorial: A soloist sings portions of the body of the pointed psalm, each portion being followed by a congregational response, perhaps using a familiar folk tune. The solo-response pattern was probably the principal way in which ancient Israel sang the psalms.

3) Anglican chant: This may be termed harmonized, accompanied plainsong. It consists of a seven- to ten-note melody, divided into two short phrases, to which the varying lengths of the words of the text are set. The reciting note (the first note in a phrase) can carry any number of syllables; the ensuing notes normally carry one each. Anglican chant is not easy to sing well; some authorities would leave it for choirs alone.

4) Responsorial after the Gelineau manner: Joseph Gelineau, in the mid-twentieth century, devised a very simple way of setting texts to simple tunes. His music and translation of the psalms are by many considered to capture the poetry of the Hebrew psalms better than any other means yet devised. The congregation, however, may find the print layout of Gelineau psalms confusing.

Melodies in all forms of chant tend to move within a relatively small pitch range, moving up or down by small steps. The number of musical notes for each syllable of text ranges—in congregational versions—from only one to five. The advantages of chant are not small. Chant recites the biblical text as is, rather than trying to make it rhyme and fit into a rigid metrical setting—a process in which both normal English language usage and fidelity to the sense of Scripture may be compromised. A psalm's poetic structure itself may provide clues to the interpretation of the psalm, and chant may better preserve that structure than would a metered version. Chant also places stress on the words, rather than the music. While some chant forms do give prominence to a soloist, the tendency of the reciting tone of the chant is to deemphasize the individual. May we say also that chanting injects a note of timelessness, of transcendence, into worship?

A metrical setting

In this case, the text of the psalm is made into a poem—the old-fashioned kind, with rhyme and meter. John Calvin and his musicians and poets did not invent the metrical setting, but Calvin adopted this form as his exclusive form of song for the church. It would be easier than chant for the common people to learn, he believed. We have seen that the church in Great Britain opted to sing just psalms with Calvin rather than psalms and hymns with Luther. Would the English and the Scots also sing Calvin's *tunes*? From Calvin's *Geneva Psalter* (1562) came what is probably the tune that has been sung more than any other in the whole world, what we today call OLD HUNDREDTH, to which we sing the Doxology. Though wildly popular elsewhere, however, only a handful of the 125 Geneva tunes made it into general usage in much of the English-speaking world. The British considered many of them, as they would the German chorale tunes, too long and wandering; the English-speaking church preferred tunes of only two lines, and in only one to three different meters—not 110! Some of the Geneva tunes that did make the transition were shortened. The Geneva tunes, moreover, were matched with the French language; fitting English words to them proved difficult and resulted in rather strange English.

Nevertheless, the psalm tunes that developed in Great Britain (ST. FLAVIAN, for instance) share certain characteristics with the Geneva tunes, and thus, to some extent, the plainsong melodies:

1) Avoid a beat; this helps distinguish church tunes from others, and minimizes any bodily movement that might result from music with stresses in the rhythm.

2) Keep things simple by employing only two note values. The beginning note is always the longer of the two, serving as a "gathering note" of sufficient duration for everyone to find the pitch (theoretically) and carry on together.

3) Tend to move step-wise (no great leaps up or down) and within a rather narrow range.

4) Are syllabic; that is, they provide one note for every syllable of text.

5) Maintain an overall flavor of the early tunes that is solemn, dignified, proper, and restrained.

Toward the end of the sixteenth century, the "common tune" appeared in Great Britain. Instead of singing a different (proper) tune for each psalm, one tune might be used for all psalms that were in the same meter. Thus many congregations got by with no more than a dozen very simple tunes. Probably the best known of these common tunes still in use today in North America is DUNDEE, to which we sing "God Moves in a Mysterious Way" and other texts. Many of the early psalm tunes in Britain are anonymous. Two highly gifted musicians who composed tunes for the psalms were Thomas Tallis, in the sixteenth century, and Orlando Gibbons, in the seventeenth. It was the less well known William Croft (1678–1727), however, who bequeathed to us the greatest of all British tunes, the stately melody, ST. ANNE, to which we sing Watts's Psalm 90: "Our God, Our Help in Ages Past."[6]

The period of composition of psalm tunes lasted in Great Britain for about two hundred years after the Reformation. Before the middle of the eighteenth century, there began the practice of setting psalms (and other biblical passages) to hymn tunes, from both Great Britain and Germany. Fresh translation of the Psalms in the twentieth century elicited the composition of a number of new tunes specifically for them. Also, some of the most appealing of the Geneva tunes for the Psalms were brought out of storage to be treasured by another generation—GENEVAN 25 and GENEVAN 47, for instance. (These tunes had remained in circulation all along in parts of Europe.) Some Geneva tunes were recirculated for use with hymns, the lovely RENDEZ À DIEU (the tune for Pss. 98 and 118 in the Geneva Psalter), for instance, to which we may sing, "Bread of the World in Mercy Broken" and other hymns.

The Church Sings Other Scripture

Though the psalms of the Old Testament constitute the lion's share of the Scripture that has been set to music and sung by the church, they have not had a monopoly. The canticles of both the Old and the New Testaments have through the centuries also been sung. Three of these have enjoyed a special prominence: the Song of Mary (the *Magnificat*, Lk. 1:46–55), the Song of Zechariah (the *Benedictus*, Lk. 1:68–79), and the Song of Simeon (the *Nunc Dimittis*, Lk. 2:29–32). Other passages of Scripture outside the Psalms have also been versified and set to music. Among the most widely used (formerly) of these are those known as the Scottish Paraphrases of the second half of the eighteenth century, consisting of thirty-two songs from the Old Testament and thirty-five from the New Testament. Already in the sixteenth century, the Ten Commandments (in an abbreviated form of the version found in Exod. 20) were sung and, from outside the biblical canon, the Apostles' Creed. (Some then believed it to have been written by the apostles.) Throughout the church today we may find in use many choruses and hymns that are settings of passages from Scripture.

THE CHURCH HAS A VAST AND EVER-EXPANDING STORE OF HYMNS TO SING

~

What Is a Hymn?

As noted in chapter 1, a good case can be made for understanding the word "hymn" to refer to both a text and the tune to which it is married—taken together. In what follows, however, I use the term in its more traditional sense, namely, a certain kind of text. The word "hymn" as used in this book may be understood to be a poem that:

1) Is of the lyrical variety; that is, a poem that by its very nature leads us to sing it;

2) ". . . expresses the worshipper's attitude toward God or God's purposes in human life" (Carl F. Price, in Eskew and McElrath 1995, 7);

3) Is divided into segments of equal length (strophes or stanzas), each to be sung to the same tune; there may be a refrain that is sung after each strophe;

4) Envisions being sung by a congregation.

The Old Testament psalms, in their metrical form, meet these qualifications; they constitute a particular category of hymn. It is helpful, however, to refer to the psalms as "psalms," in distinction from hymns. I use the word "song" to refer to either a psalm or a hymn. The word "hymn" may be heard by some today as "church-speak."

Some Milestones In the Evolution of an English-Language Hymnody

To attempt to outline the subject matter that follows is, among other things, an exercise in omission. It is also not just to risk oversimplification, but to court it. So let the reader beware: Things are more complicated than they may seem!

The English-speaking church was slow to develop a hymnody, and understandably so; Christians in Great Britain and many of those in North America had the psalms! Their canon of congregational song was, like that of the church's Scripture, complete, closed, and sufficient. (As late as the beginning of the twentieth century, there were more hymns in German than in English.) Already in the seventeenth century, however—before Watts—there were the beginnings of an English-language hymnody. Several gifted men wrote hymns or poems that were subsequently made into hymns: George Herbert, John Milton, Richard Baxter, Samuel Crossman, John Bunyan, and Thomas Ken. George Wither and the Baptist Benjamin Keach took pioneering steps toward expanding the congregation's repertory to include hymns.

The importance of Scripture for English-language congregational song did not cease when the church moved from singing only psalms to singing hymns also. The Psalter has been likened to "the womb" of the church's hymns. The hymns of Watts and his successors are replete with the thought, language, and imagery of the Bible. Just count the references to Scripture, even verbatim quotations, in one of Charles Wesley's hymns! Fast-forwarding to the work of two nineteenth-century hymn writers, compare the refrain of "For the Beauty of the Earth" with Psalm 106:1–2, and "Praise, My Soul, the King of Heaven" with Psalm 103.[7]

What follows below is a highly selective, oversimplified sampling of the mind-boggling vastness of English-language hymnody.

The glories of a sovereign God

It was, as noted earlier, Isaac Watts who opened the floodgates. Watts reacted early in life to both the theological and the literary defects of psalm singing as then practiced in the church. This Dissenter clergyman not only gave us immortal hymns such as "When I Survey the Wondrous Cross," but also psalm paraphrases such as "Jesus Shall Reign Where'er the Sun" (Ps. 72) and "Joy to the World" (Ps. 98). Watts was exceptionally gifted at choosing memorable phrases, and for compressing large amounts of thought into a very few words. He aimed to write so that the simplest person could understand. His hymns and psalm paraphrases did not need any new music; they could all be sung to already existent psalm tunes.

Ecstasy: The unfathomable love of Christ for the sinner

Watts's model of what a hymn should be inspired successors—Joseph Addison, Philip Doddridge, Anne Steele, and others. The next name comparable to that of Watts, however, is that of the brothers John and Charles Wesley. The younger, Charles, was the author of most of the hymns the brothers produced—more than six thousand! Crucially influenced by the warm piety of the Moravians, Charles Wesley added hymns about Christian experience and evangelical concern to Watts's Calvinistic hymns of objective wonder and praise. One example is "Love Divine, All Loves Excelling." Evangelical successors to the Wesleys included William Williams of Wales ("Guide Me, O Thou Great Jehovah"), John Cennick ("Children of the Heavenly King"), Thomas Olivers ("The God of Abraham Praise"—the longer of the two by this name), and Edward Peronnet ("All Hail the Power of Jesus' Name").

The ex-slaver-turned-Anglican clergyman, John Newton, who gave us "Amazing Grace," and the fragile poet William Cowper (pron. Cooper, "God Works in a Mysterious Way") together published one of the most influential collections in the history of English-language hymnody, *Olney Hymns* (1779). Somewhat apart from others in this camp was Augustus Toplady, whose "Rock of Ages, Cleft for Me" has long been a favorite. The Baptist John Fawcett is remembered for "Blest Be the Tie that Binds."

The Romantic Movement

The first half of the nineteenth century witnessed the influence of the Romantic Movement in hymnody. Reginald Heber, of "Holy! Holy! Holy!" fame, in the line of Watts, also gave us "From Greenland's Icy Mountains." James Montgomery ("Prayer is the Soul's Sincere Desire"), in the line of the

Wesleys, wrote "Hail to the Lord's Anointed," inspired by Psalm 72. These hymns of both Heber and Montgomery reflect the evangelical interest in missions—as well as the romance of faraway places and the beauty of nature.

The one ancient, holy, catholic church

Though hymns and hymns disguised as psalm paraphrases were being widely sung in England and Wales in the eighteenth century, producing and singing them was seen by the established church as a fringe movement. Only in 1820 did a British court clarify the status of hymns in the Anglican Church: They could be sung! Anglicans, both clergy and lay, increasingly began to take an interest in the hymnic enterprise. Hymns were needed to accompany the Book of Common Prayer. The Oxford (Cambridge was also very much involved) Movement, dating from 1833, sought to recover for the established church what its leaders perceived as having been lost at the Reformation. Reacting to the growth of evangelical influence, the Oxford Movement may be seen as a revival of the High Church Movement begun by Archbishop William Laud in about 1610. It was as a result of the Oxford Movement that the "High Church" or "Anglo-Catholic" wing of the Anglican Church came into being. In its infatuation with the Middle Ages (Gothic architecture, for instance), the movement shared in the romantic sentiment of the age. A flood of hymns celebrating the festival days of a bloated church calendar ensued. The movement's collective efforts eventuated in, among other things, the groundbreaking collection, *Hymns Ancient and Modern* (1861). The editors of *HA and M* arranged the collection's contents according to the order of the Prayer Book, to which the hymnal was intended as a companion. It was this hymnal that set the standard for ensuing collections, including the precedent of publishing texts with tunes that had been chosen specifically for them. (Of course, Calvin had insisted on this in the sixteenth century. German hymns were also married to their own particular tunes.)

To the Oxford reformers and members of their families we are indebted for an enormous number of our most beloved hymns, for instance, "Onward, Christian Soldiers," and "The Church's One Foundation." A female representative of the High Church wing of the Anglican Church is Cecil Frances Alexander, some of whose children's hymns (sung by adults as well) are still in common use, including "Once in David's Royal City," and "All Things Bright and Beautiful." In keeping with their purpose, members of the Oxford Movement not only wrote original hymns, but also through their work of translation (many times quite free) made a number of ancient Greek and a larger quantity of ancient Latin hymns available. The name of John Mason Neale (1818–1866) especially stands out in this regard; it was Neale who, beginning with a ninth-century Latin text, gave us the Palm Sunday hymn, "All Glory, Laud, and Honor." A number of Anglican clergy and laity moved all the ecclesiastical way to Roman Catholicism. Two of the best known were John Henry Newman ("Lead, Kindly Light") and Frederick W. Faber ("Faith of Our Fathers"—that is, in Faber's mind, the faith of our Roman Catholic fathers). It has to be admitted, not all of the reformers in Oxford and Cambridge were enthusiastic about the congregation singing. This movement that gave us so many hymns also set great store by choirs, and choirs often tended to usurp the musical role of the hymn singers—the congregation!

Hymns from the evangelical wing

At the other end of the spectrum that constitutes the Anglican Church is the Low Church, or Evangelical wing. The evangelicals were distinctively Protestant, and much influenced by Calvinism. Hymns written by those in this camp reflect an interest not in the institutional church, but in personal piety, the guidance of the Holy Spirit, missions, benevolent ministry, and propagation of the Bible. Examples are Henry Alford's "Come, Ye Thankful People, Come," and Arabella Katherine Hankey's "I Love to Tell the Story."

Hymns from those in the middle

Between the High and the Low wings of Anglicanism is the Broad Church, dating from about 1830. Its constituents held in common emphases of both extremes, but with less passion. Seeking modernization of theology, they were open to higher criticism of the Bible. Many of the Broad Church persuasion were passionately concerned with reforming the British society of their day; understandably, some of what they produced was short-lived. Two bishops in this camp who contributed enduring hymns were: William Walsham How ("For All the Saints, Who from

Their Labors Rest"), and John Ellerton ("Savior, Again to Thy Dear Name We Raise").

Persevering trust in a God who cares, passionate devotion to a crucified Christ

In the 1850s, English-language hymnody began to undertake another formidable acquisition—translations of some of the rich store of German hymns. Imagine a world in which we did not know "A Mighty Fortress," "Ah, Holy Jesus," and "Now Thank We All Our God"! Women led the way in this endeavor, the name of Catherine Winkworth being the most illustrious.

Hymns to meet more exacting standards

Dissatisfaction with the literary and musical quality of English-language hymnody at the end of the nineteenth century led to the publication of the *English Hymnal* in 1906. Purporting to give to the church "the best hymns in the English language," this collection, whose musical editor was Ralph

Williams, did indeed hold to high standards. (His first name is pronounced "Rafe" and his surname is Vaughan Williams.) Included were Henry Scott Holland's "Judge Eternal, Throned in Splendor," and Arthur C. Ainger's "God Is Working His Purpose Out," the latter set to an insistent, driving tune by the classical composer Martin Shaw.

North Americans can also write hymns

What could be the earliest (mid-seventeenth century) hymn written in North America comes from Canada, whose 1926 translation (and perhaps interpretation) of the French Christmas carol is known to us as "'Twas in the Moon of Wintertime." The original is attributed to a Jesuit missionary to the Huron people.

The transition in the English-speaking congregations in North America from exclusive psalmody to a repertory inclusive of both psalms and hymns was slow in coming. From the outset, the church in North America depended heavily on England for its congregational song.[8] In the nineteenth century, however, North American writers began to make their mark. Yale president Timothy Dwight paraphrased Psalm 137, a part of which we know as "I Love Thy Kingdom, Lord" (1800). Ray Palmer's "My Faith Looks up to Thee" (1830) continues to be well known and much loved. The church's mission to the colonially-organized world of the nineteenth century found a voice in G. W. Doane's "Fling Out the Banner! Let It Float" (1848). Two enduring, early twentieth-century contributions are Henry van Dyke's "Joyful, Joyful, We Adore Thee" (1907), and Harry Emerson Fosdick's "God of Grace and God of Glory" (1930). (The wonderful tunes to which they were matched have also contributed to their popularity.)

Seeking the lost

In the "gospel song," we have a distinctly North American contribution (though not one altogether without precedent[9]), and North America's largest. Its popularity was greatly enhanced by its use in Great Britain, in the American-led revivals of the preacher Dwight L. Moody and the musician Ira D. Sankey in the 1870s. Gospel song's roots lie in the slightly earlier American Sunday school songs, such as "He Leadeth Me" (1862). Furnishing even earlier forerunners than the Sunday school songs were the camp meeting songs—products of early nineteenth-century frontier revivalism. One such is the refrain added to the older English song, "On Jordan's Stormy Banks I Stand":

> I am bound for the promised land, I am bound for the promised land;
> O who will come and go with me? I am bound for the promised land.

The use of a refrain is virtually a standard feature of gospel song. Several individuals wrote large numbers of texts or tunes—in some cases both. By far the most prolific and successful writer of texts (some eight thousand!) for the Sunday school was the blind Fanny Crosby (Frances J. Van Alstyne, 1820–1915); her chief musical collaborator was Cincinnati businessman William Howard Doane. Among many other favorite songs of this genre is

Joseph M. Scriven's "What a Friend We Have in Jesus" (c. 1855). Many of these Sunday school songs were appropriated by the later nineteenth-century urban revivalists, and, together with more recent songs written explicitly for these mass meetings, came to be known as gospel hymns/songs. The text of gospel hymnody, like the tune, is simple, memorable, and calculated to have instant appeal for the most unsophisticated. The message is one of a salvation won by Christ on the cross, for which the singer praises God, and which the sinner is urged to receive now through personal faith in Christ.

Two of Fanny Crosby's explicitly evangelistic songs are "Pass Me Not, O Gentle Saviour" (1868), and "Rescue the Perishing" (1869). Thanks in no small part to the development of copyright law in the United States following the American Civil War, the publishing of gospel (as well as secular) songs became a commercial bonanza for several firms. Gospel songs became the stock in trade for North American missionaries, who carried them to all parts of the world.

Gospel song was created for a very specific purpose, and not intended for use in the worship of the congregation. Gospel song, when employed alone, does not provide a well-rounded diet, much of its focus being centered on an intimate relationship of the individual to God. Sentimentality (count the use of the word "sweet," for instance) pervades the genre. Many gospel songs manifest a concern, sometimes an urgent one, for personal evangelism. Whether to include gospel songs in the church's hymnals has often been controversial. Exclusion or inclusion of gospel hymnody was a defining characteristic of hymnals published in North America in the twentieth century, ranging across the spectrum from exclusion or near exclusion in the hymnals of fixed-liturgy churches to generous helpings in the collections published by free-liturgy churches and non-denominational publishers.[10]

This writer is happy for his congregation to have at its disposal some of the gospel songs—Crosby's "To God Be the Glory" (one of the very few hymns based on John 3:16! Written in 1875, it did not become popular until 1954, when sung in Billy Graham's London Crusade.), Edward Mote's "My Hope Is Built on Nothing Less" (c. 1834, a song set to at least seven different tunes, even including the grave German tune, VATER UNSER!) and, of much more recent (1923) gospel hymnody, Thomas O. Chisholm's "Great Is Thy Faithfulness," for instance.

As observed elsewhere, an awareness of the songs of the people of God in every age and place can help keep the church in any given period and place on course. What has gospel hymnody's emphasis on *taking* Christ *to* the world to say to the current emphasis in song and sermon on *seeking* Christ *in* the world? Are there emphases in gospel hymnody that may be traced to the perception on the part of their authors that such emphases were in short supply in the nineteenth-century church? What have gospel hymnody's notes of urgency and seriousness to say to the church today? Do gospel songs faithfully reflect the apostolic preaching found in the New Testament?

Refrains and Choruses

A refrain is very much appreciated by a congregation, especially when the hymn makes special demands, perhaps when it is long, unfamiliar, or text-intensive. A refrain lightens the load. When we have sung it once or twice, we can begin to ease up a bit on following what is printed in the hymnal and begin to listen more perceptively to our neighbors' voices; we can experience a heightened sense of "congregationalness" as we consciously, but naturally, seek to blend our voice with those of the others present.

Refrain or chorus? A refrain consists of a text and its music that recur after each stanza of a hymn, as "Yes, Jesus loves me" recurs after each stanza of "Jesus Loves Me, This I Know." A chorus is a short, freestanding song, most often of only one stanza, as the Taizé chorus, "Jesus, Remember Me." What was originally a chorus— "We're Marching to Zion," for instance—can become a refrain when added to a song; in this case added, in some collections, to "Come, We/Ye that Love the Lord." In common speech, we may hear a refrain called a chorus.

The God of liberal theology and the Social Gospel

The challenging "Once to Every Man and Nation" (1845) was taken from James Russell Lowell's long poem written in the face of the Mexican-American War. Though the North American Quaker, John G. Whittier, wrote very few, and not very successful, hymns (historically, most Quakers have not sung in their meetings), several of his poems have served well as hymns—the quietistic "Dear Lord and Father of Mankind" (1872) being perhaps the best known today. The Unitarian Frederick Lucian Hosmer's hymns include "'Thy Kingdom Come,' on Bended Knee" (1891). The Social Gospel of an earlier age still echoes in Washington Gladden's "O Master, Let Me Walk With Thee" (1879), and Frank Mason North's "Where Cross the Crowded Ways of Life" (1905). The emphasis on the universal brotherhood of man in a part of the church inspired Louis F. Benson's "The Light of God Is Falling" (1910), William Pierson Merrill's "Rise Up, O Men of God" (1911), and H. H. Tweedy's "Eternal God, Whose Power Upholds" (1929). From the Canadian R. B. Y. Scott we have "O Day of God, Draw Nigh" (1937).

The God of slaves and their descendants

The spirituals of the slaves in North America, however old they may be, were late getting into mainstream hymnody. Among those most often included today are "Go, Tell It on the Mountain," "Let Us Break Bread Together," and "Lord, I Want to Be a Christian." More recent well-known black gospel hymnists include Charles A. Tindley ("We'll Understand it Better By and By," c. 1906) and Thomas A. Dorsey ("Precious Lord, Take My Hand," 1938, set to Dorsey's adaptation of the nineteenth-century hymn tune MAITLAND).[11]

The God of "the Hymn Explosion"

After a relatively lean period of hymn writing in the first half of the twentieth century, the machinery of hymnic production began to whir full tilt once again in the 1960s in Great Britain, with what has been termed "the Hymn Explosion." Between that date and the turn of the century, a wealth of fresh hymns saw the light of day in Great Britain, North America, and elsewhere. Two of the best known of the new writers are the Methodist Fred Pratt Green (1903–2000, "When in Our Music God Is Glorified," 1972) and the United Reformed Brian Wren ("I Come with Joy to Meet My Lord," 1968)—both English clergymen, but the latter now resident in the United States.

The Hymn Explosion led, naturally, to a hymnal explosion, as denominations and independent publishers updated their offerings. Leading the way was the *Lutheran Book of Worship* of 1978. (Its successor, *Evangelical Lutheran Worship*, was published in the fall of 2006 in both print and electronic formats.) There appears to be no slackening in the production of new hymns. It normally takes years for a new hymn to work its way into hymnals (if it ever does), but in the meantime countless new hymns are available in published hymnal supplements and in collections featuring individual writers.

The concerns of hymnal preparation committees extend not only to deciding which new songs to include in the projected collection; the collection to be replaced probably does not contain some older songs and older kinds of songs that the current committee thinks should be in the new hymnal. My denomination's 1990 hymnal, for instance, reaches all the way back to 1664 for Samuel Crossman's lovely "My Song Is Love Unknown."

Songs of other peoples

To be sung at an internationally televised Billy Graham Crusade gives a hymn a leg up on competitors. So was it with "How Great Thou Art" from nineteenth-century Sweden. This hymn's rapidly gained popularity in North America is undeniable proof that grown people can and will learn songs that are to them new. Toward the end of the twentieth century, an interest in what has become known as "global song" became evident; tunes (sometimes adapted) and translations of texts indigenous to the church in Africa, Latin America, and the Orient have been made available to North American congregations.[12]

Global hymnody has some very capable and enthusiastic advocates. My own denomination's current hymnal includes a number of songs from this genre, for which I am very grateful and which I am glad to use. I have elsewhere written urging that several pastoral concerns should be taken into account in connection with the use of these songs.[13]

Tunes for the Hymns We Sing

Early North American Makers of Tunes

North American congregations have had to rely on the church in Northern Europe for the tunes they sang in the assembly even more heavily than for the texts. Especially was this true of the church in Canada, which during this period had not loosened its ties with Great Britain. The earliest hymn tunes produced in North America, however, flaunt the European musical conventions of their day. These were the tunes composed by untrained musicians in New England in the late eighteenth and early nineteenth centuries. The most renowned of these rustic composers was the Boston tanner William Billings (whose musical output was more choral than congregational). Hardly a handful of these early tunes are in use by congregations today. From the New England singing schools, homegrown musical creativity spread south into the mountains and valleys west of the Atlantic Seaboard—home of the "White Spirituals" ("Appalachian" or "Sacred Harp" tunes). These folk-hymn tunes, rooted in the British Isles, long continued to be sung in the rural South. They were, however, disdained by mainline denominations until their rediscovery in the mid-twentieth century.

Writing slightly later than Billings, Oliver Holden shows the influence of the European hymn tune model. His confident tune CORONATION ("All Hail the Power of Jesus' Name!") is not only still in use, but is still a favorite. It is the name of another New Englander, Lowell Mason (1792–1872) that is almost a synonym for nineteenth-century congregational song in the United States. According to Mark A. Noll, Mason was the first American to become a full-time, professional church musician—in 1827 (2006, 59). Mason worked tirelessly to improve congregational music, according to a European model. Several dozen of the hundreds of tunes he wrote or arranged were still widely used at the close of the twentieth century, for instance: ANTIOCH ("Joy to the World"), HAMBURG ("When I Survey the Wondrous Cross"), OLIVET ("My Faith Looks Up to Thee"), and AZMON ("O for a Thousand Tongues to Sing"). Many of Mason's tunes, as he acknowledged, are adaptations of older tunes.

Some common kinds of tunes in North American collections

Here is a rundown,[14] very much oversimplified, of the kinds of tunes most often found in contemporary North American hymnals, together with one or more examples:

Plainsong: VENI EMMANUEL, "O Come, O Come, Emmanuel." The melody flows with the natural rhythm of speech, pitch intervals between notes being small. This is our most distinctive form of tune, quite different from the others.

Lutheran Chorale: EIN' FESTE BURG, "A Mighty Fortress Is Our God." Employed with texts (to which the term chorale may also be applied) from Germany, and the tunes originating before about 1750.

Geneva Psalm:[15] OLD HUNDREDTH, "Praise God from Whom All Blessings Flow."

English and Scottish Psalm: WINCHESTER OLD. Such tunes are also used often with older hymns, in this case, "While Shepherds Watched Their Flocks by Night."

French Diocesan: O QUANTA QUALIA, "O What Their Joy and Their Glory Must Be." Often gentle, rather chant-like, but more congregational.

Wesleyan Revival: Athletic tunes like DUKE STREET and DARWALL'S 148TH.

Victorian Part-Song: ST. GERTRUDE (by Arthur Sullivan, who supplied the music for the comic Gilbert and Sullivan operettas), "Onward, Christian Soldiers." From the latter part of the nineteenth century, they reflect the then-popular, secular part-song, which emphasized harmony rather than melody. Also, among many others: MERRIAL, used with "Now the Day Is Over." For the same kind of tune by the same composer, Joseph Barnby, used for a secular text, see "Just a Song at Twilight."

Folk: Their widespread use with English-language hymn texts in North America began in the 1930s (following the lead of English collections).

Carol (this one from Germany): IN DULCI JUBILO, "Good Christian Friends, Rejoice." Joyful, originally associated with dancing. Not all carols are for Christmas; other festivals also have their carols, but you may well not find such in your hymnal.

English: FOREST GREEN, "All Beautiful the March of Days."

Welsh: ASH GROVE, "Let All Things Now Living."

American (but roots in British Isles): NEW BRITAIN (also called AMAZING GRACE), "Amazing Grace." Early nineteenth century.

Spiritual: SOMEBODY'S KNOCKIN', "Somebody's Knockin' at Your Door." Spirituals may be from black or white sources and often have lively rhythms. Henry Wilder Foote attributes the great power of the black spirituals not to their words, moving as they may be, but to their music (1940, 274–75).

Sunday School: JESUS LOVES ME, "Jesus Loves Me."

Gospel: CONVERSE, "What a Friend We Have in Jesus." Simple melodies, dotted rhythms, slow harmonic rhythm (the notes below the melody are slow to change).

Innovative: SINE NOMINE, "For All the Saints." Newer tunes are often more challenging for the keyboardist than the four-square hymns of earlier times; there are more notes to play. The arrangements often are written with the piano in mind, rather than the organ. More and more tunes are being arranged for all the people to sing the melody in unison.

Global: PESCADOR DE HOMBRES, "Lord, You Have Come to the Lakeshore." The music of global songs is immediately perceived as different from what has been standard hymnody in North America. Music from Asia is, for most North Americans, likely to be the least accessible, that from Africa the most. (The Ghanaian tune CHEREPONI, used with the text "Jesu, Jesu, Fill Us with Your Love," is a good example of the latter.)

The creation of good tunes in North America in the nineteenth and twentieth centuries was far exceeded by the production of quality texts. On contemporary Christian music, including the praise chorus and praise and worship music, see the following chapter. A very great number of psalm and hymn texts and tunes (played not on some glorious organ, but on a synthesizer) may be accessed on the Web. All of the Geneva Psalm tunes, for instance, are to be found.

Matching Text and Tune

Hymnals now come to us with texts and tunes already married. Sometimes hymnals offer us two or more tunes for one text. There can be occasions, however, when we want to use a text with some other tune than the one(s) with which it is paired in the hymnal—perhaps a tune that is more familiar to our congregation. In such a case, we must remember the four things that are necessary for a proper marriage between text and tune:

1) Both must be in the same meter. A text that has four lines of eight syllables each must be matched with a tune that has four lines with notes to fit eight syllables per line. The metrical index of your hymnal can be of help in this connection.

2) Both must have the same accentual pattern, that is, have the same poetic meter. "Joy to the World" and "Amazing Grace" have the same musical meter, but try singing the first line of one of these to the other's tune! On poetic meter and its implications for how a text is experienced, see Lovelace in Useful Resources.

3) Both must share the same mood. "Amazing Grace" is not in the mood for any of the tunes commonly used with "All Hail the Power of Jesus' Name," which is in the same meter.

4) Many would say that a tune must not be associated too closely in usage with another text. "Blessed Assurance, Jesus is Mine" could be sung to the tune used for "Beautiful Dreamer, Waken to Me," but perhaps should not be. It is unfortunate that "How Firm a Foundation" is often sung to ADESTE FIDELIS, the tune for the Christmas text, "O Come, All Ye Faithful," rather than to the especially appropriate American folk tune, FOUNDATION.

Using an alternate tune does come with a slight price: Singing and playing a tune from one page and reading the text on another page can complicate things a bit. One wonderful gift that hymnal preparation committees now and then give the church is the divorcement of a text from the tune to which it had been married, and remarriage to another tune. Recent gifts of this kind include "Love Divine, All Love Excelling," divorced from BEECHER and happily remarried to HYFRYDOL; "O Jesus, I Have Promised," long partnered with ANGEL'S STORY, has been given a new start with the Finnish folk tune, NYLAND; "Amazing Grace, How Sweet the Sound" would probably never have gained the traction it has, had it not been separated from ARLINGTON and joined to NEW BRITAIN.

SERVICE MUSIC

~

"Service music," "liturgical music," and "ritual music" are terms used to refer to music that invariably accompanies the rites or actions that contribute to making the worship service what it is. Service music is found in a good number of hymnals, both Protestant and Roman Catholic, usually the rubric over a collection of musical items grouped together in the front or rear of the hymnal. Service music, as sung prayer, not only makes a statement; it also serves to make a transition in the service to or from prayer, the confession of sins, the assurance/declaration of pardon, the offering, the parts of the Lord's Supper, and, in some traditions, still other rites.

The songs in view are very ancient texts that the church has found useful at specific places in the service. This category may include, among other items, the three-fold *Kyrie* ("Lord, Have Mercy"), sung in connection with the confession of sin; the Trinitarian *Gloria Patri* ("Glory Be to the Father"), commonly sung after assurance of pardon has been declared, or after Scripture has been read; the *Doxology* ("Praise God from Whom All Blessings Flow"), often sung at the presentation of the offering; and, in the celebration of the Lord's Supper, the *Sanctus* ("Holy, Holy, Holy") and the Memorial Acclamation ("Christ Has Died"). Singing an "amen" may at times be appropriate.

In many churches there is a liturgical conversation carried on between pastor and people. The pastor's "The Lord be with you," for instance, is answered by the people's "And also with you." Such exchanges may be sung. Fixed-liturgy churches sometimes employ unaccompanied, monotone chant for reciting prayer or Scripture; the text is sung on only one note at a pitch slightly higher than that of normal speech; higher and lower voices will, of course, be an octave apart. A leader singing alone may sing an inflected monotone, in which he or she occasionally deviates slightly from monotone in order to indicate divisions within the text.

Some traditions employ little or no service music other than the *Gloria Patri* and the *Doxology*—if even those items. Other communions, the Roman Catholic, Episcopal, and Lutheran, for instance, employ more service music—because there is more fixed ritual to accompany, or more fixed ritual best expressed by singing. In some traditions, this sung part of the liturgy is, at least in theory, more important than the congregational hymns. The worship renewal movement in the 1960s and following brought to many churches an increase in the amount of service music used.

SINGING "SPIRITUALLY"

~

When we sing, is our mind engaged with the text? With the tune? Or with something else? We noted in chapter 1 that one reason for ambivalence about music in the worship service is the tendency of music to dominate any text that is set to it. Benson was aware of this risk confronting us, and met it head-on: ". . . any theory of hymnody that subordinates the hymn to the hymn tune is definitely unchristian . . . any tendency . . . to treat the words of our hymns as a mere libretto of the music . . . should be dealt with frankly" (1927, 229). But how deal with it? How can we prevent the tune from lording it over the text? (I am referring here to music that is familiar to the congregation; obviously, in attempting to sing an unfamiliar tune, people must focus a large part of their brain power on the music.) What Benson and those mentioned in chapter 1 who share this concern have in mind seems to be an engagement on the part of singers that favors the music of a song at the expense of the song's words. In this scenario, the mind of the singer is engaged, albeit not altogether as it should be.

In another (and perhaps far more frequently occurring) scenario, we have singers whose minds are truant and not engaged with either music or words! In both scenarios, the net result is the same: The verbal message of the song is dead on arrival. When Augustine said that one who sings well prays twice, surely he was in the realm of theory; observation and reflection might well have led him to declare that one who sings does not pray at all!

Or maybe we need to emphasize the word "well" (often omitted in citing this aphorism), understanding it to include the requirement that the singers keep their minds on what they are about! Alas, the music may indeed seduce us; it is so easy for our singing to be nothing more than a mindless mouthing of the words as we allow ourselves to get caught up in the sound. Augustine expressed his concern about this possibility. And just maybe even the music does not hold our attention. The apostle admonishes us to sing "from the heart" (Eph. 5:19; Col. 3:16, author's translation). In practice, we might be inclined to settle for less; if people would at least keep their minds on the sense of what they sing! In response to this concern, several things may be said:

- Engaging the mind and keeping it engaged is surely one of the critical problems that plague not only the congregation's song, but all parts of the worship of the church.[16]

- Whose private devotions are never plagued by attention deficit? And in society at large, distraction is an ever-present demon. It is likely the culprit when we lock ourselves out of our homes, and when we fail to check the rearview mirror when we change lanes. What percentage of our attention do we give to those who are conversing with us?

- Abelard's "Oh, What Their Joy," from the High Middle Ages, reminds us of both the antiquity and the future demise of distractions in our worship. In the New Jerusalem, "We, where no trouble distraction can bring, Safely the anthems of Zion shall sing."

- Even mindless singing can have an impact on others present in the assembly—as pastoral care and as witness to the faith and to the distinctiveness of the church.

- Even mindless singing is a communal endeavor with the potential for strengthening the unity of the body of Christ and our consciousness of that oneness.

- Even as our earth may, as some think, borrow gravitational force from some other body, it is just possible that our mindless singing may borrow from the larger context of worship in which it takes place, a context rich in meaning and in associative potential.

- Is it too much to think that mindless singing may be like the rather mindless depositing of a check in our bank account, and later being able to draw out cash that can mean a great deal to us?

- We do not know how to pray as we ought (Rom. 8:26–27), but the Spirit intercedes with sighs too deep for words on behalf of us. Is it too much to hope that that same Spirit might make of our mindless singing something helpful to us, something acceptable to God?

- A few well-chosen words about the message of the text spoken by the worship leader, just prior to singing a hymn, have the potential for making the difference between mindless mouthing of the words and a beneficial engagement with the message. In the last analysis, as in all matters pertaining to all of life, vigilance and discipline are indispensable. The seventh of John Wesley's "Directions for Singing"—"Sing spiritually"—is as important today as it was in 1761.

WHO OWNS THE SONGS THE CHURCH SINGS?

~

"I am not a crook!" How about "scofflaw"? The ubiquitous equipment for reproducing printed material has presented to church staffs a temptation that countless clergy and musicians have found irresistible: the unauthorized, illegal copying of words and music that are under copyright. What is called copyright stems from the humane recognition that the creators of intellectual property, such as music and literature, are the owners of such property, and have exclusive say as to its use. Being owners of the property, they are entitled to compensation for any use of it.[17]

That a given piece of music is protected by copyright is normally indicated on the title page or first page of the piece or collection. In hymnals, such information is to be found at the bottom of the page or collected together in the rear of the hymnal. The name of the holder of the copyright and a date are included.

Note that none, or any part or parts, or all of the material on a page may be under copyright—thus only the words, only the music, only the arrangement of the music, only the descant—or any combination of these. If, for instance, the music on a page is anonymous American traditional whose harmonization is under copyright, we are free to reproduce the melody, but not the harmonization (which requires some cutting and pasting)—unless we secure permission.

Note these key provisions of the current U.S. copyright law:

1) No work created before 1923 is any longer protected by U.S. copyright law. This probably means that at least one-half of the material in your hymnal is not under copyright, but in the public domain.

2) All material copyrighted in the U.S. on or after January 1, 1978, is protected for the life of the composer/author plus seventy years.

3) Material copyrighted after 1922 and before 1978 is protected for ninety-five years. Copyright in Canada remains in force for fifty years after the end of the year in which the originator died. Copyrights may be sold, transferred, or inherited. For a work created in a country that is party to the Berne Convention for the Protection of Literary and Artistic Works, international copyright protection is automatic.

Like all law tends to be, copyright law is complicated; its interpretation and application may require a court ruling. Many attorneys make their living by dealing with copyright and patent matters. I have heard two

veteran publishers of church music who disagreed on certain details of
interpretation. There will be gray areas, especially as technology continues
to develop, and at times we may be cast upon our own best judgment—and
that of colleagues. One basic underlying principle that can guide us is this:
that we not deprive the laborer of what he or she deserves. In concrete terms
for us, this means that we not illegally reproduce material in order to avoid
the just compensation due owners of the copyright.

Common Copyright Questions
(For much of what follows, I am indebted to Dean B. McIntyre.)

Here are some common questions about reproducing copyrighted material, with answers given by some in the know (none of
the answers, however, should be considered court-proof).
Is it legal to:

1) make transparencies for projection? Not without permission. If
   you own the material, however, you may project an image of it
   using an opaque projector.
2) alter an author's words? Not without permission.
3) copy hymns for choir members so that they will not write in
   hymnals? Yes, if you have already bought enough hymnals for
   the choir, but some would say that you should ask permission
   from the publisher.
4) make a copy to avoid a page turn? Yes, without asking
   permission.
5) make a second copy so both keyboardist and soloist will each
   have a copy? No, buy a second copy.
6) reproduce out-of-print music without asking permission? No.
7) reproduce one or more hymns for a special program, if church
   has enough hymnals for the assembly? Request permission.
8) print text of anthem choir is to sing? Yes, if this is for a service
   to which admission is free. But print copyright data in bulletin.

9) reproduce material for which permission has been requested of owner, but owner has not replied? No.

10) reproduce copyrighted material whose creator is deceased, and whose estate does not respond to request for permission? Yes, indicating copyright, year, and name of owner, with intent of paying royalty if and when owner is located.

11) make needed additional number of copies of out-of-print, copyrighted material, if an insufficient number are already on hand? Seek permission to print the additional copies. If no response from owner, go to press prepared to pay royalty.

12) record audio or video or to broadcast music under copyright? Seek permission and be prepared to pay royalty. For broadcasting, also contact the station.

Permission may be requested by telephone, e-mail, or post. A file containing requests and authorizations should be maintained and kept current. Your church might benefit from the services of a licensing company. Such a company has contracted with a large number of copyright holders, and can authorize your church regarding all the music under its control. Annual and one-time copyright permissions are available. The fee charged is likely to be based on the size of the church.[18]

– Useful Resources –

Lionel Adey, *Class and Idol in the English Hymn* (Vancouver: UBC Press, 1988).

Albert Edward Bailey, *The Gospel in Hymns: Backgrounds and Interpretations* (New York: Charles Scribner's Sons, 1950).

American Guild of Organists, "U.S. Copyright Law: Guide for Church Musicians." Free.

Horace C. Boyer, *The Golden Age of Gospel* (Chicago: University of Illinois Press, 2000).

Harry Eskew and Hugh T. McElrath, *Sing With Understanding: An Introduction to Christian Hymnody*, 2nd ed. (Nashville: Church Street Press, 1995).

C. Michael Hawn, *Gather into One: Praying and Singing Globally* (Grand Rapids: Wm. B. Eerdmans, 2003).

John Julian, ed., *Dictionary of Hymnology: Origin and History of Christian Hymns and Hymnwriters of all Ages and Nations* (Grand Rapids: Kregel Publications, 1985). Reprint of 1892 original and 1907 supplement. Two large volumes.

Austin Lovelace, *The Anatomy of Hymnody* (Chicago: G. I. A. Publications, 1982). Reprint of 1965 edition by Abingdon Press.

Madeleine Forell Marshall and Janet Todd, *English Congregational Hymns in the Eighteenth Century* (Lexington: University of Kentucky Press, 1982). Analysis of poetry of Watts, C. Wesley, Newton, and Cowper.

Madeleine Forell Marshall, *Common Hymnsense* (Chicago: GIA Publications, 1995). A literary analysis of thirty-six well-known hymns.

Dean B. McIntyre, "Copyright and Licensing: Questions and Answers about Hymns, Public Domain, and Copyright," "How Do I Research a Music Copyright?" Music articles on Web site of The United Methodist Church.

William McNeil, ed., *Encyclopedia of American Gospel Music* (New York: Routledge, 2005).

David W. Music, *Christian Hymnody in Twentieth-Century Britain and America: An Annotated Bibliography* (Westport, CT: Greenwood Press, 2001).

Millar Patrick, *Four Centuries of Scottish Psalmody* (New York: Oxford, 1949).

David Poultney, *Dictionary of Western Church Music* (Chicago: American Library Association, 1991).

William Jensen Reynolds, Milburn Price, and David W. Music, *A Survey of Christian Hymnody,* 4th ed. (Carol Stream, IL: Hope Publishing Company, 1999). The 1963 edition updated by Price and David W. Music.

Erik Routley, *The Music of Christian Hymnody* (Chicago: G. I. A. Publications, 1981).

Erik Routley, *A Panorama of Christian Hymnody* (Chicago: GIA Publications, 2005). An edited and expanded version by Paul A. Richardson of the original 1979 work.

Erik Routley, *An English Speaking Hymnal Guide* (Chicago: GIA Publications, 2005). An updated version by Peter W. Cutts of the original work published in 1979 and republished in 1984.

S. Paul Schilling, *The Faith We Sing: How the Message of Hymns Can Enhance Our Faith* (Philadelphia: Westminster Press, 1983).

George H. Shorney, *The Hymnal Explosion in North America* (Carol Stream, IL: Hope Publishing Company, 1988).

James Rawlings Sydnor, *Hymns and Their Uses: A Guide to Improved Congregational Singing* (Carol Stream, IL: AGAPE, 1982). The 1976 list of ecumenical hymns is given on pages 46–72.

James Rawlings Sydnor, *Hymns: A Congregational Study* (Carol Stream, IL: AGAPE, 1983).

J. R. Watson, *The English Hymn: A Critical and Historical Study* (Oxford: Clarendon Press, 1997).

J. R. Watson, ed., *An Annotated Anthology of Hymns* (Oxford: Oxford University Press, 2002).

Web sites dealing with copyright issues: The text of the entire United States Copyright Law may be found at http://www.copyright.gov/title17/. See http://www.cb-cda.gc.ca/info/act-e.html#rid-33225 for the Canadian Copyright Act. See http://www.pdinfo.com/copyrt.htm, the Web site of Haven Sound.

Carlton R. Young, *My Great Redeemer's Praise: An Introduction to Christian Hymns* (Akron, OH: OSL Publications, 1995), 41–128.

N. B.:

Handbooks are published for a number of hymnals. These give information on authors, composers, texts, tunes, and historical and biographical circumstances. Is there one for your hymnal?

CHAPTER
SIX
CONTEMPORARY CHRISTIAN MUSIC

~

The facilitator at a workshop on contemporary worship began with a question: "When you hear the words 'contemporary music,' what comes to mind?" I shot back, "Some other church!" Perhaps that would have been your response. It requires no great theological reflection, however, to bring us to the admission that we do not own the church, that we do not even own ourselves, that we are only servants, people under orders. How might the servant, how should the mind of a servant, respond to the phenomenon of Christian worship that is so different from what we know and love?

WHAT IS CONTEMPORARY CHRISTIAN MUSIC?

~

What is termed contemporary Christian music is a world unto itself. It is for this reason that I am devoting a separate chapter to the subject. Even so, I am dealing with the subject in a very summary form, for CCM, as it is universally abbreviated, is a very big world. Depending on how CCM is defined, it can also be a very diverse world. In addition, CCM is a rapidly evolving world. CCM makes no claims about being built to last; what goes around does not necessarily come around. To begin to do justice to our subject would require all the space in this book. The emphasis in this chapter will not be on CCM as such, however, but on the question of how best to respond to it.

I am no happier than many other people with the use of "contemporary" in CCM, as though CCM had a corner on all Christian music that happens to be contemporary. CCM is contemporary, but it is far from being the only music for Christian worship that is contemporary. Also, CCM includes music that is much older than contemporary. The praise chorus, for instance, was in use before World War II.

One obvious characteristic that distinguishes contemporary worship from traditional is the fact that the former is generally performed or led by an ensemble of vocalists and players of various instruments. Another is the substitution of the hymnal by the CD (compact disc) and the projector screen.

The Genres of Contemporary Christian Music

To attempt to develop the taxonomy of CCM involves shooting at a moving target or targets. Any shooters, moreover, are more than likely to arrive at widely differing results.

> One common mistake made by people who plan worship is to assume that contemporary music generally all sounds the same and reaches the same kinds of people. As a result, many worship planners have chosen music that completely mismatches the musical languages of those they intend to reach. (Glaeser and Webb 1998, 84)

Mark Glaeser and Richard Webb (1998, 84–86), writing near the end of the twentieth century, identify six genres of CCM:

PRAISE AND WORSHIP:
The most widely encountered sub-group.

ALTERNATIVE:
The most recently developed; a local phenomenon; rarely uses keyboard.

CONTEMPORARY LITURGICAL:
Mainly Roman Catholic in origin and written to serve the rites of the Mass [but otherwise like praise and worship].

ROCK 'N' ROLL:
An adaptation of secular rock 'n' roll, music of the boomer generation.

JAZZ AND BLUES:
Not generally congregational, used mainly in instrumental numbers.

COUNTRY:
Increasing in popularity, very diverse!

Group Magazine's Youth Ministry Resources[1] divides the pie this way, with descriptions of each of twelve genres:

Modern Rock, Rap, Electronic, Heavy, Rap Metal, Pop Rock, "Christian-y" Mainstream, Pop, Urban, Pop Punk, Worship, and Random ("music that doesn't fit into the other categories").

Margaret Leask divides what she terms "Christian pop music" into:

1) CCM, which specializes in individual artists and groups who tour and who produce CDs, paralleling the secular rock industry; and

2) Praise and Worship Music—groups specializing in materials for worship and Christian education.

"Both streams adapt multiple forms of pop music to express Christian lyrics." (2004, 12)

Since CCM artists have been more recently involved in cross-over songs which have worship in view, however, this distinction is no longer very helpful.

Robb Redman, writing in a 2003 publication, distinguishes two broad categories:

1) Contemporary Christian Music, CCM, "message music," generally aimed at listener, headquarters in Nashville. Its purveyors include Amy Grant, Michael W. Smith, dc Talk, Jars of Clay, and Steven Curtis Chapman, all successful "pop" recording stars;

2) Contemporary Worship Music, CWM, directed primarily to God. Lion's share produced by "The Big Three": Maranatha! Music, Integrity Music, and Vineyard Music Group.

This distinction between message music and worship music is a more recent development. (2003, 75)

In this chapter I shall consider two genres of CCM: praise and worship and rock.

Praise and worship

The praise chorus is one of the older genres, and the most widespread and least sophisticated genre of CCM. The text of the praise chorus is short, consisting of words taken from Scripture or Christian experience. Many young people learned praise choruses at camps and conferences and helped spread them on their return home. An example of a somewhat more recent, very popular, and enduring chorus is Karen Lafferty's "Seek Ye First," whose two-stanza text is from Matthew 6:33 and 7:7. This chorus is included in the 1990 hymnal of my mainline denomination. Other choruses that have known widespread use have been Jerry Sinclair's "Alleluia," Terrye Coelho (Strom)'s "Father, I Adore You," Merla Watson's "Jehovah Jireh," and Jack Hayford's "Majesty, Worship His Majesty."

Such a praise chorus may be sung straight through at some point in a very traditional worship service. Praise choruses may also be repeated any number of times, and sung one after another for several minutes. The fact that the last line of the music of the praise chorus does not bring us to rest disposes us to continue singing indefinitely. This more extended use of the praise chorus has, in charismatic and neo-charismatic circles, been termed praise singing, or, more recently, the praise and worship service.

The leadership for the praise and worship service may consist of the pastor and a worship leader, who seek a balance between spontaneity and a certain amount of guidance. Musical accompaniment ranges from a minimal use of instruments to a full array of drums, piano, synthesizers, guitars, and occasionally wind instruments. Amplification can provide as much volume as desired.

Consistent with the impulses driving the creation of CCM, the use of the hymnal in worship services has given way to the practice of projecting the texts on a screen, from which all present can sing in unison— assuming they know the tune or that the tune is projected as well. Familiarity with the simple, oft-repeated lyrics may also render the screen unnecessary, of course.

Rock 'n' roll—or just rock

The second half of the twentieth century saw successive waves of change washing through North American churches. Perhaps none of these forces had more impact than those that affected the way the church worships. Leaders in mainline Protestant churches sought renewal of worship by a critical reincorporation of ancient church tradition. In contrast, a host of young evangelicals began constructing their worship services out of materials imported from outside the church, from the contemporary world. The world's music was their music, the music they had grown up with, music that distinguished them from their parents— and the establishment—and through which they bonded to their peers, music that came to be available 24/7, music called rock.

This genre is not the most widespread type of CCM. It is, however, the genre that comes to mind for many of us when CCM is mentioned. Rock 'n' roll gets your attention! The music is dominating and overpowering. It is generally agreed that this music is derived from the secular style known by the same name. It has thus been called "Baptized Rock." The heart of rock, whether played both in or out of the worship service, is not melody or harmony, but *rhythm*, or more pointedly, the beat. It has been said, "The drum has the melody." And the drum has lots of help—from an electric bass and, to some extent, keyboards and other instruments. All this is more than enough to sound forth an indisputable beat. But to make sure the music gets our attention, electronic amplification is another sine qua non.

The Larger World of CCM

CCM would not have developed without the recording industry, television, and other technologies. Nashville is home to CCM, as it is to so much other music. Greenville College in Greenville, Illinois, and North Central University in Minneapolis are two schools offering majors in CCM. The San Francisco State University's College of Extended Learning offers, under the umbrella "Gospel Music," a three-hour course called "Praise and Worship." Of the music used by CCM, Maranatha! Music, Word/Integrity Music, and Mercy Publishing (Vineyard Ministries) are three well known suppliers among many. The world of CCM is larger, however, than even the proliferation and scale of such institutions may lead us to believe. Like the music of the earliest church, much of it never gets beyond the local congregation where it originated.

HOW SHALL WE JUDGE CCM?

～

For those of us who have a deep appreciation for the disciplines of academic theology, it can be difficult not to be predisposed against a populist movement like CCM. The sixteenth-century reformers learned all they could about the church's tradition, and then set about seeking to reform what they had inherited according to their understanding of the Gospel. Many contemporary proponents of CCM worship, on the other hand, show little regard for all that stands between them and the Bible—including the church. Their program is not to reform so much as to reinvent. The disciplines of the academy—the shared, accumulated knowledge of nearly two millennia of the worldwide church's life—have little to teach. The untutored are the equals of the tutored. Academically trained musicians may feel similarly about many of the advocates and practitioners of CCM.

There seem to be within the church three major responses to the phenomenon of CCM: whole-hearted embrace; an openness to consider it critically; or whole-hearted rejection. At the risk of losing some readers without further ado, I shall say here and now that I consider myself to be in the middle camp. So open, yes—but critically; as in all matters, here too, the spirits must be tried. Any church that confesses that the earth is the Lord's, that God loves the world, and that takes seriously the mandate to disciple the people of every nation is under obligation to look into CCM. In addition to concern for the missionary mandate, a church may also want to consider CCM with a view to enriching and enlivening its current worship services, and making them more generally appealing, more inclusive, and more catholic.

By what standards shall we judge CCM? For many who prefer the kind of music I do, it is tempting to call out our aesthetic criteria; that would make short work of it. This music is just not ours, period! At least, for the worship service, it is not. As I tried to make the case early on in this book, however, literary and musical standards and tastes cannot be allowed the last word on music in the church. As noted above, CCM is evolving; much of the early CCM was produced quickly to meet an urgently felt need. In assessing the movement, we do well to judge it by its later, more mature fruits. In what follows you will find listed some possible strengths and weaknesses of CCM. The ultimate question for CCM, however, is the same one to be asked of all music used in the church: What kind of fruit does it bear? The measure of all Christian liturgical music is whether it functions, how well it serves, to what extent it enables Christian worship to take place, worship that issues forth in holy living and kingdom seeking (Ps. 40:6–8).

POSSIBLE STRENGTHS OF CCM

~

CCM Is an Example of the Vernacular Principle in the Service of Evangelism

The proponents of CCM, critics say, confuse worship with evangelism. CCM and the post–World War II Church Growth Movement do share an evangelistic agenda. Reaching the unreached and the dropouts is often explicitly stated as the driving motivation for initiating worship services whose music features CCM. But must we draw such a sharp line between worship and evangelism? Yes, the focus of worship is God; worship does not have to justify itself by producing any by-products. As Ronald P. Byars says, "Worship finds its power when we set aside all other concerns, and lose ourselves, as Charles Wesley [who got it from Joseph Addison] put it, 'in wonder, love, and praise'" (2002, 28). Yet, as we saw in chapter 2, something besides worship does take place in worship; the worship of the assembly must be edifying to those present, or it is not acceptable to God. Congregational worship necessarily involves the horizontal as well as the vertical (see Pss. 22:22, 25; 26:12; 35:18; 40:9–10). If edification of others present must take place when God is worshiped, then surely evangelism may take place. Of evangelistic efforts in another culture in another land, an inculturational (culturally adaptive) approach is nowadays considered sine qua non. The use of CCM in domestic evangelism involves the same respected principle; the vernacular of the target population, in this case the boomer culture, is adopted. I see this as the time-honored vernacular principle at work, not "taste-generated worship," as someone has called it. Plantinga and Rozeboom see inculturation not merely as desirable, but as inevitable:

> Cultural adaptation of worship is inevitable, even as we are "inevitably subject" to culture. So if worship isn't adapted to this culture—including, to some measure, contemporary culture—it's not that it is being adapted to no culture, but to some other one. Worship doesn't take shape in a cultural vacuum, for culture is the gospel's atmosphere, worship's habitat. (2003, 63–64)

Brian Wren suggests: "Perhaps contemporary worship is like a foreign language, which we, as liturgical missionaries, need to learn," citing Acts 2:11 and 1 Corinthians 9:20–23. And further, ". . . one purpose in using contemporary worship music is to invite people into the drama of Christian worship, and win a hearing for a Christian message, by using culturally familiar forms: visual, dramatic, and musical" (2000, 152–54). James White puts it like this: ". . . suddenly we have found that the real problem of indigenization is right here at home" (1997, 73). The 2003 Chirograph of Pope John Paul II, while holding firmly to the innate and universal superiority of Gregorian chant, acknowledges the rightness of compliance "with the legitimate demands of adaptation and inculturation."[2]

CCM Helps Us to Worship with Our Whole Being

We have already dealt with this topic in chapter 2, and can be brief here. It is true that the worship described in Scripture tends to be, as is much of CCM worship, more physical than the worship found in many churches. The Hebrew and Greek verbs for "worship," etymologically at least, contain the notion of bowing or prostrating oneself. The element of praise is indeed dominant in connection with the worship referred to in the Bible, and it is often loud and exuberant, involving the whole assembly. The congregation shouts (Ps. 33:3; Zech. 9:9), shouts for joy (Pss. 32:11; 132:9, 16); their shout is great (Ezra 3:11). Many of us would appreciate some ardor added to our order.

> . . . sometimes, when the music resonates in my body as well as in my soul, I would like to sway just a little as we sing. In fact, I would like to sing more, and sometimes engage in prolonged singing. . . . There are times when I would like to cast aside my northern European tradition and raise my hands. . . . I want to be bodily present in worship, and not just intellectually present. (Byars 2002, 35)

The lively rhythm that characterizes much of CCM conduces to increased physical involvement. Not having to concentrate on more complicated texts and tunes also frees us to think about blending our voices with those around us, engaging in *una voce dicentes*, practicing the oneness of the body.

Those Who Accept Global Music Should Welcome CCM

Michael S. Hamilton (2001) points out that some who reject CCM may accept global music without question; after all, global music is folk, non-white, non-Western. But, in Hamilton's view, much CCM also has a claim to being folk music—both in its origin and its development—and should be welcomed as such. (As for CCM being commercialized, most kinds of music are, sooner or later.)

CCM Worship May Flow

Even though invalid distinctions may be involved, the sequence from thanksgiving to praise to worship followed by some in the world of CCM, it must be granted, does embody an important liturgical idea. This idea is one that many pastors do not seem to grasp, that is, that the elements in the service of worship are not just so many things that have to take place, but that good worship is sequential, one element leading to the next.[3]

POSSIBLE WEAKNESSES OF CCM

~

Is CCM Congregational?

In some CCM worship, the role model of the musician(s), the very large number of people present, together with the design and the acoustics of the building, may contribute to anonymity and nonparticipation on the part of any but the performers up front. Sometimes at least some of those present do not know the music, at least at first. It must be remembered, however, that traditional worship in a church of any size gives a part of the vocal music to a choir or soloist.

The Questionable Literary Quality of the Lyrics

Repetition is one of the basic devices of musical practice. The lyrics of some CCM, however, tend to be excessively repetitive. How much is too much? Ravel's "Bolero" was deemed on its first hearing in Paris to be intolerably repetitive. How about Pachelbel's "Canon in D"? Or "Behold the Lamb of God" in Handel's *Messiah*. (Admittedly, in these classical numbers we are talking about some rather sophisticated music, and, in *Messiah*, a repetition of elements of the text, not necessarily the music.) The short musical items of Taizé are most often repeated mantra-like. Repetition is a feature of gospel hymnody, the spiritual, and a number of psalms—none more than Psalm 136. "Alleluia" appears four times in every stanza of "Jesus Christ Is Risen Today," seven times in every stanza of "All Creatures of Our God and King." (Of course, in these hymns there is some very rich text between the alleluias.) Just reading the same words again and again, or even hearing someone else singing them over and over again, may not do much for us. But singing them ourselves may be something else! This is not unlike the contrast between merely listening to very repetitive country dance music and actually dancing to it!

Much of the language of CCM lyrics is trite. The user must discriminate.

What May be in Short Supply

In some CCM, lyrics have tended to dwell on certain attributes of God (not unlike scholastic and neo-scholastic theology!), rather than, as does biblical praise most often, on God's mighty, redemptive acts in history. CCM lyrics may dwell on certain aspects of God's timeless being, not God's timely doing. Why should praising God for what God is be thought more exalted than praising God for what God has done, or is expected to do, as we encounter most often in the biblical psalms? It often remains unclear why we should be praising God. (See Hull 2004, 18.) Mary does not stop with praising God, but proceeds to tell us why she is so engaged (Lk. 1:46–55; cp. Ps. 40:1–10).[4]

A common criticism of CCM lyrics has been that social concerns get short shrift; there is in them typically no hungering and thirsting after justice in society. (Matt. 6:33 does appear in one of the best-known CCM songs. Do those who sing "Seek Ye First" understand the reference here to be to social righteousness? Or to the individual's justification before God?) However true this may have been, a cursory examination of some of the most recent Roman Catholic collections, for instance, will reveal a very respectable quantity of songs whose theme is the longing and quest for social righteousness. It is also important to remember that the whole of the church's agenda does not have to be carried by our songs.

Some proponents of CCM have claimed that the biblical psalms show us that the dominant note of worship should be praise. We are tipped off to expect this to be the case by the very name commonly given to those who lead a CCM service: Not "worship team," but "praise team." (I am not sure we can attach much weight to this.[5]) Praise is what worship is all about. Confession of sin and sorrow for sin are scarce in some CCM, as is an awareness of real-world trials, pain, suffering, hard questions, and death.

In response to this emphasis, the following may be noted:

- Lament may also be scarce in mainline, traditional worship. Pastors know all too well that their congregations much prefer to sing happy songs in church!

- Where lament is lacking, petition may also be in short supply. Psalm 25—which is not short of the element of praise—is an example of how lament can lead to petition.

- Over against so many "I-centered" lyrics, "Keeping God as the subject and object of our worship enables us to deal with the darkness by lamenting it, by complaining about it" (Dawn 1995, 91). (But is it not possible for a lament also to be "I-centered," to be overly preoccupied with self?)

- The ancient rabbis did indeed refer to the book of Psalms as "Songs of Praise." It is also the case that each of the five divisions within the book of Psalms concludes with a doxology. About a third of the psalms, however, are laments. Two of the three psalms of the Old Testament most often cited in the New Testament (22 and 69) are psalms of lament. (In the New Testament, however, these psalms are applied not to the church, but to the suffering Christ or His enemies.) The church that knows the Hebrew Scriptures is aware of how sad the songs of God's people can be. "A funny thing happened when we were in captivity. Our captors taunted us, 'Sing us one of the songs of Zion!' 'How can we?' we replied. 'It's hard to sing the Lord's song in a strange land. Tell you what we'll do: We'll sing about how hard it is to sing here in the exile.'" (Ps. 137)

- The New Testament also knows weeping for sin (Matt. 26:75) and the song of lament (Matt. 2:17–18). Not all the prayers of the church are happy prayers (Acts 4:23–30). The faithful church in a broken world joins voices with the martyrs' "How long will it be, O Lord?" (Rev. 6:10). The Christian faith is realistic; its expressions are as multifaceted as life itself.[6]

- As is true with respect to the theme of social righteousness, newer collections of CCM serve up generous helpings of lament. In both of these categories, a debt to the songs of the church in Latin America is obvious.

Scarce in some CCM lyrics have been mentions of covenant, church, and the sacraments. (These themes may be rather scarce in some non-CCM worship as well.) In this case, too, the force of a criticism of CCM is blunted by some recent Roman Catholic collections—collections that offer a large quantity of material written for the liturgy.

To omit completely the vast treasure of the church's music accumulated over the centuries is to deprive people of an incalculably rich and varied heritage, and to reduce "the communion of the saints" to nothing larger than fellowship within a local congregation at one point in time. CCM alone does not provide a balanced diet, and must be supplemented. If the reading of the present church music scene by Christian music's leading lady, Amy Grant, is on the mark, perhaps hymn lovers may take heart. Grant believes she sees the pendulum swinging from so much emphasis on the praise chorus back to standard hymns. The March 2005 issue of *CCM Magazine*, in which she is quoted, featured the subject of hymns, as rendered though, not by congregations, but by (mostly) young soloists and ensembles, all with several CDs to their credit. Hymns are made not to be heard, but to be sung, and that by congregations. Hymns hardly lend themselves to being sung straight through, one stanza after another, by a soloist; therefore such renditions, when they do occur, tend to be highly stylized and idiosyncratic. Otherwise they would be pretty ho-hum. (It has to be acknowledged, of course, that even recordings of hymns sung by non-CCM choirs and soloists are also likely, and for the same reasons, to be treated in very creative, noncongregational ways.) On the positive side, I was encouraged to learn the names of some of the hymns that had been recorded.[7] The issue also contained an article on lament—inspired by the book of Job!

POSSIBLE ERRORS OF COMMISSION

~

The Use of the Old Testament

An understanding of ritual in the Old Testament is of enormous value to anyone who would understand the worship of the early church. Whereas, however, most liturgical scholars look to the New Testament for basic elements in Christian worship, some proponents of CCM have concentrated on the Old, raising the question of normativity. Some have combined CCM with the "dominion" motif, the result of selective use of Old Testament texts that link material prosperity with the right kind of worship; the Old Testament's laments and questions tend to be neglected. The New Testament, in particular the cross, should dispel this kind of thinking.

Some CCM has employed a large measure of battle language. The reason for this has been attributed by some to CCM proponents' fondness for the book of Joshua. (Or is it the other way around?) As I indicated in chapter 4, while the use of such language is not to be ruled out, a pastoral sensitivity is called for. Balance must be maintained. (Certainly CCM is also not short of the hierarchical language we deal with in Useful Resources. This usage involves not only the Old Testament, of course, but the New as well.)

Does the Old Testament distinguish so clearly between praise and worship that follows it? Some proponents of CCM point to Psalm 95. But what about Psalm 66? And 99? Does Psalm 100:4 really have in view a movement from thanksgiving to praise to worship? Our English Bible reflects a variety of Hebrew terms used to express the proper stance before God, for instance: praise, worship, extol, give thanks, bless, confess, serve, bow down, ascribe, render, acknowledge. It would be a mistake to attempt to distinguish too precisely among these. Liturgical language tends to be effusive, redundant. Among CCM advocates themselves, there is discussion as to a distinction made between worship-oriented song (song *to* God) and praise-oriented song (song *about* God). I do not think that such distinctions can possibly claim any biblical or lexical support. Many individual hymns and psalms combine both orientations.

Is CCM Narcissistic?

According to Kenneth Hull, the praise chorus and alternative music have appealed most to the white middle class, a part of North American society that is especially vulnerable to the alienating forces of contemporary North American culture. These people have a deep hunger for intimacy, a need that is met through CCM, with its emphasis on an emotionally-suffused relationship with God. In this matrix, a narcissistic worldview is nourished. Infatuation with feelings substitutes praise that is focused on God.[8] When the worship at one address no longer provides the infatuation, worshipers move on, seeking their emotional high at some other.

CCM has indeed been faulted for being narcissistic, for emphasizing the "I." Some CCM lyrics do focus on intensifying the individual's experience of God as the be-all of worship (Hull 2004, 18, 21–22). Songs cannot be ruled out, however, just because they are first person singular; it must be granted that Psalm 23 and other psalms and many first-person-singular hymns are acceptable in worship, even if sung by a soloist.

$\sim$

Some of the shortcomings of the lyrics of CCM can be addressed by seeing to a balance through the judicious use of standard hymns. Again, let it be said that the music of the worship service does not have to bear all the church's freight; the church has other means of edification at its disposal.

The Music

Much CCM music has been musically impoverished and, like the lyrics, repetitive. I have just listened to a CD's worth of praise choruses that came with a collection published in 2005, and found most of the music to be insipid and unappealing; one CCM number does, indeed, sound like so many others. Perhaps this is what might be expected, for many of the choruses are written by only a few people; irrespective of whatever talent they may possess, they must know that they are not writing music for the ages, but rather tunes of the throwaway variety. It may, in any case, be helpful on the consumer side to bear in mind this ephemeral nature of much of CCM. The praise chorus is, we hope, not the meat-and-potatoes of the musical diet we are offering the congregation. Our investment of time and energy in what is so very transient will be in proportion to the expected shelf life of the music involved, and to the role given this music in our overall program. This does not mean that in looking for music in this genre we should not seek out the best that CCM has to offer. CCM is, of course, far more than the praise chorus, and quality and variety may be sought among other genres of CCM.

The very thing that particularly characterizes some CCM, the amplified beat, can be off-putting for both the musically unsophisticated and the trained musician. The music is just too audible! How loud is that? A common answer is: "If you have to shout to be heard over the music, the music is too loud." Commonly mentioned in connection with high-decibel rock music is a drug-like high, a sensation that is pursued by turning up the volume. Whatever else may be said about such overwhelming loudness, hearing loss—temporary or permanent—is guaranteed. A very high volume of sound may also make it difficult for the praise team to hear the singing of the congregation. If this kind of CCM is not amplified, will it be authentic? Will it attract and hold the interest of its fans?

The music of traditional congregational song is like a time-release capsule: The music of a particular song has the potential for continuing to work its effect in us long after the congregation has stopped singing it. Such music has this ability because it is melodic; it is the melody that persists, that we carry away—stored in our brain—from our singing. At some later time, our mind and perhaps our tongue may recreate the song. If there is any truth in the saying that in some CCM, the drum has the melody, what is there to take away that might lead to such re-creation?

Liturgical Considerations

The notion of liturgical flow found among many planners of CCM worship is in the movement's favor. Questionable, however, is the stress on the preparatory nature of music. Every musical item in the service, rather than being appreciated as itself worship, seems to be valued largely because it serves to prepare the assembly for what follows. In a letter from a correspondent, I am told that what is prepared for in the writer's service is the sermon—an agenda shared, regrettably, with a very large body of non-CCM worship!

A second liturgical concern about CCM has also been raised. Paul W. Wohlgemuth, who is sympathetic toward CCM, writes: "No worship movement in recent years is so dependent upon music for the heart of its expression" (in Young 1985, 90). One of the criteria for worship music set forth by Ronald Byars is particularly apropos in connection with CCM: "Does the music dominate the service, drive it, overpower it, or serve it?" (2002, 62). As I maintained in chapter 1: The calling of music in worship is to be *servant*.

OPTIONS FOR YOUR CHURCH

~

Faced with CCM and having examined it as it might relate to your congregation at this time, what are your options?

Stay the Course

Resolve to continue worshiping as you have been doing. Some congregations that do this schedule some time (ten or fifteen minutes) just before the worship service for the singing of CCM. Is this worship, or just singing? How is it related to what follows? One congregation known to me indicates that this singing of praise songs is "*to prepare* our hearts and minds for worship" (italics mine). The same thing is often said in defense of the organ prelude! Whatever it is, like all other music in the congregation, it should be under the authority of the governing board of the church, and its music subject to approval by that board.

Move from Traditional to Contemporary

Michael S. Hamilton (2001) offers a thoughtful "go with the flow" position with regard to Christians grouping themselves with the musically like-minded. He calls this the "new sectarianism," the sectarianism of worship style. Hamilton is not embarrassed by this development. On the contrary, he points out that the Christian faith is thriving precisely where denominationalism has thrived—in the United States. So bring on your differing worship styles! There is one for every taste. Those concerned with the visible unity of the one body of Christ, of course, will have to swallow very hard before acquiescing in this de facto balkanization of the church— even after the battering that the post–World War II ecumenical dream has suffered in more recent years. It was in no small measure the development of alternative, niche worship styles that brought about the separation of Methodists from Anglicans in America and Great Britain, and that of similar pietistic movements on the continent from their Lutheran moorings.

Moving to CCM guarantees that all your worshipers will be deprived of the musical treasure of the church. It risks alienating some. Is there enough liturgical CCM to supply what may be considered a complete order of service? Beginning and continuing contemporary worship requires a heavy investment of time, energy, and money. It requires leaders who are knowledgeable and enthusiastic with regard to CCM; doing CCM must be for them not a chore, but a calling. People who hear expertly performed music outside the church are not likely to be enthusiastic about amateurishly or unenthusiastically performed music in the church. There must be sustained effort, not just playing other people's music long enough to get them inside.

Many church musicians have experienced pressure from pastors who, understandably, are concerned with the statistics of membership and attendance. The well-intentioned pastor believes that a change in the kind of music employed in the church would make its worship more attractive to nonchurchgoers—especially the younger ones. Contemporary Christian music, the pastor suggests, could be just the ticket. How is the more traditionally trained musician to respond? (Let us assume that the musician is being treated as a fellow professional, that his or her expertise is being shown the respect it deserves.)

Increasingly, church musicians are being pushed to consider styles of music that are to them like new languages. Contemporary music relies heavily on improvisation (a skill recommended in classical training also, but by no means acquired by all classical musicians). Other kinds of sounds are called for, other instruments are employed, a percussive beat may be front and center. For musicians to make a new style their very own, they must not only invest the time required for learning new ways of making music; they must also summon up the nerve necessary to question deeply held convictions about what is very dear to them. In such circumstances it is not hard to imagine discomfort and insecurity setting in. Could it be that some church musicians need to undergo conversion from their view that there is only one proper style of music for the church? Such openness is very much in line with what was said in chapter 1 about the servant role of music in worship. Once musicians have opened themselves to embracing a new style, they can help the rest of us not only to accept the new styles, but also to distinguish within that style between the good and the inferior.[9]

Traditionalists who are considering CCM may be encouraged by learning of classically trained musicians who are seeking to build bridges to the oh-so-different world of contemporary Christian music. The American Guild of Organists is not known for cherishing plebeian musical tastes. Yet in the Guild's monthly journal, *The American Organist*, organists such as Cheri Sykes and Marilyn Gonzáles have published articles that point out in practical ways how their classically trained colleagues can learn what Sikes and Gonzáles are willing to term the "new performance practice" of CCM. Brian Wren, though not himself a musician, gives suggestions to classically trained musicians who want to make the crossover (2000, 159–62). The organ, especially one with MIDI, can find a home in CCM, and the organ's use in such a different context has bridge-building potential.

For those committed to implementing CCM, there is no shortage of help available. See, for instance, Lynn Hurst, under Useful Resources. Lee Orr recommends buying some new music and tapes—from a source other than the musician's normal supplier—and listening to hear what is currently popular elsewhere (1991, 37). Without leaving your computer station, you can have a look at (and a listen to) CCM on the Web. Classically trained musicians need not be on only the receiving end; they may well have opportunities to upgrade CCM musicians and music.

Go Blended

Marva Dawn reflects a concern of Paul Westermeyer: The church's music should express the broad inclusiveness of the church, not the narrow focus of any particular sector of society (1995, 178). Applied to the local congregation, this can be seen as favoring blended worship—blending traditional music with praise singing at one or more spots in the service.

(Does the result of inserting into the traditional order of service one or two praise choruses, led/accompanied by the usual organ or piano, qualify as blended?) The blended approach keeps the congregation together. It has been remarked, supposedly jokingly, however, that a guaranteed way to make everyone mad about something is to go blended. Engaging in blended worship does indeed call for the practice of Christian charity. Blended worship leaves space for the balancing, deepening, and broadening influence of the church's store of hymnody. It may require knowledge and skills not yet possessed by current staff. Blending the music of the service does not mean that time allotted for prayer and the reading of Scripture, for instance, has to be reduced. All music should be selected not because it happens to be either traditional or CCM, but because it works well for a particular place in the order of worship and contributes to moving the service along.[10]

Offer Both Styles of Worship at Different Hours or in Different Venues

Sunday morning need not be the only option to consider in scheduling a CCM service. The afternoon or evening of Sunday or even some other day may be best. Offering additional services does mean added work for the staff, or adding staff. It divides the congregation into two or more parts, perhaps separating some generations from others. Perhaps surprisingly, CCM sometimes draws a higher percentage of the seniors than it does the middle-aged. The younger generation, when not present, will be missed. (My experience in several pastorates led me to conclude that very few members of an urban congregation of more than two hundred people know very many of their fellow worshipers anyway. Smaller units within the one congregation might foster more intimacy and knowledge of others.) Offering multiple services can result in demoralizing empty spaces in the sanctuary. Should a worship space other than the one used for the traditional service (even if this latter is available at the desired hour) be sought for the CCM service? The symbols of pulpit (and open Bible), font/baptistry, and table should, in any case, be present.

Offer an Occasional Alternate Service

Many churches designate at least one Sunday in the year Youth Sunday, Senior Sunday, or the like. So there might be offered an occasional Contemporary Music Sunday.

∼

Whichever of the above-mentioned courses is followed, it is crucial that every service be complete, that appropriate attention be given to all the parts of the public worship of the church—word, prayer, and sacrament. Also, all of the assembled must be given the opportunity to participate actively.

MOVING TOGETHER

∼

What applies to all considerations of possible changes in the church's (the *people's*) worship applies with special force in moving from what is for us traditional toward a style of worship so very different: Go slow! Study, look around, discuss, pray. (See John Witvliet, "The Virtue of Liturgical Discernment," in Kroeker 2005, 83–97.) Genuine, ongoing, two-way conversation is of the highest priority. In designing a new service, it is important not to be guided too largely by complaints that have been made about the traditional worship service, resulting in the new order being a sort of "anti-service" (Byars 2002, 102). Every effort must be made to get everyone on board. In the meantime, this somber reminder:

> The realization that any one church cannot be all things to all people is often painful, especially if we care about the community and are willing to bend to keep it from coming apart. (Doran and Troeger 1986, 146)

In all the study, decision making, planning, and implementing, there is one particular matter that has special potential for disaster: the clergy-musician relationship. This relationship always carries within it the seeds of conflict. Moving into CCM is most often clergy-initiated, and it can be next to life-threatening for the musician. He or she may in this context see the pastor not only as a Philistine with no appreciation of the finer things, but also as one idolatrously consumed with increasing the numbers. The pastor may view the musician as an esoterically preoccupied elitist who has no knowledge of the real world, one who loves a rare kind of music more than people. The pastor can all too readily forget that the musician also is a fellow image bearer, one who also is called, one who also is a professional.

It will be well for all of us, as we face the future, to remember these words of James F. White: "There has never been a period in church history when worship remained absolutely unchanging" (1997, iii). "If we look a little further back in religious history [prior to 1950], we discover that 'contemporary worship' is . . . something of a recurring phenomenon in the Christian church" (Plantinga and Rozeboom 2003, 35). And as we face one another in the church, it is imperative that we remember the words of the apostle: "Each of us must please our neighbor for the good purpose of building up the neighbor" (Rom. 15:2 NRSV).

– Useful Resources –

Barry Alfonso, *The Billboard Guide to Contemporary Christian Music* (New York: Billboard Books, 2002).

Paul Baker [Frank Edmondson, a.k.a. Brooke Chamberlain], *Contemporary Christian Music* (Westchester, IL: Crossway Books, 1985). A revised and expanded edition of the author's *Why Should the Devil Have All the Good Music: Jesus Music—Where It Began, Where It Is, and Where It Is Going* (1979).

Andrew Donaldson, "CCM Artists and Hymn Recordings," *The Hymn*, 57.4, Autumn 2006, 25–29.

Lynn Hurst, "How to Start Contemporary Worship." Article on Web site of The United Methodist Worship Web site. http://www.gbod.org/worship/default_body.asp?act-reader&item-id-9295.

Donald P. Hustad, *Jubilate II: Church Music in Worship and Renewal* (Carol Stream, IL: Hope Publishing Company, 1993).

The Hymn, 55.3, July 2004. An issue devoted to Contemporary Christian Congregational Song.

Terri Bocklund McLean, *New Harmonies: Choosing Contemporary Music for Worship* (Bethesda, MD: Alban Institute, 1998). A reasoned presentation of the case for consumer-driven music. Criteria for assessing theology and music. Opts for blending of old and new.

Terri Bocklund McLean, *Choosing Contemporary Music: Seasonal, Textual, Topical, Lectionary Indexes* (Minneapolis: Augsburg Fortress, 2000).

Robert H. Mitchell, *I Don't Like That Music: Why Don't We Sing the Good Old Hymns Anymore? Why Don't We Sing the New Songs to the Lord?* (Carol Stream, IL: Hope Publishing Company, 1993).

Robb Redman, *The Great Worship Awakening: Singing a New Song In the Postmodern Church* (San Francisco: Jossey-Bass, 2002).

Robert E. Webber, *Blended Worship: Achieving Substance and Relevance in Worship* (Peabody, MA: Hendrickson Publishers, 1996). Originally published as *Signs of Wonder: The Phenomenon of Convergence in Modern Liturgical and Charismatic Churches* (1992).

Robert E. Webber, *Planning Blended Worship: The Mixture of Old and New* (Nashville: Abingdon Press, 1998).

John D. Witvliet, "The Blessing and Bane of the North American Megachurch: Implications for Twenty-First Century Congregational Song," *The Hymn*, 50.1, January 1999, 6–14; also in *The American Organist*, May 2000, 51-56. Generous bibliography.

John D. Witvliet, *Worship Seeking Understanding: Windows Into Christian Practice* (Grand Rapids: Baker, 2003). On the lament in the psalms and in liturgical prayer, see pages 39–63; on the relation between liturgy and culture, see pages 91–125; regarding the challenge to relate to megachurch music, see pages 263–65.

CHAPTER SEVEN

MUSICAL INSTRUMENTS IN THE WORSHIP SERVICE

~

FROM NO INSTRUMENTS TO A VARIETY OF INSTRUMENTS

Like a number of other questions asked within the church, the question of the validity of musical instruments in the worship service has spawned a generous serving of legalism and biblicism. In my last pastorate, I lived next door to a Church of Christ. On some Saturday afternoons, a pickup would arrive with an electronic organ to be unloaded in time for a scheduled wedding. I have already referred to a theological professor in my own tradition who would sing only unaccompanied psalms, but who on occasion was moved to sway ever so slightly by a hymn played on a piano and sung by others. I attempt here to arrive at a position resting on certain broad principles.

Over the Course of Time

It should be granted that in the New Testament there is not to be found prescription, proscription, precedent, or disparagement regarding the use of musical instruments in the worship service.[1] There would have been no need for instruments; any singing could be accomplished a capella. The absence in the earliest sources of any reference to the use of instruments in the service may well be due simply to their nonuse; their use or nonuse was not an issue.

Post-apostolic references to instrumental usage run the gamut of attitudes, from cordial approval to the severest condemnation. Among both rabbis and church fathers, however, the anti-instrumental polemic is 1) from a later period; and 2) is not directed against worship, but against extra-liturgical instances.[2] Clement of Alexandria (*Prot.* I) and others occasionally speak figuratively: The believer is God's instrument. The music of the medieval church was unison, unaccompanied choral. (In the worship of the Orthodox Church, noninstrumental music has long prevailed.) Organs and bells, however, began to be used in the ritual of the Benedictines as early as the tenth century. By the fifteenth century, organs were in widespread use in the churches in Western Europe, to support the choir or to substitute for a sung part of the service.

In the sixteenth century, the Calvinists in Switzerland stripped organs from the church buildings they had claimed from the Roman Church. Any reservations Luther had about the use of the organ in worship may have been owed not to the organ as such, but to the particularities of the organs which he heard. The reformer did appreciate the use of wind instruments in conjunction with choral music (not the song of the congregation) in large churches with trained choirs. Though some Lutherans had reservations, they came to accept the use of the organ and other instruments in their reformed Mass. Until the late 1700s, however, though the organ played, among other things, the introductions (intonations) to the hymns to be sung, and also alternated with the congregation on some stanzas of the hymns, Lutheran congregations sang without the organ. Calvinists in the Netherlands eventually found the sounds of their wonderful organs irresistible, and admitted that instrument to lead the song of the congregation. An organ might be heard in the larger and wealthier churches in England, but in Scotland, noninstrumental Calvinism would prevail until well into the nineteenth century. In the latter half of the eighteenth century, musicians playing from a rear gallery came to be used in England in churches without organs. Their chief function was to reinforce the choir, especially the bass voice part. Barrel organs were also used in the eighteenth and nineteenth centuries. (Such organs employed, to direct the wind to a particular pipe, a mechanism similar to that found in music boxes. They could thus play only a limited number of tunes.)

In North America, the superior musical culture of Moravians and other German immigrants included widespread use of the organ and other musical instruments in worship. These immigrants also gave North America some of its first organ builders. By the middle of the nineteenth century, use of the newly developed harmonium (reed organ) spread among smaller English churches and chapels and in the churches of North America. The use of the harmonium in the Moody and Sankey revivals in Great Britain persuaded even some Scots that organs were not necessarily of the devil. In 1882, the subsequently very influential introduction to the hymnal of the Methodist Protestant Church (in the United States) published in that year specified that "An organ and a choir are essential to the proper maintenance of singing as an element of worship in church service." The same introduction also gave detailed instructions regarding the organ, choir, and congregation.

In his chirograph of November 22, 2003, Pope John Paul II gave this cautious directive on the use of musical instruments in worship: "Care must be taken . . . to ensure that instruments are suitable for sacred use, that they are fitting for the dignity of the Church and can accompany the singing of the faithful and serve to edify them."[3]

My own tradition has moved over the centuries from the use of no instruments of any kind in public worship to affirming in my denomination's current *Directory for Worship*: "Instrumental music may be a form of prayer since words are not essential to prayer." (How shall we relate this to the criterion of mutual edification set forth in 1 Cor. 14 and implied in Col. 3:16? And to the relation of music to word traced at the end of chapter 1? Perhaps only along associative lines.)

Theory and Present Reality

I have said that the role of music in the worship service is to serve the word, or, more comprehensively stated, serve the liturgy. Also to be noted are the prominence and fundamental significance in Scripture of terms such as "voice" and "word" (admittedly embracing much more than mere words spoken and heard), both divine and human, and with respect to "word," both spoken and written. This phenomenon creates a strong presumption in favor of vocal music, as opposed to instrumental. And by vocal, I mean words sung to express and communicate ideas. This does not include vocalise.

The presumption favoring vocal music can claim allies in these historical facts: In Western society, the role of instruments historically has tended to be that of accompanying the human voice—until as late as the Renaissance. Until the modern age, most congregations that sang did so without instrumental accompaniment. Our very term for unaccompanied singing, *a cappella*, refers to singing "as in the chapel."

> In the church, the primary musical instrument is the human voice, given by God to sing and proclaim the word of God. . . . The use of the human voice is basic to communal worship. Christian proclamation is based on spoken, sung, and heard words that bear the Word Incarnate. (Evangelical Lutheran Church 2001, 26)

Whatever the theory, whether musical instruments may be used in the Christian service of worship is a nonquestion for most of the Western church. Exceptions include the Free Church of Scotland, the Presbyterian Synod of North America, and the Churches of Christ.[4]

In the worship service of the contemporary church in North America, we are most often dealing with several possible sources of music: congregation, choir, pastor, worship leader, cantor, song leader, and instrumentalists. Several chapters in this book at some point address the question of how these sources relate to one another and to the whole. Reason would seem to indicate it to be true, and experience does indeed confirm what we learn from the long history of congregational singing, that is, someone, somehow, must lead the singing. If this is not done by a song leader (called by whatever term) or a choir, then it must be done by one or more instrumentalists.[5]

The role of instruments in the worship service is twofold: 1) To support song, most importantly that of the congregation, but also that of choir, choral ensemble, or vocal soloist (as just noted, in the case of congregational song, unless there is a song leader, one or more instruments do the leading); 2) To provide appropriate solo or ensemble instrumental music. Following is an overview of the instruments commonly used in the service.

THE ORGAN

~

The Organ and the Church

For several centuries, the organ has held pride of place among instruments associated with Christian worship in Europe and North America.

> The pipe organ is to be held in high esteem in the Latin Church, for it is the traditional musical instrument, the sound of which can add a wonderful splendor to the Church's ceremonies and powerfully lifts up people's minds to God and to higher things. (Vatican, *Constitution on the Sacred Liturgy*, n. 120)

Similar praise for "the king of instruments" is commonplace among Protestants. The organ is not more holy than other instruments, but because of its power and variety of sound, it is superior to all others for energizing and leading the song of a congregation of any size in a worship space of any size. People unsure of their own vocal capabilities may be more inclined to join in singing with an organ than with a piano because the organ gives their voice more "cover," and the organ can produce sounds more nearly resembling singing than can the piano.

Though the organ is widely found outside the church, and much of its repertory has nothing to do with the church, it is likely that mention of it will make us think of church. If people hear an organ played at all, it is most likely to be in a church. It was not always thus. The organ not only originated outside the church, but even before the church, and served secular purposes. The earliest form of the instrument is known today as the hydraulis. Though this ancient instrument, just as the modern organ, used air to produce sound, the weight of water was used to regulate the wind pressure, thus the name. By the advent of the Protestant Reformation, the instrument had developed to be essentially what we know today as the organ, and was in widespread use in cathedrals and monasteries across Europe. In addition to the large, stationary instruments, there were smaller, portable or semiportable models. The modern organ may well be the most expensive piece of equipment a church may own. It is also one of the most complex devices in common use; a description of its workings is beyond the scope of this book, but may readily

be found in books named in Useful Resources following this chapter, and on
the Web.

Has the Organ a Future?

For years, the demise of the organ and organists in North America has
been predicted. Like the large symphony orchestra and grand opera, the
organ is viewed by many as a relic on the way to extinction outside
museums. The number of organ majors in schools is down. Even organists
stay away from programs of organ music. Much of the repertory for organ
seems to hold little or no perceptible melodic interest; the music appears to
have been composed to demonstrate the capabilities of the instrument and
the virtuosity of the performer. The promotional piece for a recent, church-
sponsored youth retreat proclaimed what its designers assumed would be
perceived as good news, that is, that "there would be no organs or other dull
music here." On occasion, a large organ may sound uncomfortably loud or
shrill. Many of those churches where organs are most likely to be found are
churches in decline.

Against such a backdrop, the amount of activity in the organ world is
truly amazing. Every issue of *The American Organist* brings news of new
installations, restorations, and additions across the continent; advertise-
ments of several dozen builders of organs in the United States, Canada, and
Europe also appear. The Web site of the Associated Pipe Organ Builders of
America in 2004 included twenty-five of the fifty or so builder firms in
North America. There is also an International Society of Organ Builders.
Organs are imported from the Netherlands, Germany, Italy, Austria,
England, the Czech Republic, and Denmark. At the turn of the century,
from 100 to 120 new organs were being installed annually in North
America, about 85 percent of them in churches. Organs are being restored,
built, and installed even in Europe, where church attendance is abysmal.
Across North America, "Pipe Organ Encounters" acquaint children and
youth with the organ. For churches that use the organ in worship, an
encouraging sign is that organists and the schools where they study are now
placing more emphasis on the role of the organ in the church's worship than
was formerly the case. In the same vein, a good number of gifted composers
are writing appealing hymn-based music for the organ.

Care and Repair of the Organ

Being the expensive, long-lasting, conspicuous, space-taking, wonderful thing that it is, the organ merits the most careful consideration—whether we are concerned only with maintaining what we already have, upgrading the present instrument, or undertaking the purchase of another organ. Fortunately, help is not hard to find. Each issue of *The American Organist* lists practical literature for people in every situation with regard to an organ. In the meantime, here are a few pointers.

If you have an organ, you likely have had contact with an organ technician, someone who lives within your region, if not in your city. You know how to reach this person and he or she will try to come quickly in emergencies. This is a person who should have the know-how necessary to do at least the routine maintenance and very often more. A service contract with such a technician is recommended. It should cover both routine service and emergency calls. Before contracting for the more serious matters, do some checking of the references the technician gives you. If your church has not engaged a service technician, you may get help in securing one by enquiring at sister churches, colleges, or the firm that built your organ.[6]

Alternatives to Any Organ You Now Have

Before any major move with regard to an organ, a dedicated committee must be assembled. (There is helpful literature for this, also.) All options need to be considered. Is your present instrument satisfactory? Does it simply need minor surgery? Does it need something more major, like another manual (keyboard) or a few more ranks of pipes? (Pastors: Explaining what a "rank" is can become a bit involved; if you do not know what the term means, ask an organist to explain.) The every-forty-years reconditioning needed by some of its components? Would your worship be helped by the acquisition of a new instrument? Would your congregation at this juncture be served as well or better by a high-quality piano rather than an organ? The committee studying the options needs to understand that its agenda does not include mastering the intricacies of how an organ works, but getting to know who's who among organ builders. A guided tour through an organ can be both interesting and helpful. Hiring a consultant may be in order; this is normally a well-known and experienced organist.

A new organ

Though not an organist, I am from my youth a lover of the instrument. I attend more organ recitals than any organist I know—with the possible exception of my wife. I currently serve as chaplain of the area chapter of the American Guild of Organists. It does not, however, take a very large instrument to meet the needs of the average congregation. This means that I cannot in good conscience challenge the members of a church to give sacrificially toward the purchase of the kind of organ I would like to have where I worship. One organist has written: "Our wholesale endorsement of the organ as the instrument of sacred music is a curious one, given its expense, its problems of placement, balance, and repair, and the great skill that is needed to play it musically" (Parker 1991, 96).[7]

In planning for a rebuild of your present instrument, or for the purchase of either a used or a new organ, one of the most important decisions is whether your church wants an instrument only for the worship service, or an instrument that is adequate also for recitals—occasional events only rarely well-attended. The latter will have more resources, require more space, cost more, and will certainly make an organist happier. Most churches need only the former, however. In this case you are not looking for an organ that can imitate all the instruments in the orchestra, nor one that can play all of the standard organ repertory. What you want is an organ that "sings," one that makes beautiful sounds to invite, encourage, accompany, and lead singing. Capabilities for accompanying a broad range of choral music, including that sung by children, should also be borne in mind. Focus on the long-term needs of the congregation, not the personal tastes of the current organist (which, like mine, just might be idiosyncratic)—though by all means he or she should be involved, as should be the choir directors.

The size of the organ needed will be determined by the volume of the worship space, its acoustical properties, where the organ is placed, and the size of the assembly present. The average number of ranks in new installations in North America in 2001 was twenty-five. As for the number of manuals, an organist in my last pastorate was, I believe, on the mark when she said that all organs need three, none more than three. It is true that some organ music, even some that, being hymn-based, is not part of the classical repertory, cannot be played on an organ of less than three manuals. An exciting, articulate organ with only two manuals, however, is much to be preferred over a dull one with three. Bigger is by no means always better.

A poll of organists may net you very divergent opinions about this or that in the design of such a complicated instrument as the organ. Not all organs are created equal! One example: A particular question that has divided organists for the last half-century has to do with the manner in which the keys on the manuals and the pedals are connected with the inner mechanism of the organ; some organists have argued stoutly that the linkage should be mechanical—the far older style of linkage known as "tracker action." Others have insisted on some combination of electrical/electronic and pneumatic. In the final analysis, however, what matters is, as the organ builder Walter Holtkamp Jr. put it, ". . . *how an organ sounds in the room and how it responds to the needs of the player*" (in Ferguson 2001, 58; italics mine).

If planning a new worship space in which an organ will be used, it is of the utmost importance that the architect consult with a potential organ builder, even if the organ is not to be installed immediately. Except for some smaller instruments, no two organs are alike, but each is tailor-made for the space in which it is installed. Both aural factors and visual integration into the whole must be taken into account.

A rebuilt organ

Rebuilding the instrument you now have is much cheaper than buying a new instrument. Every year, there are about one hundred major rebuilds in North America. In addition, many organs have pipes added or the manuals upgraded or increased in number. Also, electronic additions to existing pipe organs have become rather common. Especially in view here are electronic substitutes for the pipes that are lower in pitch, those pipes that require more room and are more expensive.

A used organ

Your (or your neighbor's) organ technician may know of instruments that are for sale. Another option is the classified advertisement section of *The American Organist* or *The Diapason*. Still another is the Organ Clearing House (in Useful Resources).

Financing an organ

How to finance such a major expense as the purchase of a new organ, or even the rebuilding of, or adding to, an older one? Normally such expenditures are in the "over and above" category in a church's budget. Costs can be wrapped into the budget for a new worship space. Major gifts may be sought from well-to-do members. Life insurance is one way in which members can leverage their gifts into larger sums at the time of their deaths. An "adopt-a-pipe" campaign is sometimes mounted. In both new installations and rebuilds there are sometimes tasks that church members can perform that trim a little from the costs. Some strategies not only help financially; they can lead to more personal interest in the organ. A new instrument does not need to be all installed at once; often churches will install only a part of what has been planned, completing the design as funds become available.

An electronic organ

In 1935, Laurens Hammond made the first electric organ; its tone was generated by electromechanical means. Subsequent developments led to the electronic organ, whose tones were generated electronically, without any mechanical aid. In the seven decades since Hammond made his first organ, enormous strides have been made in improving the quality of tone produced by the electric or electronic instrument. Current state-of-the-art technology is called digital sampling—the recording and storage of a sample of the sound produced by an organ pipe, to be summoned forth by the organist. Optimum sound from this process depends on the storage capacity of the computer, the quantity and quality of the speakers, and the room into which the sound is emitted. Large electronic instruments with many resources are marketed by several firms in North America and Europe.[8]

Without question, the electronic organ is here to stay. It and electronic additions to pipe organs are increasingly getting the nod from organists who have undergone a conversion experience. What matters, of course, other things being equal, is not whether the instrument has pipes, but the quality of the sounds it can produce. The quality of the sounds of electronic instruments continues to rise, although some kinds of sounds are of higher quality than others. Before anyone today is qualified to make a judgment as to the worth of the electronic organ, he or she must seek out one or more of the very best, latest installations in acoustically optimum spaces. Most people in the pews, in any case, could never tell the difference between the sounds of pipe ("butter") and electronic ("margarine") organs, and it is not the mission of the church to bring them around. It may help to remember, also, that the latter does not have to sound like the former (though some manufacturers of electronic organs themselves encourage people to make this comparison). What matters most is the instrument's capability to lead and support the song of the congregation.

Arguments in favor of the electronic organ include: they are generally far less expensive to purchase; less space is required; and they are probably less expensive to maintain. The question of the relatively rapid obsolescence of anything electronic versus the anticipated long life of a pipe organ is to be considered. (Just because some pipes in European organs are still sounding after a few centuries of use, however, does not mean your pipe organ will not need regular and emergency servicing and replacement of parts.) To make helpful comparisons when shopping for an electronic instrument, you may need to become familiar with some of the technical terms used.

A combination organ

These instruments make use of both pipes and electronic sound sources. Thus far, there seem not to be many builders of this hybrid instrument, but at least one such builder is currently advertising in *The American Organist*.

THE PIANO

~

A grand piano can be very useful in the service of worship. Sizes range from the baby grand (four feet, eleven inches long) to the concert grand (nine feet or, rarely, more). Below are listed some advantages to using a piano instead of, or with, an organ.

1) The piano's percussive quality (not possessed by the organ) is a definite plus in leading hymns. On the other hand, whereas the volume of the sounds made by the organ remains constant as long as the key is depressed, that of the piano begins to decay immediately. Moreover, the sound produced by an organ pipe is much more like the human voice than is that emitted by a vibrating piano string.

2) A good share of the choir's music and an increasing number of new hymns envision the use of a piano rather than an organ.

3) The piano sound can provide a pleasant contrast with that of the organ.

4) The piano can, at least on occasion, be played in tandem with the organ in leading and accompanying congregational song. Unless the gathering is a large one, however, it is all too easy for organ and piano together to overpower the congregation's song.

5) The piano is the preferred instrument for accompanying some instruments.

6) If your organist is unavailable and no substitute can be found, a pianist may be available to fill the bill.

7) Though the initial outlay for a piano is not small, pianos require relatively little maintenance beyond the twice-yearly (or less often) tuning.

There are limits to the size of worship space and assembly beyond which the piano's sound will be insufficient, unless it is amplified. If the piano is to be used with the organ, they should be fairly close together, never at opposite ends of the room. Does it need to be said that the two instruments need to be tuned together if they are to be played together?

In deciding on the purchase or restoration of a piano, competent and trustworthy judgment should be sought. In the case of restoration, seek a professional appraisal and estimate. It is to be hoped that your church will not be offered the gift of a piano that a pianist would not consider desirable. Contrary to violins, pianos—like the human body—do not improve with age.

MISCELLANEOUS ELECTRONIC INSTRUMENTS AND AIDS

Several electronic instruments, in addition to the familiar electronic organ, are available. Here, too, the current word for the most advanced method of sound production is "digital." Things to look for include quality and volume of sound, the touch or feel of the keyboard, and the instrument's ability to sustain a sound. Electronic keyboards can be split, so that the lower half, for instance, may be made to give forth the sound of a string bass, and the upper the sound of a piano. The biggest plus that electronic instruments give us is their ability to create sounds that acoustic instruments cannot make. Here follow the basic types of electronic instruments.

The Electronic Piano

Much less expensive than the acoustic piano, the electronic piano requires less space and is portable. Some offer alternative sounds—that of the harpsichord, for instance. For Sunday school classrooms, the electronic piano is definitely to be preferred over the old, hand-me-down, often small and not maintained, acoustic pianos found in so many classrooms.

The Portable Keyboard

Available in various sizes, the portable keyboard is smaller and less expensive than the electronic piano. It is capable of imitating various instruments. It is also self-contained and easily moved about. Most contain an amplifier and a speaker system.

The Synthesizer

The synthesizer is capable of producing a wide variety of sounds, both like and unlike those made by acoustic instruments. It may be used as a solo instrument—as an organ, with an organ, or to imitate other acoustic instruments; or to accompany organ or choir (Munro 1997c). If used primarily with the organ, it may be wise to situate the synthesizer's speakers inside the organ.

MIDI

The Musical Instrument Digital Interface, or MIDI, was developed in the early 1980s. Added to the organ, it enables the organist to play one or more synthesizers from the organ bench, creating sounds that no acoustic instrument could make. If integrated into the organ, the playing can be done through the organ's keys and pedals. Otherwise, a small keyboard to the side of the console is used. This is less convenient. Connected to a sequencer, MIDI allows the organist to record his or her playing, then to move to some other part of the room and hear what that music sounds like. What has been recorded can be edited, and can be heard at a later time— not as a recording, but as the instrument itself playing in real time. More important, a MIDI and synthesizer can add endless new sound capabilities to the organ. MIDIs are manufactured and marketed by several firms.

Electronics and the Integrity of Worship

"The very concept [of prerecorded accompaniments for choirs and congregations] is antithetical to the most fundamental understandings of prayer as openness to the sovereign Spirit of God" (Doran and Troeger

1992, 87). I mentioned above that there have been objections to the use of electronic devices as additions to, and especially as substitutes for, pipe organs. Not surprisingly, questions have arisen about the larger use of electronics in the musical part of worship. That to which the most strenuous objections have been raised regards the substitution of canned music for the live musician. Opponents of any such substitution often insist that the integrity of worship requires the physical presence of the musician.[9]

Jayson Rod Engquist writes: "As long as a live person is playing the instrument in 'real' time, I have no objection to their [electronic instruments] use in worship" (1998, 3). Does the fact that there is neither any living person nor real time involved preclude our being drawn into drama or music or a worship service mediated to us by means of TV or DVD? I know of a church pianist in one town and a church organist in another who prerecord the keyboard music for their services when they have to be away. (What the congregation hears on Sunday morning are not recorded sounds, but live sounds in real time. However, important defining characteristics of those sounds were determined outside of what is real time for the congregation, determined in isolation from the worshiping congregation.) In their towns there are no substitutes. Are there more appealing solutions to the problem? Would it be better to ask a violinist in the congregation to lead the music? Find a song leader and sing unaccompanied? Pay for a musician to come from another town and play?

A well-known scholar in the field of Christian worship, Don Saliers, after considering the questions raised for some by the use of electronic sound production, concludes: "I see no reason to reject what sophisticated technology may do for music in liturgy provided that the living presence and collaborative sense of worship itself is not impeded or distorted" (1995, 32). The American Guild of Organists, understandably concerned about its members being electronically substituted, in 1996 adopted "A Position Statement . . . on the Use of Prerecorded Music for Worship," which reads in part as follows:

> Prerecorded substitutes cannot replace living, breathing worship leaders who interact with living, breathing congregations. The use of recorded choirs, organs, and cantors, although it may seem to serve an immediate need, has the effect of discouraging the local community from marshaling the resources necessary for authentic celebration.

The Guild urges churches and synagogues to resist the temptation to replace the offering of the community with such impersonal devices as taped accompaniment tracks, instrumental reproductions, prerecorded sermons and prayers, and the like. Rather, the Guild advocates the cultivation of live music making, preaching, and praying in communal worship. (*The American Organist*, April 1996, 23)[10]

I believe that certain words in three of the statements just cited contribute to making a strong case against the substitution of live musicians in the worship service by canned music. It is not enough that there be present "a live person . . . playing the instrument in 'real' time." Something else is essential. All leaders of worship, including musicians, must during the service be open to the sovereign Spirit of God; they must interact with the congregation; the collaborative sense of worship itself must be upheld. Any worship leader who fails these tests is a candidate for electronic substitution. I have not come across any reference to the relevance of the musician's faith or non-faith for collaboration in the leading of Christian worship. Worship is to be sincere—in the words of the apostle, "from the heart." What bearing does integrity have on this aspect?

HANDBELLS AND HANDCHIMES

~

The employment of a bell (not handbell choirs!) in the Christian worship service goes back to the Middle Ages. The twentieth century witnessed the introduction of handbell choirs into North American worship, and their use is now widespread. Churches and schools normally begin with a set of two octaves (twenty-five bells) or three octaves (thirty-seven bells). Bells are also sold in four-, five-, and six-octave sets, as well as individually. Handbells are of bronze, and are made in the Netherlands, England, and the United States. Most bells are of very high quality and should last for years. The number of ringers needed depends, of course, on the number of bells, though by some ringers ringing more than two bells, the number can be kept to a minimum. Usually, eight to fifteen people plus the director are involved. Though some ringers happen to be trained, even professional, musicians, ringing handbells is essentially an endeavor for amateurs, which is one of the instrument's appeals. Some large churches maintain more than one bell choir, all using, at different times, the same bells. Cases, tables, and other accessories are necessary. Domestic handbells cost less than imported. One North American maker currently advertises on the Web a thirty-seven-bell set for just over $8,700.

Where to situate the ringers and their tables in the worship space for playing during a service can be a little tricky. If the ringers are in front of the congregation, bell-ringing is as much a visual as an aural phenomenon; potentially enjoyable to watch, it can become a sideshow, especially if one (or more) of the more athletic ringers is responsible for more than two bells. Any grimness or evidence of anxiety on the part of ringers about their missing a cue is also counterproductive. Spatial and visual considerations must be taken into account; the tables that hold bells at rest take space and may appear intrusive in the worship space. Some choirs ring from a rear gallery or some other location out of sight, where they, among other things, do not need to wear vestments.

There is a large and ever-growing supply of music available, as is training for directors and ringers. Bells can lead a processional; be used with or without other instruments; substitute for the organ or piano on the prelude, offertory, and postlude; and substitute for the voice on descant parts. In the worship service, bells are best reserved for occasional use. By no means should their use be allowed to encroach on the song of the congregation. Difficulties may arise when a set of bells is given as a memorial and the memorialist expects the bells to be rung often.

Handchimes are a less expensive alternative to bells. A five-octave set may be found for a little less than $5,000.

Apart from whatever use is made of them in the worship service, bells may serve as a means of fostering community (every ringer is important); in developing the gifts of the ringers, including skills useful in other musical activities; as a ministry to nursing homes and other institutions; and as a means of involving nonmembers.

OTHER INSTRUMENTS

⁓

Perhaps one reason many churchgoers pay so little attention to the service music played in worship is because one week's service music seems, at least to them, so similar to another week's. Functioning like Muzak in the dentist's office, the music is, like the air-conditioning, just there; people hear it, but do not listen to it. Some variety in instrumentation can cause woolgathering people to sit up and notice, and chatterers to shush and listen—though it is not guaranteed to do so. In some circumstances, not only preceding a worship service, the only way to make listeners out of talkers is for someone to get the attention of those present and say something.

Plucked string instruments such as the guitar, harp, and autoharp can complement a simple vocal solo in a most appealing way. Another plucked instrument, the harpsichord, may on occasion serve to enrich musical worship. Orff and percussion instruments merit occasional use with certain genres of music. None of these instruments is adequate, however, for leading the song of the congregation. All instrumentalists leading or accompanying congregational singing should be aware of what is involved in that unique task. On those rare occasions when a bagpipe is used indoors, the smaller instrument with less volume should be sought. If used with the organ or some other instrument, be certain both are tuned together! The above-named instruments, in addition to standard instruments like the violin, flute, clarinet, oboe, recorder, and on grand occasions, brass instruments, can be used in all kinds of ways to enhance our service of worship. (Every effort should be made to avoid all but the most necessary tuning of instruments during the service.) Unused talent may be lurking among the membership. When the budget allows, guest musicians may be summoned.

A CAVEAT

⁓

This caveat as we conclude this chapter: The song of the congregation has ever been an endangered species. This should be borne unyieldingly in mind as we consider the use of musical instruments, including the keyboard variety, in the worship service. Too easily, without so much as a bow to critical reflection, a very large part of the church in North America today—that part not involved with CCM—assumes that the musical practices it has inherited from the twentieth century are of the essence of what it means to be the church—and this in the context of a massive rethinking of worship in general. But this does not stop me from dreaming my dream of a singing congregation, the kind described thus by Mark Sedio:

> The [music] leader should always begin with the idea of unaccompanied singing as the model for all congregational song. When a congregation is asked to sing without the aid of instrumental forces, the individuals making up the congregation listen to themselves and to others. It is here that the congregation can best become aware of and find its true voice. Something happens when a group of people joins their voices in song, especially in unison song. Voices, each with their own character and timbre, come together. Barriers drop. The individual gives way to the corporate. The singing takes on a life of its own. The group "gels." This is the goal of the leader of the people's song. (1998, 21–22; see also 14–15)

This dreamed-of reformation cannot happen without musicians, but it will not likely be initiated by them; their training has in all likelihood not prepared them for it. Nor do they have the authority. Only clergypersons do. Working together, musicians and clergy can move toward the goal.

– Useful Resources –

The American Guild of English Handbell Ringers Web site is http://www.agehr.org/.

The American Guild of Organists Web site is www.agohq.org. Helpful material may be sought there and in any issue of *The American Organist*.

John T. Fesperman, "Organ," in Randel, 600–12.

Herbert Gotsch and Edward W. Klammer, "The Music of Instruments," in Halter and Schalk, 172–216. Describes the organ and the role of organ and other instruments in worship.

Carl Halter and Carl Schalk, eds., *A Handbook of Church Music* (St. Louis: Concordia Publishing House, 1978).

Orpha Ochse, *The History of the Organ in the United States* (Bloomington and Indianapolis: Indiana University Press, 1975).

John K. Ogasapian, *Church Organs: A Guide to Selection and Purchase* (Grand Rapids: Baker Book House, 1983).

The Organ Clearing House, Box 290786, Charlestown, MA 02129-0214; 627-241-8550, 617-241-8551 (fax); john@organclearinghouse.com, for information on available used organs and restoration of organs.

Barbara Owen, Bibliography for "Organ," in Randel, 611–12.

Don Michael Randel, ed., *The Harvard Dictionary of Music*, 4th ed. (Cambridge, MA: Harvard University Press, 2003).

CHAPTER EIGHT
MUSIC AND THE WORSHIP SPACE

~

The design of a church confronts the architect with unique challenges. Spatial, visual, and acoustical considerations in the design of the ideal church all distinguish the worship space from every other kind of gathering place. In the worship service, all participate, not just those up front. A sound from anywhere should be heard everywhere. Our concern in this chapter is how to maximize the quality of the musical part of worship. It will be noted that the same considerations that tend to maximize our consciousness of community are some of the very things that maximize our experience of the musical parts of the service.

THE SIZE AND SHAPE OF THE WORSHIP SPACE

~

Is there a pastor or church musician who has not experienced the demoralizing effect of a wee congregation huddled in a capacious sanctuary? Is there one who has not known this firsthand, compounded by the fact that those who are present seem to take their places as far from their leaders as possible, and may be scattered from one another as well? The same phenomena take their toll in equal measure on the congregation's singing. If we are to practice the communion of the saints by means of our singing, we must be able to hear one another. This requires that we be physically close to one another. Ideally, the congregation should, under normal circumstances, almost fill the worship space. In the second place, no one should be farther than about four feet from the person nearest to him or her.

> If people sit more than four feet away from each other, they won't sing in case they are heard. If they sit less than four feet away from each other, they will sing because they hear others singing. It is as simple as that, and has to be taken very seriously. (Bell 2000, 128–29)

If we are unable to fill our meeting space and cannot find a smaller space that might serve, perhaps the best thing we can do is to arrange for the congregants to sit reasonably close together on one side, near the front. (I realize that this may require the threat of excommunication.)

One other consideration in seeking to maximize the song of the congregation (and the sense of community in worship) has to do with what, to borrow a term from the world of electronics, we may call interfacing. As we have noted, while worship is indeed oriented to God, we are not worshiping alone, but together—at the same time, in the same place, in the same way. Worship at the table of the Lord's Supper, assuming we do not remain in the pews, but go forward to participate, very clearly shows both of these simultaneously occurring orientations. So should the congregation's prayers, sung and spoken, and also the confessing together our faith—if we include a creed in our service. My praise of God strengthens you, and yours contributes to my being encouraged and built up in the faith. Now, we can accomplish this mutual edification much more efficiently if what I can see is not your back, but your face. Carry this logic to its conclusion and you will understand that the ideal gathering is one in which all the gathered are arranged in a circle or a square.[1]

One unfortunate configuration of the congregation is the type found in some concert halls and cinemas (and also in Gothic cathedrals)—a space generally longer than it is wide, with parallel rows of seats or pews across the width of the space from front to back. This configuration, though it fosters neither community nor good singing, has been widely adopted. In some situations it may be possible to angle the seating to achieve something approaching a semicircle. One tactic that involves no rearranging of the furniture is to have the members on either side of an aisle turn ninety degrees to face those across the aisle when singing and reciting the creed. (This does presuppose that there is sufficient distance between the pews or rows of seats for the people to stand comfortably.)

The interior of both the church of my boyhood and that in which I last ministered followed, to some extent, the nineteenth-century Akron Plan—a space wider than it is long, a floor that slopes downward from the rear of the congregation to its front, pews that radiate in a little less than a semicircular arc around a raised platform. On the platform were placed the pulpit and its chairs, behind which was space for the choir and organ console. The seating was divided into three parts, giving a total of four aisles. Both of these churches also had rear balconies. This floor plan undeniably promotes community and, ipso facto, congregational singing. If the curvature of the arc is somewhat reduced, the preacher will not find it difficult to share face-to-face contact with all present. (The cruciform floor plan does present problems in this regard, as well as dividing the congregation—visually and aurally.) Some critics find anything approximating the Akron Plan to resemble too much a lecture hall, or to foster a feeling of spectators-performers—more so than in other configurations. A larger and lower dais may relieve this a bit.

Other configurations have been adopted. Alas, none is perfect. All architecture is a compromise. What matters most is that the people are able to participate as fully as possible—visually and aurally—with those leading in worship and with the other members of the congregation.

Obviously, balconies do have their merits. Some object to them because they divide the congregation. The degree of feeling of isolation we may experience in a balcony turns in some measure on our ability to see those below us, not only when we are standing, but also when seated. A shallow balcony presents less difficulty than a deep one. I for myself have found balconies to be very congenial; they can give an inspiring view of a large part of the congregation at worship, and I do not feel isolated or second class. One disadvantage, if people are seated under the balcony, is that the sound under a balcony is never equal to that elsewhere in the room, nor is the sense of participation.

WHERE TO PUT THINGS: THE LOCATION OF CHOIR AND INSTRUMENTS

~

Spatial, aural, and visual considerations must all be taken into account when deciding where the choir, organ, piano, and other musical instruments can best be located. As in other matters, here too there is no arrangement that is perfect from every standpoint, and compromises will have to be made. Here follow some basic considerations.

Wherever They Are Put

Choir and instruments

1) Choir and instruments are two distinct sound sources that must blend their sounds together. They must therefore be close to one another. This holds true not only due to aural considerations, but also because the director of the choir is very often the organist or pianist; the keyboardist, director, and singers must be in one another's lines of sight. Also, the keyboardist, even if not directing, should be able to hear the choir; for this reason the keyboardist should be in front of the choir that, in turn, is in front of the organ pipes.

2) Dividing the choir and dividing the organ, as in a divided chancel, is less than ideal.

3) Movable seating in the musicians' space allows for flexibility.

4) Provision should be made for access and space needed for disabled musicians.

5) Avoid locating musicians next to high-traffic areas where they may be disturbed by passersby, for instance: the organ console near and on the same level as an entrance to the worship space.

6) The music program of many churches suffers because planners were too stingy with space, and there is not any room for instrumentalists or for numerical growth in the choir.

The choir

1) A choir's sound and singers' ability to see the director both benefit from the choristers being on a tiered floor.

2) Wherever the choir is situated, its members, when singing, should face the congregation.

The organ

1) For several reasons, it is imperative that in planning to build or remodel a worship space, the architect have input from the organ builder. More than any other instrument, an organ is part of the room in which it stands. We may even say that the organ and the room in which it is located together form one instrument, for it is impossible to separate the sound of the organ from all that makes the room what it is—size, shapes, and surfaces.

2) An organ's sound is maximized by being focused along the long axis of the worship space. This is difficult to achieve if the organ is located at the front or the rear and if the worship space is wider than it is long. The sound should not have to suffer going around a corner, as often happens in divided chancel sanctuaries. The sound of the organ is optimized if all the different sounds that constitute it are blended and focused. To this end, the organ as a whole is best situated in a sound-reflective housing, or when the separate divisions are enclosed (except on the front) in resonant cases.

3) The divisions of the organ should all be on the same level, and close to one another—except in the case of an echo organ. They should not be located directly behind the singers. A trompette en chamade (trumpet in façade) may, like the echo organ, also be at the opposite end of the space—and thus not in the organ's façade.

4) Façade pipes (whether working pipes of the organ or just for show) and decorative grilles must not be allowed to hinder the sound of the pipes behind them.

5) Locating the console even a small distance from the rest of the organ may help the organist better judge how the organ sounds. "... the organist needs to be out from under the organ to hear it and the congregation. . . . It is in the hymns that the members of the congregation stand and state their faith. The organist must be in a position to hear them and lead them" (Walter Holtkamp, Jr., in Ferguson 2001, 56).

6) The organ should not be placed in front of or near a window. Even if this arrangement should pass muster visually, a window does not provide the needed reflective surface, it will not be the same temperature as the walls around it, and a broken window may admit water that can seriously damage the organ. Some windows permit sunlight to shine into musicians' eyes.

7) An organ cannot function without blowers, and blowers cannot function without making at least a certain amount of noise. Blowers need a supply of clean, temperate air—not cold, damp, unfiltered air from basement or street. Decisions regarding the location of the blowers should bear both of these facts in mind. Noise from air-handling equipment must also be considered.

8) If the organ is located anywhere in the room but to the rear of the congregation, then how the instrument relates visually to

other parts of the room and its furnishings becomes more critical; the visible part of the organ is part of a larger visual whole, and should be integrated into it. The case and pipes of an organ can present a rather glorious face, but it is most unfortunate when the presence of the organ visually overwhelms pulpit, table, and font—as does happen. Remember, music's role in worship is to serve.

9) The use of the organ in the worship service takes priority over its possible use in recitals or concerts. (For the latter, closed-circuit television is used in some cases to make visible an organist otherwise unseen, and to give an up-close look at the organist's feet and hands.)

10) A movable console for the organ and wheels on the piano make for flexibility in positioning the console and the piano. While the console of a tracker organ cannot be moved about, it does not have to stand next to the organ.

A variety of arguments have been put forth to justify placing the musicians in the front or in the rear. Here follow the most important ones.

Put the Musicians in the Front[2]

1) The choir, while in its song addressing God, at the same time has a message for the congregation. Like all music in the service, choral song partakes of this double orientation. A vested, capable choir can be inspiring visually as well as aurally. Choristers may, through facial and bodily expression, reinforce their audible proclamation of the Word. These advantages are, of course, compromised if the choir sings from a divided chancel, in which case the congregation has only a side view of the choir. Vocal soloists are most often situated with the choir, and the soloist's contribution greatly benefits from the singer being visible to the congregation. Contemporary North

Americans are oriented to visual communication; we want to see the action, not just hear it. This argument applies both to the choir's singing of choral music and to its singing in support of congregational song.

2) A children's choir, when singing, will invariably stand in front, facing the congregation. It is important that the children be seated, before and after singing, where they will not distract the congregation.

3) The organist's chief function is to lead the singing of the congregation. To do this most effectively, the organist needs to be able to hear that singing—when it occurs, not later. If located to the rear of the congregation, there will inevitably be a time lag between the singing of the congregation and the organist's hearing of the sound. By the time the organist hears something, the congregation will have moved on to something else.

Put the Musicians in the Rear

1) Optimum sound from the choir, the organ, and other instruments will be obtained when these are behind and on a level above the congregation, close enough to the ceiling so that sound is reflected from it very soon after its production—but not closer than fifteen feet.

2) The presence of the musicians in front can easily upstage the primary symbols of word, font (or baptistry, if this be visible), and table.

3) Musicians located behind the liturgist-preacher are consigned to seeing only the back of his or her head, and miss the facial expressions and hands and body language. If the musicians are unable to see the preacher's face, they may be more readily distracted by

what they can see—the congregation. In some situations, they may not even be able to hear well what is being said. Some churches have alleviated this problem by using speakers and closed-circuit television. Or the choir (and hence also the organ) may be located to the side of the preacher-liturgist. This placement, however, may not be ideal for the sound of the organ and vocalists; it may also make it difficult for the congregation to see the musicians.

4) Bodily movements—in playing, making adjustments to the instrument, changing music, a nodding head, the suppression of a yawn, or the blowing of a nose—on the part of the musicians can be distracting, as can be the movement of the swell shades on the organ.

THE ACOUSTICS OF THE WORSHIP SPACE

~

The Importance of Good Acoustics

"Perhaps the greatest challenge in architectural acoustics is the worship environment" (Fleisher 1990, 7). A good acoustical environment is essential for us to experience the reality of the community that is Christ's body, as opposed to being just so many individuals. "A bright, lively, and reinforcing acoustical environment is important, therefore, primarily for the sake of the congregation" (Schalk 1983, 270).

To hear or not to hear is a huge problem in contemporary North American society—especially for us presbycusis-afflicted seniors (those with age-related hearing loss). Regrettably, many churches build without considering the question, confident that they can amplify their way out of any difficulty. That amplification can help is cause for thanksgiving. But amplification is at best helpful only for making heard the word spoken into the microphone. Many amplifying systems do give a helpful volume of sound, but it is not authentic sounding.

Our concern here is how the musical parts of the service fare in the worship space. Acoustics are a function of the volume, shapes, and surfaces involved. In an already-standing building, it is the surfaces that are most amenable to acoustical improvement. Remember that our goal in this regard is to keep the sound going without distortion for the optimum length of time. This is accomplished by excluding or minimizing some things, and including or maximizing others. What we seek is a space that is acoustically "alive," not "dead" or "dry." "Vigorous corporate worship is impossible in a dry room" (Alec Wyton).

Acoustics 101

What we perceive to be sound in our worship space is a quantity of mechanical waves which travel from one or more of the sound sources (preacher, choir, instrument, etc.) through air to reach our ears and set our auditory mechanism going. Altogether a most wonderful phenomenon! The sound we hear as music begins as vibrations in a human body or some musical instrument. These vibrations are then transmitted to us by particles of air banging into one another until the vibrations reach our ears. These vibrations, or sound waves, do not all reach our ears by the same route. The same vibration comes to us directly, by simply banging its way through all the particles between the sound source and us; and indirectly, by traveling first to one or more reflective surfaces (the ceiling and the walls, for instance), which reflect(s) the vibration to us.

It is obvious that those waves that take the direct route from the sound source to our ears will reach us a wee tad sooner than those that take the roundabout route. This means that we hear each feature of the sound not all at once, but more than one time in very close succession. It is this perceived fusion of sounds coming by differing routes to our ears that gives the sound a richer, fuller quality. A room in which this happens is called a live, that is, a resonant/reverberant room. When potentially reflective surfaces, however, do not *reflect* the sound that strikes them, but *absorb* it, most or all of what we hear is merely the sound that comes to us directly. This kind of room is acoustically dead, or dry.

The contribution made by reflected sound waves to the final product is termed reverberation (or resonance), and it is an acoustical property we

very much desire—for the sake of music. Reverberation is the "prolonga-
tion of sound within a space after the sound source has stopped" sounding
(Shade 2002, 18). Reverberation increases the loudness, and blends, to a
certain degree, one sound with the next. Though beneficial for music, reverberation can be detrimental for speech intelligibility. Reverberation can be
excessive, and is undesirable when it tends to distort both speech and
music. Excessive reverberation is rare, however, in churches smaller than
cathedral size.[3] It is easier to reduce reverberation time than it is to increase
it. In addition to optimum reverberation time, *The Harvard Dictionary of
Music* mentions as acoustically desirable: freedom from external noises, even
distribution of sound throughout the room, balanced response between
high and low frequency sounds, and a sense of "acoustical intimacy"
(Silsbee, in Randel 2003, 12).

Improving the Acoustics of the Worship Space

Down with absorption!

Some years ago, I was presiding at a monthly meeting of the
governing board of a small congregation without an installed pastor. The
church is a lovely antebellum structure brought brick by brick from its
original location and erected anew in a property awash with very old and
large live oaks. At the meeting of the board, concern was voiced about
the wall-to-wall carpet in the sanctuary. It was showing its age. The
sunlight that streamed in though the tall, clear glass windows had accelerated the fading of the carpet's deep red color. I suggested that instead
of replacing the carpet, they might expose the concrete on which it lay,
and greatly enhance the acoustics. If desired, the concrete could be given
an attractive treatment with paint or some other finish coat. Other, more
costly alternatives might include parquet and quarry tile. I could see
immediately that such a proposal could only be considered zany by those
present, even if it meant saving a bundle of the church's money. Sure
enough, when the vote was taken at our next meeting, no discussion was
necessary; it was apparent that discussion had already taken place. The
otherwise lovely worship space would continue to be as sound-dead as a
funeral parlor.

As noted in chapter 2, people need to get over the idea that our worship space is a place for our private devotions, and that we want, therefore, to muffle as much sound as possible. Someone has said, "The sound of the footsteps of our fellow worshipers should be music to our ears." The worship space is not our living room. If concert halls where the audience does not participate are not carpeted, why would we install carpet in a worship space where the congregation *does* participate? If your worship space is carpeted, there probably is no single thing you can do to improve congregational singing more than to remove the offender. If your governing body has to pay too high a price for this in terms of relations with people, a fallback step might be to apply or leave carpet only in the aisle(s). You should also be aware that carpet is available that has a significantly reduced sound absorbency.

Carpet is lavishly applied to worship spaces not only for aural reasons— to reduce the sounds of foot traffic, but also for visual—because some people have it in their minds that carpet is the most attractive floor covering. Even the dais, where there is relatively little sound of foot traffic to muffle, must project the appearance of quiet, warmth, and comfort. Just as many homeowners have rediscovered flooring they find much more interesting than wall-to-wall carpet, it is not too much to hope that the decision makers in our churches may make the same happy discovery. I know of one congregation that is delighted to have exposed the heart pine flooring in their historic worship space.[4]

Surfaces that absorb sound: That is an acoustical no-no. (Some absorption may be necessary in very large spaces to prevent echo. Variable acoustic curtains, blankets, and baffles have been installed in some spaces. They can be adjusted to give optimum quality to both spoken word and music.) The most significant offender in this regard is one we can do nothing about: the human body and the clothing that covers most of it.[5]

But another gross offender is, like carpet, one over which we do, to some degree at least, have control: the pew or seat cushion, loose or attached to the furniture. Carpet and cushions not only absorb sound, stopping it dead in its tracks; they also cancel out the potential benefit of otherwise reflective surfaces of floor and seating. It is true that a very few people have physical conditions that make a cushion almost mandatory.

But it is also a fact that a well-designed wooden pew or chair, one that is ergonomically contoured to accommodate the human form, can be quite comfortable, far more comfortable than the bleachers people sit on for longer periods of time at ball games. It is true that when people are seated, their bodies cancel out most of the absorbency of as many cushions as are occupied. Most often, however, people stand to sing, and a good part of their song travels no farther than the nearest cushion. (European Christians did not sit on anything until about the fourteenth century; Eastern Christians still stand for the entire service.) Again, if it costs too much in terms of relations to remove or never install cushions, in this matter too, material is available that absorbs significantly less sound than does the material used for the average cushion: vinyl or fabric with latex or vinyl backing for the covering, and, for the padding, closed-cell foam. An encouraging story from one church: After some discussion, it was resolved to remove the cushions that covered every pew seat, with this proviso: that individual cushions would be available at the entrances to the sanctuary for those who wanted them. Word is that few people bother to avail themselves![6]

Carpet, cushions, and other fabrics are not the only undesirables that rob us of the sounds of instruments, choir, and congregation. In the mid-twentieth century, many churches mistakenly thought their worship spaces would be more congenial if steps were taken to reduce sounds as much as possible. (The preacher could, of course, be heard by using an amplification system.) To this end, sound-absorbent material was liberally applied to ceilings and walls! Acoustical tiles began showing up in churches in untold number. More recently, churchly authorities have come to their acoustical senses, at least in part, and at least temporarily; the once-prized acoustical material has been excommunicated, uncovering a more reflective surface, or has been sealed, covered, or plastered over to render it less sound absorbent.

Other possible offenders may masquerade as reflective surfaces: thin gypsum board applied to studs or furring strips, plywood, porous concrete block, and window glass. Good sound reflection, especially of low frequency sound, requires not only a hard surface, but mass behind it—such as a brick or stone wall.

Up with reflection

Let the sound go! Minimizing the barriers to its trajectory is one side of the equation. The other is enhancing the sound by maximizing those things that foster good sound. Here are some:

1) A large room. The larger the volume of the room the better.

2) A high (minimum thirty feet), vaulted ceiling (and thus tall walls), not flat, not concave (like the dome in St. Paul's Cathedral in London), but coffered or sloped, or otherwise sound-diffusing. A high overhead allows sounds to move and mix. Volume and height make for long reverberation and supportive reflections of sounds. Volume and height do cost— up front, for maintenance, and for cooling and heating.

3) No wide, fan-shaped floor plans.

4) No deep transepts, no deep balconies.

5) Opposing walls not precisely parallel.

6) Irregular, uneven, undulating surfaces, and molded details help ensure diffusion.

7) A floor of concrete, stone, or brick.

8) Sound benefits from being projected from an elevated location. Thus chancel, organ, choir, and any loudspeakers should be elevated. Congregational sound may benefit from tiered or sloping seating.

9) A choir's sound will benefit from a solid, reflective wall behind it, a sloped ceiling (at least fifteen feet above choir), and angled side walls. Overhead reflectors and choral shells can sometimes assist the projection of the choir's sounds.

It seems to be rather well agreed that a room that is acoustically satisfactory for congregational song will also be satisfactory for an organ or other instruments. An expert organ technician may be able to voice the organ in such a way as to compensate (with regard to the organ) for some acoustical deficiencies of the room.

Achieving the amount of reverberation that is optimal for music is almost certain to render speech less intelligible. A compromise may have to be made. Acoustician Neil Thompson Shade tells us that in a space that is desirably reverberant for music, a voice reinforcement sound system [professionally designed and expertly installed] will be necessary, and that the hearing impaired will, in such a space, benefit from an assistive listening system (2002, 4). Acousticians have standards and means of testing the acoustical properties of a room, but, as noted above, the acid test is how well sound is heard by the human ear.

The Name of the Game Is Sound

Worship is an experience in sound—spoken, sung, played. The worship space is an acoustical environment. Good acoustics means more than being able to hear the sermon, more than the uplift that comes from hearing the choir do its best. Good acoustics fosters good congregational singing. Public worship is something we do together. Our sense of worshiping together is never stronger than when we sing. Just as when we are in the shower, so in the acoustically-alive worship space we sound better than we thought we ever could, because here, too, we have help. The sounds we make are being enriched by the reinforcing reflections. This may even give us confidence to turn up the volume, and it will help us reach even those notes at the extreme ends of our voice range. Singing in an acoustically-friendly environment begets singing.

Do you remember the thrill of entering a room (perhaps an empty one) and suddenly discovering how acoustically live it was? Suddenly you found yourself smiling, and you were all ears. Why must we settle for so much less in our worship spaces? How long shall we keep at bay that "new dimension in the world of sound" that we sing about in Fred Pratt Green's "When in Our Music God Is Glorified"?

Being convinced of the truth of three very specific propositions is sine qua non for any committee that wants to make the very best choices with respect to planning for the building or renovation of a worship space:

1) There is no property of the worship space more important than the acoustical. Worshipers should be able to hear intelligibly and naturally all sounds in worship: spoken, sung, and played.

2) Handsome, comfortable, ergonomically-designed wooden seating (pew, chair, and pew-style chair) is available.

3) Sound-reflective material for flooring ranging from the merely attractive to the positively sumptuous is available.

The people skills of pastors and church musicians will probably never be more severely tested than when they become involved in planning a new worship space, or for the renovation of an existent one—assuming that they themselves have some strongly held beliefs about what makes for the ideal worship space. In this context, too, we must pray for grace to bear in mind that our people are number one on our list of priorities. Of the visual, liturgical, and acoustical considerations involved in such planning, it is the visual that will tend to take center stage at the outset. "What will it look like?" And of course that is an altogether legitimate concern. But how can we lead the committee to appreciate also the crucial importance of acoustics? To understand that worship is all about sound? To ask the question, "What will it sound like?" How can we get them to understand that hearing is more important even than carpet and pew cushions and drapes? Do you have within a reasonable distance of your church a space (other than the rest rooms) that is acoustically alive? An Episcopal or Roman Catholic sanctuary may be your best bet. One that is really dead? (How about a funeral parlor?) Would a visit by the committee (including some musicians) to the two contrasting spaces help them to appreciate the importance of good acoustics? A second option involves learning of a church that is planning to replace carpet and cushions. Arrange to visit the space between the removal of the old and the installation of the new—and give a shout. You could also locate one that has just been constructed, with carpet and cushions not yet installed; sing away! Any members of that congregation who are with you might be converted! Still another option is to contact an acoustician and ask for a simulated demonstration. And if it takes prayer and fasting. . . . It is important that, very early on in the acoustical education program, all musicians, both paid staff and volunteers, are on board, and that all of the decision makers take acoustics as seriously as does this chapter.

TEMPERATURE AND HUMIDITY IN THE WORSHIP SPACE

~

In my last pastorate, a couple in the congregation pulled out all the stops for the wedding of their eldest daughter. They paid the florist to move enough greenery into the sanctuary to accommodate Tarzan and Jane. All the activity back and forth meant that the outside doors were open for a considerable amount of time. Our organist was upset because, she said, all the cold air had "distuned" the organ. Should she have been upset? Ask any two organists about the effect of temperature and humidity on the organ, and you well may get two very different answers. What follows here is chiefly from the late, well-known organ builder Walter Holtkamp, but for which I accept full responsibility.

Lowering the thermostat setting in unused space in the winter and raising it in the summer can result in substantial savings. Altering the temperature of the sanctuary will indeed put the organ out of tune. But restoring the temperature to what it was when the organ was in tune should retune the instrument. If the organ is not enclosed in chambers, then ten to twelve hours at operating temperature prior to service should be sufficient. Organs that are enclosed require a longer period of time to return to tune; for these organs the temperature should be returned to operating level twelve to sixteen hours prior to use of the worship space. Exhaust fans can be used to force out cold air and introduce warm air. Keeping the swell-shades open helps equalize temperature in the organ chambers. The welfare of the organist during practice time or lesson time on the organ must also, of course, be taken into account. An electric space heater and circulating fan near the organ console can be useful.

It is very important, and should be understood by all whose impossible task it is to see to everyone's comfort during the worship service, that, for the organ's sake, the temperature in the worship space needs, for whatever time before the service is required to bring the organ into tune, to be what it will be during the worship service. Changing the temperature in the worship space during this period or during the service itself can wreak havoc with the organ's tune before the service is concluded!

In the long run, it is not temperature per se, but fluctuations in the humidity within the worship space that can impact negatively on the organ. An organ is very largely wood, and radical changes in humidity can result in the wood splitting and in glued joints separating. (This applies to the piano and other wooden furniture as well.) Our aim then is to stabilize the moisture content in the air in the worship space. Whether high or low is not as important as is stability.[7] Generally speaking, it is more economical to add moisture to the air in the winter than to reduce moisture in the summer. Optimum moisture content can be achieved with the help of a humidifier controlled by a humidistat. If condensation gathers on the windows in the winter, an exterior thermostat can be installed to override the interior humidistat, shutting down the humidifier when the temperature outside drops to very low levels.

LIGHTING IN THE WORSHIP SPACE

Though worship is an experience in sound, singers will not make much sound if they cannot see the words they are to sing. Sufficient lighting to illumine adequately the printed page for all who are to sing, at least when they are to sing, is imperative. Having sufficient lighting, however, isn't always practiced. Optimum illumination also enhances morale. Avoid noisy filament lighting that buzzes.

– Useful Resources –

American Guild of Organists, *Planning Space for Pipe Organs*, free. The Guild makes available a number of resources on architecture, acoustics, and disposition of the organ.

André Biéler, *Architecture in Worship: The Christian Place of Worship* (Philadelphia: Westminster Press, 1965).

Donald Bruggink and Carl Droppers, *Christ and Architecture* (Grand Rapids: William B. Eerdmans Publishing Company, 1965).

The Hymn, 41.3, July 1990, issue dedicated to the acoustics of the worship space. Articles and annotated bibliography. Available from The Hymn Society as a reprint: *Acoustics for Liturgy*.

Donald Ingram, et al., *Acoustics in Worship Spaces*, available from American Guild of Organists. A four-page pamphlet.

Hymn Society in the United States and Canada, *Acoustics for Liturgy* (Chicago: Liturgy Training Press, 1991).

"Internet Resources in Church Architecture," Worship Web site of The United Methodist Church. http://www.gbod.org/worship/worship/articles.asp ?act=reader&item_id=12340&loc_id=1048,1053

Lonnie Park, *Church Sound Systems* (Milwaukee: Hal Leonard Publishing Corporation, 2001).

Physics Classroom, "Waves, Sound and Light," at www.physicsclassroom.com.

Scott R. Riedel, *Acoustics in the Worship Space* (St. Louis: Concordia, 1986).

Sauder Manufacturing Company, of Archbold, Ohio, is a large and well-established firm that supplies ergonomically-designed wooden furniture. Contact sales@sauderworship.com.

Neil Thompson Shade, *Electronic Sound System Design* (Ruxton, MD: ADC Press, 2002). You may contact Mr. Shade to ask about a simulated demonstration: neil@akustx.com. His Web site is www.akustx.com.

Edward Anders Sövik, *Architecture for Worship* (Minneapolis: Augsburg Publishing House, 1973).

James F. White, *Introduction to Worship* (Nashville: Abingdon Press, 1980). Rev. ed. 1990. Includes a chapter on acoustical environment.

James F. White, *Christian Worship in North America: A Retrospective 1955–1995* (Collegeville, MN: The Liturgical Press, 1997), 211–91.

CHAPTER
NINE

IN THE SHOES OF THE
CHURCH MUSICIAN

~

This chapter is more about church musicians than it is about pastors. But it is a chapter as much for pastors as for church musicians. In what follows, I want to help pastors walk just a little in the shoes of musicians, and to help both pastors and musicians walk together. My prayer is that both may grow in their sense of being in a shared ministry, and that this may be a source of great strength for both.

What comes to mind when musicians think about church? If what we read in *The American Organist* is any guide, the organists' professional relation to church translates very often into these three issues: compensation, staff relations, and what to do about the prelude-postlude question. Church musicians other than organists could probably identify with the first two of these. Pastors and musicians may find it easy to identify with one another as fellow sufferers, sharing some of the same frustrations and hearing some of the same complaints. Pastors and musicians alike may, at least on occasion, perceive the church as unfair and unloving. It is also possible that musicians see the pastor as part of the problem—even the major problem. The musicians envisioned in this chapter are those for whom making music in church is more than just a job. They are the musicians who are more likely to experience difficulties in their relations with the church.

A Church Musician's
Vocational Hazards

~

Their relationship with clergy is not the only potential problem facing church musicians. Before we look at that often-troubled relation, we shall note other areas in which the musician may encounter difficulties, none related specifically to the clergy, but associated with the profession itself, and the workplace—the church.

Compensation

In this world, the issue of compensation, like sin, is pandemic. It extends across a wide spectrum, from minimum wage worker to what the public sees as the grossly overpaid CEO. Judging by what I hear and by the classified advertisements in *The American Organist*, the compensation church musicians tend to receive in the early twenty-first century, relative to hours worked, lags considerably behind that of the pastors. (By pastors' compensation, I mean all the financial benefits that accrue to pastors, however they may be labeled in the church's budget.)

Social Status

Not unrelated to the issue of compensation is the social status of a musician. Historically, musicians have been considered to be of the servant class; entertaining is what they are paid to do. ". . . the unspoken presupposition is that musicians are entertainers" (Westermeyer 1988, 6). Indeed, a search of the Web will turn up, for instance, "Music and Entertainment," "Musicians and Entertainers." (Not to disparage entertainment, but may we not claim that it is uniquely the worship service, more than any other format, that provides the musician an opportunity to transcend this classification?) In the great houses of past societies, musicians were expected to enter through a side or even a rear door—certainly not the front. They may have already been in the house, as servants assigned this or that nonmusical duty, for servants who could also sing or play an instrument were preferred. While musicians have always been meant to be heard, they have very often been expected not to be heard too much; their contribution was, and in many situations continues to be, a kind of sonic tapestry furnishing a pleasant background for what really matters when people get together—food, drink, and conversation. (We of course are not referring here to that select company of stellar performers.) You can for sure amaze at least some of your friends by telling them that, when you play a recording of one of Bach's Brandenburg Concertos, you lay all else aside, and concentrate on listening. Until modern times, of course, music was not an art form, to be appreciated for its own sake, but was most often subservient or backdrop to some activity, such as dance, marching, work, dining, or ritual.

Because they often do their work hidden from the congregation's view, the organists' faces may go unrecognized by those for whom they play. For an entire year, my wife played an organ located in a rear gallery, but many in the congregation must have never known she was the organist; their ignorance got an assist from the fact that her name never appeared in the bulletin or in the church newsletter. While newspaper wedding announcements often name the officiating clergy, mention of the musicians' names is not much more likely than is that of the sextons'. So much of what the church musician does is behind the scenes; how many in the congregation have any idea how much time the musicians may spend on staff meetings, selection of music, rehearsal or practice, and administration?[1]

Professional Status

Being a musician is one thing, but being a church musician is in a category all its own. Some music students have been told that they did not have what it takes to concertize, that all they could hope for was to be church musicians! And one who plays an organ, an unpopular instrument in our society, is usually associated with institutions like churches that are in decline! Even some musicians may think an organ is weird. It has been remarked that, as theology was once "queen of the sciences," so the organ was "king of instruments," but now both have been dethroned. Every Sunday, the "Arts and Leisure" section of the *New York Times* informs its readers of the rich musical diet that awaits Gotham's public in the upcoming days—a never-ending feast of instrumental and vocal fare served up by some of the world's most acclaimed performers. The offerings are as likely, however, to include a program of music played on the kazoo as on the organ. If an organist is degreed, chances are he or she did not spend all those years and all that money in anticipation of playing hymns for a congregation to sing! Being part-time, as the majority of church musicians are, does not increase one's stature; it makes the position sound like an "odd job," something done on the side of a real job, even a hobby. A question for the pastors: There are a large number of nationally and internationally known organists; can you name one? You have doubtless read or heard from time to time of the death of a great musician. Was one of them ever an organist?

Low Self-esteem

By no means do all musicians suffer from an underdeveloped ego. Some may seem to overcompensate for what they think society thinks of them. Nevertheless, low self-esteem among their ranks is not unknown. Judging from articles and letters in *The American Organist*, what musicians think of themselves is evidently a more serious problem than what society may think of them. How others see the musician, however, is bound to influence the way musicians see themselves. Pastors do little to raise the musicians' self-esteem, for instance, when they ask the secretary to call the musician; a clergy colleague would rate a collegial call from the clergy him or herself. Church musicians may find themselves navigating in that old sea of ambivalence regarding the role of music in worship and in society in general. Just what is the musician's contribution? Surely pastors should know. But do they? Do musicians? Even people who dedicate their lives to music and are quite secure in that career choice may have little or no understanding of the vital role of music in worship. Those musicians who did receive academic training in classical music may well be evangelistic about it; their zeal to win converts to such music may be impossible to combine with what they in fact are expected to do in church. Some musicians may depend for their sense of self-worth on their attainment of perfect performance, or on lavish praise from the pastor (who may not really be interested in music—even of any kind) and others. This makes them highly vulnerable to feelings of inferiority. People can suffer from their failure to have found meaning and mission in their lives. Various factors may conspire against there developing on the part of church musicians a sense of calling, of professionalism. This, in turn, readily leads to their being treated in unprofessional ways.

Ideals Versus Reality

The trained musician will have certain standards; he or she will listen, moreover, for things that may escape others. The gap between the musician's inclination and training and what is expected by others may surface in a particularly unpleasant and friction-producing form in the matter of style or taste. Over the course of time, the musician may have developed a deep appreciation for the music of the late Olivier Messiaen. Her fondness will not likely be shared by very many, if any, of the congregation she has come to serve. They would find the devout Frenchman's music boring and unmelodic. The musician in this case will have to adjust to reality—or resolve to change reality through her educative efforts; she will teach the people to like Messiaen! Such a goal may be next to impossible to reconcile with what is maintained throughout this book about the role of music in the church.

Performance Anxiety

Church organists are on trial in every service. When they fumble, it does not go unnoticed. Even the most competent will inadvertently strike a manual or a pedal now and then, or forget that a certain piston was on. Preachers' fumbles may be more readily overlooked, but then preachers have probably not rehearsed the sermon as much as organists have the music. In addition, when the preacher errs, the congregation can still get the point, which is what matters most; when the musician makes a noticeable error, the very raison d'être of the musical offering is threatened. After all, the piece the musician is playing attracts us because, in contrast to our experience in the larger world, everything in the work of art is just as it should be. The musician

knows that the preacher or lector can stumble over a word here or there, and still the message will have its impact. To stumble over a note is much more dangerous; the message's impact will dissipate much more quickly when there is a musical error, partly because there is more of art. (Westermeyer 2001a, 52)

Tied Down

One inconvenience that comes with the church musician's turf is easy to understand, the inconvenience of being pretty well tied down, not only on Sundays, but midweek also. In this matter, too, the pastor can readily identify. It is hard for church musicians, including those who only serve part-time, to get away at any time other than the stipulated vacation. Responsibilities in connection with funerals and weddings can result in a part-time musician being on call every day. Like pastors, it can be hard for church musicians to find Sabbath time in the week.

Do the church's musicians ever have the privilege of corporate worship? Sitting with their family in worship? Pastors know that it is not easy for people to give themselves over wholeheartedly to worship when they are the leaders who have to call the shots. It is hard to be both Mary and Martha at the same time. That it is the head of staff that is, in many cases, the musician's pastor is also less than ideal—something akin to the position of the spouse of the pastor.[2]

Health Concerns

Musicians may experience certain health problems that are less common among the population in general, or are more likely when they do occur to affect the musicians' work performance. Carpal tunnel syndrome is perhaps more likely to result from playing the piano than the organ. Handicapping or crippling arthritis can affect anyone's limbs and extremities, as can gout. Organists whose benches have no backs may experience back pain. Organists may suffer discomfort and fatigue because the organ bench is too high or too low. Keyboardists who wear bi- or trifocal glasses may experience tiredness and pain in the neck from straining to see the music, unless they have a special pair of glasses for playing. Many organists know the discomfort of practicing in worship spaces that are uncomfortably warm or cold.

Singers are vulnerable to the variety of maladies that afflict the throats, and the nasal and sinus passages of us all. What is an inconvenience for most of us, however, may put the singer out of commission—at least temporarily. Aging affects voice production. The voice can become breathy, rough, hoarse, weak, and characterized by tremolo. Women find it harder to sing high notes than formerly, men are unable to sing the low notes they once could.

Hearing loss is regrettable wherever it occurs, but it can be career-threatening for the musician.

Some organists can practice on the instrument only after hours; they may be understandably concerned for their safety when alone in churches located in decaying neighborhoods.

Anxiety About the Future of the Profession— and the Job

The Web site of a thriving Presbyterian Church in New York City that showcases a professional-caliber program of music indicates that occasionally a pianist or organist is called on to help! The use of nontraditional music calling for a variety of other instruments has in many cases rendered any kind of keyboard unnecessary. Organists may feel that they are an endangered species, as schools of music report declining numbers of organ majors.[3]

In the local congregation, when a change in pastors is taking place, will this mean a change in musicians also? Is it to be expected that a new pastor will have the privilege of replacing the musicians on the church's staff with his or her own choices? If kept on, how will the musician on hand get along with the pastor just coming on board? Will their understandings of the role of music in worship match? Will they share the same tastes? In the interim between pastors, of course, musicians may enjoy a rare degree of freedom—tempered with anxiety about relations with the next pastor.

Relational Hazards: Getting Along

~

Although we know of some excellent professional collaboration between pastors and musicians, that has been more the exception than the rule in our experience. Every time we offer a workshop we discover again the gulf that exists between most worship leaders and musicians. (Doran and Troeger 1992, 80)

In lists of complaints drawn up by church musicians, the matter of relations with clergy is an ever-recurring theme. Why should this be so?

Predisposed to Conflict?

"The theologically trained person tends to favor the sophisticated use of language. The training of the musician is primarily focused on aural, sonic qualities" (Doran and Troeger 1992, 80). Probably no one would dispute this. Articles that I have seen on the subject of clergy-musician conflict, however, tend to emphasize not the differences, but the similarities between those in one profession and those in the other. For instance, both clergy and musicians:

- may have larger-than-average egos, may treat one another as functionaries;

- are creative persons;

- tend to be highly intuitive, highly motivated self-starters, conflict avoiders, people pleasers, and vulnerable to misplaced and mistimed criticism;

- work alone much of the time;

- preside over mysteries and produce products that are unquantifiable and intangible;

- are heavily involved emotionally in what they do;

- think of their work not as a career, but as a calling, and of themselves as professionals.

Do these similarities predispose the clergy-musician relation to conflict? Surely some would seem to. Other similarities might be thought to make for mutual understanding and positive relations. Linda J. Clark's survey indicated "a remarkable agreement between clergy and musicians on a majority of" a wide variety of questions. But the same author tells us of areas in which her survey indicated significant disagreement between clergy and musicians: Who makes the decisions regarding the worship service? Should the director of music choose the hymns? Of the clergy, 75 percent said no; of the musicians, 58 percent said yes. We have already cited the disparities Clark found with regard to what music in the service is considered the most important. Clark points out that in our therapeutic society we tend to see difficult relations as personality conflicts; she acknowledges that while personality issues may indeed be involved, other factors must not be overlooked. Difficult relations "can also be the product of badly managed or poorly thought out planning structures that distort or disrupt the capacity to accomplish tasks" (1994, 54). From my own observations, I believe that poor relationships between clergy and musicians are very often the result of there being no relationship in the first place. Pastor and musician move along unthinkingly on parallel tracks without communicating with one another. What one does that hurts the other stems not from malice, but from ignorance.

Responsibility and Authority

The flashpoint of clergy-musician relations, of course, is planning and leading in worship. It is in this connection that some of Clark's findings are especially apropos. "What the data of the project suggest is that issues of power—patterns of accountability and responsibility—and the lack of a shared understanding of worship among leaders and lay people in a congregation may lie behind much of the bad feeling between clergy and musicians" (1994, 54).

The issue of power, of final authority in matters pertaining to worship, is, in all church polities known to me, settled: Musicians are to be consulted regarding musical questions, but ultimate authority and responsibility for a particular service rest with the pastor. No matter their superior expertise in matters musical, musicians are in no position to overrule the pastor. In discussions about clergy-musician relations, this may be the elephant in the room that goes unremarked. Discussions most often proceed as though the relationship between clergy and musician were simply one of one professional with another—period. But the larger context forbids this. The playing field is not level. In contrast to the musician, the clergy is the bearer of an office rooted in the New Testament and almost two thousand years of history. (Larger congregations in the fourth century, especially in the East, did often include singers as one of several minor offices.) In a certain sense we may say that, within the clergy-musician relationship, the pastor is the church. In many polities, clergy authority extends even beyond the local congregation. The musician, even if he or she serves on the church's governing board, as a musician is only an employee of the church, or if you prefer, a self-employed person who contracts for his or her services. (Qualifications being met, musicians may, of course, be ordained to clergy status. Also, in 1996, the United Methodist Church created the office of a specialized diaconate which, among other things, opened the way for musicians to enjoy clergy status.) Clergy are far more likely to be considered essential for the life of a congregation than are musicians, and project a much more prominent presence. It is the clergy's name that appears on the church sign and stationery, and in advertisements of the church. It is the clergy who interfaces with all the members of the congregation—in connection with all kinds of matters—and who represents the congregation in the larger community. Even in the worship service, the musician may be unseen by the members of the church. Whereas the clergy's concern and responsibility extend to every aspect of the life of the congregation, the musician's is restricted to only one specific area: music.

Not least of all, clergy, in contrast to musicians, are not only office bearers; they must be people of faith, people committed to a specific faith. The church is all about faith. Though I can guess that most church musicians are people of some kind of faith, that they be Christian, and especially that they share the particular faith of the church they serve, may well not be taken into account at all when they apply for employment in the church. Nothing more may be required of them than that they perform dependably, with a certain level of competence. The vulnerability of musicians, even the most accomplished veteran, in this arrangement is obvious, and it is not hard to see how ill-feeling and conflict may result.

In addition to musicians being under the authority of the clergy, and their consequent vulnerability, there is another complicating factor—on the side of the clergy: The clergy may feel threatened by the musicians. This may be because the musicians are more gifted, or because they have more attractive personalities than the clergy or, much more rarely, because the musicians are better compensated. (In my last pastorate, the choir director probably received more compensation per hour than I did.) In many cases, a musician, in contrast to a pastor with less time on board, has through long, faithful service endeared himself or herself to the congregation—and even to the larger community.

The music of the worship service can itself be a threat to the clergy. During the anthem, the clergy is reduced to the status of the humblest worshiper. The preacher's sermon may seem quite pedestrian compared with the glorious anthem the choir has just rendered. No one likes to be upstaged. Even if the choir's performance is not so memorable, all music that is part of the service means that for its duration the clergy are out of control, that they must share the spotlight with others—even with the whole congregation during the singing of a hymn! It is not, moreover, just the pastor's ego that may suffer. Clergy may feel that time given to music threatens their divinely given agenda—that part of the worship service led by the clergy and only the clergy. The musician may be seen as a competitor rather than a partner.

I am ready to declare that there is no more serious threat to the relations of clergy and musicians than this. Until clergy and musicians understand and appreciate the potentially vital role of music as servant of the Word, of the liturgy (all of which is seen as vital, not just the sermon), the failure in this area is going to continue to be a very large pothole in the road that is clergy-musician relations.

Professional Lacunas

Another source of relational hazard is the musical lacuna on the part of the pastor. "Much of what we [church musicians] face is not conscious manipulation and grabs for power, though there is plenty of that. Much of what we face is ignorance. In the face of such a circumstance we are called to teach" (Westermeyer 2001b, 73). Since music plays such a vital role in what is central to the life of the church, namely worship, we might think that candidates for the ministry would be exposed to at least some musical training.[4]

Alas, such is not the case. The normal three-year seminary course is so full of other disciplines deemed more important that there is most often no place for instruction in any of the arts, even in the one most useful in the church. Relatively few seminaries offer a course in church music/hymnology; in some of these instances it is only an elective. "The musician finds it difficult to view his or her terrain as important when it is neglected in the training of the full-time leaders" (Westermeyer 1988, 8).

Matters are not made better to the extent that there is also a lacuna on the part of the musician. Whether academically or more informally trained, musicians are not likely to know much about theology, church history, pastoral care, or worship. Only a handful of institutions in North America seek to integrate instruction in these subjects with training in music. Some denominations offer a certification process that aims at enhancing a musician's qualifications to serve in the church. The musician's problem is not always only a lack of knowledge or skills, however; views regarding the role of congregational song, and attitudes toward accepting and learning new performance practices may be out of sync with a church's convictions and goals.

> Pastor and musician both need to possess an elemental knowledge of the assumptions, skills, and vocabulary of each other's respective disciplines. Without this knowledge, communication becomes difficult, and even the best intentioned efforts at collaborative ministry become strained. (Doran and Troeger 1992, 79)

Whoa Before Woe

Relations between clergy and musicians can, it happens, be too good. Two people who have so very much in common, who are working together to accomplish shared goals, and who are often alone together can all too easily drift from a lofty feeling of intellectual, aesthetic, and spiritual kinship and appreciation to physical intimacy. The outcome, if either party is married or engaged, is never life-giving for anyone; the end of the course is disaster—compounded if knowledge of the relationship comes to public notice. It may be small comfort to the musician to know that in this case, too, the clergy bears ultimate responsibility. Even if both parties are free, such a liaison may not be in the best interest of all concerned.

Musician Versus Musician

In some situations, friction may develop between two or more staff musicians. The advertisement under "Wanted" read: "Male choir director. Will have assistant to play organ." Two things are plain: No females need apply, and the choir director, who does not need to have any keyboard skills, ranks higher than the organist, who is his assistant. It is advisable not to refer to the keyboardist as assistant to the choir director. The keyboardist is an equal partner with the choir director, possibly even surpassing him or her in training and competence. People skills are often rewarded more generously than is work done by people whose work requires little or no interfacing—like the keyboardist. It is also the case that, in the execution of choral song, it is the choir director who leads; the keyboardist follows. Therefore, some might argue, a choir director merits higher compensation than the keyboardist. Keyboardists are likely to resent this, and will remind us that they put in far more time practicing and contribute far more music to the worship service than do choir directors. In most situations, it is the keyboardist who leads the most important music of all: the song of the congregation. In an emergency, moreover, an organist is more likely to be able to conduct the choir than is a choir director to be able to play the organ.

TOWARD SHALOM

~

What to Call the Musicians

Music staff positions may be full-time or part-time. How many musicians are there on the staff of the church you serve? Commonly, there are two basic musical functions to be discharged: playing a keyboard instrument and directing the choir. One person may fill both positions, and often does, even when financial resources could underwrite the compensation for two people. Some musicians are unable or do not want to do both tasks. Appropriate titles may be "choir director" and "organist," or if only one person, "choir director-organist." The titles "minister of music"/"music minister" and "director of music"/"music director" are generally applied to someone who is over all the music. The generic term "pastoral musician" is a favored term in Roman Catholic circles. Episcopalians may refer to members of the music staff as "parish musicians." Churches with larger staffs may have a "director of music ministries." These persons may be ordained clergy. Psalm 68:25 notwithstanding, pastors and others should take care not to make the gaffe of speaking or writing of "singers and musicians." Singers also are musicians!

The Church Musician's Church Membership

Should musicians be free to be members of the congregation they serve? Opinions vary. Some churches require that musicians and some other staff not be members. The rationale often seems to be that any difficulties arising in connection with staff can more easily be dealt with if the staff persons are not members. (Especially, this may lighten the burden for the pastor.) Very often, however, a touchy situation would not be any less delicate if the staff member involved were not a member of the congregation served. When I arrived at my last pastorate, the long-serving husband and wife musician team had not been permitted to unite with that congregation; I can imagine the brouhaha that would have ensued, however, had their continuance been questioned. By closing the door to membership for their musicians, churches are denying them freedom of choice in a terribly significant matter. Congregations may be effectively denying musicians the benefits of church membership altogether, for, given their responsibilities, it would be very hard for them to participate in the life of any other congregation. Perhaps the most fundamental consideration of all: Has the church the authority to deny membership to any who meet the criteria?

Compensation: How Much?

Beyond cash remuneration, what benefits do the staff musicians enjoy? Social Security? Medical coverage? A pension plan? Unemployment insurance? The fact that a musician may be only a part-time employee of the church does not lessen the church's obligation to seek his or her well-being by considering all such benefits. "But she lives at home with her mother and has very low expenses," "But she does it because she loves it," "But he won't find such a wonderful instrument to play on anywhere else in town," "He does it for the Lord," "They would be offended if we offered them money," even "Soli Deo gloria"—none of these has any legitimate place in considerations regarding the musician's compensation.

A church that preaches social righteousness will certainly be expected to practice it with regard to its musicians. Guides for the compensation of church musicians may be secured from the American Guild of Organists, and from some local chapters of the Guild. You may also be able to secure information regarding compensation from area churches—for whatever that might be worth. An oft-recommended practice in determining what may be considered fair compensation is to consider what those in comparable professions, such as teaching, are making. Lack of formal training may be offset by natural gifts and by experience. It may also be helpful to consider what other church staff members are receiving, remembering to include all benefits. The amount of time the musician gives behind the scenes to practice and rehearsal, the selection and ordering of music, meeting for planning, and communications must be borne in mind. Compensation for part-time service can be calculated as a percentage of what full-time compensation is determined to be. Whether the compensation in question be that of musician, pastor, or anyone else contracted by the church, any committee that finds itself thinking "How little can we get by with?" needs to be born again.

Getting It in Writing

A contract between the church and its musicians is strongly recommended. Such an instrument is in the interest of both the church and the musicians; it can also have a fundamental importance for clergy-musician relations. A contract spells out in writing what both parties have agreed to concerning the musician's duties, specifies the agreed-upon compensation, and makes clear who it is to whom the musician is responsible. The contract can reduce misunderstanding—or at least make the misunderstanding inexcusable. It can be helpful when changes in responsibilities or compensation are being considered. A contract offers the musicians some protection in the case of serious disagreement, at least slowing things down to allow time for them to seek employment elsewhere. "Job creep" is common, especially in connection with part-time work; having a contract to consult now and then can help avoid abuse of the musician's good will. An annual or even more-frequent review of the contract and the musician's on-the-job performance is recommended.

Marion J. Hatchett recommends that a contract should address the following: salary and fringe benefits; fees for weddings and funerals; time and financing for continuing education; vacation; use of instruments for practice, teaching, and students' practice; availability of choir room; heating and cooling of worship space and choir room; selection of music for choir and congregation; selection of assistants and substitutes; relation to any committee [on worship, for instance]; number and nature of services with music; number and nature of choirs; number and time and duration of rehearsals; budget for singers, music, and supplementary instrumentalists; and for tuning and care of instruments (1989, 33). I would add use of premises for recitals, compensation for substitutes, sick leave, and retirement. Other items to consider include:

1) Knowledge by the pastor of anything that the musicians would not be willing to do—such as play or sing show tunes at weddings, or play a duet with a bagpiper. Has the clergy the right to insist that certain pieces be played or sung?

2) It should also be understood by both parties whether or not the church's musicians are routinely given first option with regard to playing or singing for weddings and funerals.

3) With respect to part-time musicians, what is understood about their responsibilities for music at weddings or funerals scheduled at a time when the musician is elsewhere engaged?

4) Not only might it make for good relations between clergy and
   musicians if both swapped brief statements outlining their
   respective understanding of the role of music in worship; it
   could also be very salutary for both.

5) Who has authority to terminate a musician's employment with
   the church? Such authority should not be vested in only one
   person acting alone, and certainly not the pastor or the director
   of music alone. Also, how much advance notice must be given?

6) How will a change in pastors affect the musicians on staff? At the
   very least, the current musicians should be considered on a par
   with any possible replacements. If a pastor is being considered by
   a church with a view to being called, and that pastor knows a
   priori that he or she would, if called, want to choose member(s) of
   the church's musical staff, he or she should communicate this to
   the church's committee.

The Musicians' Professional Organizations

Potentially supportive of the church's musicians is a professional or
denominational organization. The professional organizations of organists in
North America are the American Guild of Organists, and, in Canada, the
Royal Canadian College of Organists. Choir directors are also accepted as
members in both organizations. Local or area chapters of these organizations
gather on a regular basis for programs of mutual interest, exchange of information, and fellowship. The Guild publishes an attractive monthly of
something over one hundred pages, *The American Organist*, sent to more than
twenty thousand addresses. (Just browsing through an issue would increase
the average pastor's knowledge of the world of organs, organ builders, and
organists a thousand-fold!) Members of the Royal College of Organists receive
The American Organist and also *Organ Canada/Orgue Canada*. How many organists in North America are AGO or RCCO members? According to an estimate
in 1981, only 5 percent were (*The American Organist*, December 1981, 4).

Choir directors may also participate in the American Choral Directors Association. The *Choral Journal* is the Association's monthly publication. Given that the organ is more likely to be found in a church than in any other venue, and that very many choral organizations exist independently of the church, it is not surprising that the music of the church figures much more prominently in *The American Organist* than in the *Choral Journal*.

Musicians have also organized themselves denominationally, holding conferences (sometimes in conjunction with clergy of their denomination), publishing journals, and offering certification (which may well involve not only matters musical, but also theological and liturgical).

Sharing Life Together

Adalbert Kretzmann gives us a salutary approach to clergy-musician relations. He does this not by showing us how to deal with problems, but by setting forth positively what makes for a wholesome and productive working relationship. The key word is "together." Kretzmann uses it in five major section headings:

"Together in Dialog and Understanding"
"Together in Proclamation"
"Together in Ministry"
"Together in a Growing Understanding of Liturgy"
"Together in Planning"

All these culminate in "A Constant Doxology" (1978, 217–31). The emphasis falls not on psychology and techniques that may result in getting a job done, but that leave people unchanged; the focus rather is on theology, on an earnest, sensitive, and caring living out of the Gospel together in a shared ministry.

It is this writer's fond hope that this little volume you are reading may be shared between clergy and musicians, and that this may help clarify and strengthen the clergy-musician relationship of which you are a member. We have looked at some very important matters, and it is more than likely that there is room on the part of both or all of you for growth in some of these areas. Two bottom-line issues regarding which understanding and agreement are absolutely essential are those of authority and the role of music (especially congregational song) in worship. I have already indicated that the ultimate responsibility for decisions regarding music in the worship service is virtually always vested in the clergy. Musicians must acknowledge this. As for the clergy, it is incumbent upon them that they treat musicians as fellow-professionals whose special expertise should be respected—not only for the sake of the well-being of the musician, but also for the sake of the church's ministry. "Ministry," another keyword! That is what both clergy and musician are all about—serving people. "Minister and cantor [musician] need to begin with the fundamental presupposition that they are in this together for the people" (Westermeyer 1988, 101). For both clergy and musician, the service is one of mutuality, as Kretzmann and Westermeyer both put it, serving together. Both clergy and musician need the affirmation of one another and of the congregation. Pastors will relate to musicians who are Christian, of course, not only as the respect-deserving human beings and professionals that they are, but as brothers and sisters in the Lord. The ideal has been termed "partnership" (a term used in the New Testament in connection with both commercial and gospel endeavors), the pastor being understood to be the senior partner. In practice, this will translate into planning together and communication—both timely and both executed in mutuality. The spirit of 1 Corinthians 12–14 should permeate all relations in the church, including those of clergy and musicians.

– Useful Resources –

The American Choral Directors Association Web site is www.acdonline.org.

The American Guild of Organists has several publications, a few of which are free, that can give guidance in the matter of finding, selecting, and compensating church musicians. See the Guild's Web site: www.agohq.org or any recent issue of *The American Organist*. Included recently are:

AGO Model Contracts

"Documents Regarding Professional Conduct"

"Music in the Church: Work and Compensation"

"Points of Consideration for Churches and Church Musicians"

"Professional Concerns Handbook"

"Resources in Professional Concerns"

"The Work and Compensation of the Church Musician"

"What the Clergy Should Know about the AGO"

The Diapason, published since 1909, and formerly the official journal of the AGO, is another monthly for organists. Address: 3030 W. Salt Creek Ln., Suite 201, Arlington Heights, IL 60005.

Carol Doran, "Syllabus for a Foundational Church Music Course for Seminary or Continuing Education Use." Available from AGO and from Web site of AGO. About eight pages.

Joy E. Lawrence and John A. Ferguson, *A Musician's Guide to Church Music* (New York: Pilgrim Press, 1981). Focus is on the part-time musician without benefit of extensive academic training for church music ministry.

Karen A. McClintock, *Preventing Sexual Abuse in Congregations: A Resource for Leaders* (New York: Alban Institute, 2004).

The Music Commission, Diocese of Connecticut, *When a Church Calls a Musician: A Handbook for Parish Churches and Pastoral Musicians* (1992). 35 George Washington Highway, Ridgefield, CT 06877, (202) 792-5266.

N. Lee Orr, *The Church Music Handbook for Pastors and Musicians* (Nashville: Abingdon Press, 1991), 41–70. Orr stresses the partnership relation of clergy and musician.

The Royal Canadian College of Organists: http://www.rcco.ca/membership%20info.html.

Paul Westermeyer, *The Church Musician* (San Francisco: Harper & Row, 1988).

CHAPTER TEN

GROWING A MUSICAL CHURCH

~

There are within the congregation three ongoing tasks in the area of music that need to be accomplished: 1) Planning and choosing the music for weekly worship; 2) In the worship service itself, helping the congregation to engage in the most fruitful way possible in the musical parts of worship; 3) The development and implementation of the congregation's overall music program—the subject of this chapter.

DEVELOPING AND ADOPTING THE PROGRAM

~

Congregations differ widely as to the extent to which music is a part of their life. The difference may be traceable to just one person, one person convinced of and enthusiastic about the importance of music in the life of the church, one person dedicated to making it happen in her or his congregation. That person will need lots of help, but it starts with him or her. In your congregation, who will it be? You? If not, then who? Whoever it is will see to it that certain things get done.

The Needed Spark

At some point, a sufficient number of the congregation's decision makers must be convinced of the importance of music in the life of the church. The church's leaders also need to understand that if anything musically significant is going to happen in the congregation, the church itself, in most situations, must take over the role of music educator; it cannot depend on any other institution to do the job.

Our concern in this chapter is not just music in church, and certainly not just music in the worship service, but music in every corner of the life of every member. At the heart of a church's overall music program, however, is the song of the congregation, and that will be at the center of our attention in this chapter, too. I have tried to flesh out a bit the theory of what can happen when a congregation sings. How can you make this theory come contagiously alive so that your congregation can experience the reality for itself? Is it feasible for some of your members to visit a congregation in which music is emphasized? A well-done hymn festival can spark enthusiasm. At a series of midweek gatherings, a musician with the right personality can accomplish a very great deal toward generating enthusiasm for singing. Have you a children's choir that can lend a hand? Helping the congregation to sing can have a domino effect; what is taught about one song transfers to another. Simply to know musicians are interested in and trying to help them conduces to greater effort on the congregation's part.

Determining Where You Are Now

Those of the staff who share responsibility for the overall music program of the congregation should include at least the senior pastor and the musicians. At least one influential member of the governing board could prove valuable. Other members of the congregation can be enlisted as the opportunity arises.

It is probable that early on you will discover that there will have to be a certain amount of education; your goals may, to some, seem overly ambitious—even needlessly so! There will be skeptics who have to undergo conversion. Surely there will be room for growth on the part of all. At the outset it is well to begin to look at where you and the congregation are at present. What do you understand the role of music in the life of the church to be? Do you have a pretty good idea of how important music—of all kinds—is in the overall life of your people? What is the importance of music relative to other aspects of the church's life? What do you really know about your congregation, in terms of music of course, but also more generally? Dean McIntyre, Linda J. Clark, and Gordon Truitt (1991, 95), all stress the importance of "understanding congregational identity." The music program of the church must be in sync with all that makes a particular congregation what it is, otherwise the music will be found irrelevant. A congregation should also seek to reach out beyond its present members—to the faculty and students at the local college, for instance, or to a growing community of recent immigrants. It is important that the identity of any such specific target population also be taken into account. Though the writers just mentioned have in view specifically planning for the worship service, the concern that we know well our own congregation (and the larger community) is just as important for the more general planning discussed in this chapter. For ascertaining where a congregation is musically, Ronald P. Byars argues for the use of focus groups rather than questionnaires (2002, 59–60).

"At the center of a successful music program is a vital connection between music and the life of faith of a particular congregation" (Clark 1994, 3). In developing a plan for your congregation's musical life, it is important to remember that there is no one-plan-fits-all. As for what is specifically musical, for sure you will want to inventory your congregation's working repertory of congregational song at present. You will want to discover what in the worship service is thought meaningful. What is considered not helpful? Are many people allergic to music in a minor key? Do many people have a problem with a small ensemble substituting for the organ now and then? What hymnic repertory have members brought with them from their childhood and youth or from congregations where they previously worshiped? How strongly attached to it are they? Beyond the worship service, what is going on musically?

Deciding Where You Would Like to Be

Having determined where your congregation is musically, you are ready to plan where you would like to be, and how you can get there. Study, discussion, sharing, and prayer should, over a period of time, bring into focus some definite goals. Then the concrete steps necessary to reach those goals should be determined. A few suggestions are mentioned here, and many more will be found later in this chapter.

One very basic goal might be to enlarge and deepen the repertory of the congregation's song. Steps to achieve this might include congregational rehearsals at midweek gatherings, adoption of a hymn-of-the-month program, and teaching certain hymns to the children which they, in turn, can help the adults learn. Congregational song, the heart of the church's music, may well be the area of musical concern that is most vulnerable to the time constraints of both pastor and musician. You may want to develop a task force with the one responsibility of developing the singing of the congregation. With preparation, patience, and perseverance, your people can become a singing congregation.

Some churches with more-than-average resources have embarked on more ambitious undertakings. A series of sacred music programs over the course of several weeks may be offered. A few churches expand their programs to include drama, dance, painting, and sculpture, offering a festival of religious arts to the community. Beginning small, they have expanded over time to include a full week of activities. All such programs should, of course, be evaluated not only in the light of what resources the church has at its disposal, but also in terms of its understanding of the mission of the church in the larger world. Has the church a mandate to promote the arts in general? Can such efforts be understood (and thus justified) as a kind of pre-evangelism—as some Latter Day Saints justify their promotion of the Mormon Tabernacle Choir? Princeton sociologist Robert Wuthnow draws out an implication of the correlation between contemporary spirituality and the role of the arts in religion: The arts may well be a source of renewal and outreach for the church.

Not all musical happenings require major investment of resources. In my last pastorate, the congregation joined every other year or so with a couple of churches of another denomination to present a hymn festival. Another project involved even less effort, but was found to be very meaningful. After every Easter Sunday morning service for several years, our congregation gathered in the street at a nearby intersection and joined with two or three neighboring congregations to sing "Jesus Christ is Risen Today." This was followed by the benediction/blessing and greetings. A little creative thinking will yield a good number of possible musical goals for your congregation, both long- and short-term.

Once a program has been settled upon, it can be presented to the governing board for its consideration and approval. You may want to formulate your plans in terms of a mission statement that sets forth goals and, at least in general terms, tactics. Again, some amount of educative effort is in order. More than in certain other matters dealt with by the board (paving the parking lot, for instance), you in this case want not mere formal passage of your proposal, but endorsement that is as informed and enthusiastic as can be; what is needed is an ongoing commitment. Once the governing board's approval has been secured, at the first opportune time you are ready to take the next step: enlisting the support of the congregation.

GETTING ALL ON BOARD

~

Communication

No matter what your church's polity, you want the congregation to experience all programs of the congregation as their program. It is important that all see the program as a collaborative effort. Unless your congregation's polity requires it, there is no necessity for the congregation to vote on the adoption of the plan. It is important that the congregation as a whole willingly accept the plan as a challenge. This adds up to communication—the enthusiastic presentation of the plan to the congregation.

It will help if the plan is presented not by any member of staff, but by one of the congregation's own. The presentation of the plan to the people may take place over the course of time, employing various tactics, making use of a wide variety of presenters, and asking for feedback. Both written and spoken communication will be involved. It is important in the presentation to take small steps, to think not revolution, but evolution.

A role that has a make-or-break potential for the proposed musical program is that of what we may call advocate for music in the life of the congregation. An advocate may be a staff musician or some member of the congregation. This person will have a passion for seeing to it that music is taking place in every corner of the congregation's life. He or she will "bird-dog" the plan relentlessly—not just at the outset, but over time. The advocate will be concerned to discover and develop musical interest and talent within the congregation. The leaders of every department of the congregation's life will in due course come to think "music" whenever they see this person—because this person is doing his or her job—tactfully and unobtrusively, of course. If not already somewhat knowledgeable about music in the church, an advocate must be willing to bone up on the subject. The advocate can be helpful also in providing feedback and in communicating—in all directions. It is of the utmost importance that any such advocate have no private agenda, but work in the closest possible relation to the staff and any relevant committee. Though the advocate will ever be seeking new avenues to explore, and will make recommendations to the proper party, his or her task is not to initiate program, but to implement it.

Attitudes That May Need Changing

It is time now to remember the first rule of pedagogy: Begin where the people are. We have already noted the importance of ascertaining where the people are, what the identity, musical and otherwise, of our congregation is. Perhaps we have already discovered that the task before us is not the mere passing on and learning of text and tune; before that and other things can be accomplished, there are probably also some attitudes that need to be changed. We shall encounter musically challenged people, people who tell us they cannot sing. Quite often such people may tell us that years ago one of their teachers heard them trying to sing and told them the world would be a better place if they just did not try—maybe simply pantomime the words if they were in a children's choir and just appear to be singing. Sometimes the offending party is a spouse who laughs at or jokes about his or her mate's attempts to sing. Voice teachers tell us that people who really cannot sing are few and far between, that almost everyone, with a little help, can make what passes for a joyful noise. A session or two could be offered by a staff musician, billed as being for all who think they cannot sing.

We noted in chapter 2 that singing in the assembly renders us vulnerable to the others present. It is not just that those around us may discover that our voice is not one to be envied; in singing, our defenses come down, we are engaging in a communal activity that we do not control, but that controls us. Some people may experience self-consciousness, intimidation, even fright. Wise and compassionate leaders will recognize the understandable reticence that such people have and deal with it accordingly.

Something else we may encounter is very definitely an attitude problem: the unwillingness to learn a new tune. Every tune anyone knows was at some point new to that person. When did that person stop learning anything new? Again, we must remind ourselves that education begins where the people are; what they already know must be honored. People will surely feel threatened if they perceive they are being called on to jettison the old and familiar to make room for something that is new. Old dogs can learn new tricks! How many parents of the boomer generation late in life not only learned, but waxed enthusiastic about hymns that were new to them, like "How Great Thou Art," "Great Is Thy Faithfulness," "Gift of Finest Wheat," "Here I Am, Lord," and "Lift High the Cross." All appealing tunes, all in major key, and all with refrain!

Some of your people's favorites may include texts and tunes that strain the integrity of theologian and musician. You may feel called to educate people out of some texts and some tunes. You do not have to campaign against such songs. Offering something better in their place may make such explanations unnecessary. Of course, if people do want to know what is wrong with this or that hymn, you may have a teachable moment in your lap. As indicated in chapter 4, we do want, in worship, to mean what we sing and to sing what we mean. The musical choices of some people are driven by sentimentalism, by association of a particular piece of music with memories of childhood, or some experience later in life. Their favorite music is that which above all else produces feeling. Feeling has its place; heaven forbid that we should sing without feeling. But not feeling that is valued for its own sake and unrelated to faith and duty.

Since music is associated with the divine, it often becomes the arena in which we manifest our ambivalence toward God. Our responses to music bear the weight of our spiritual struggle. This helps to explain the passion that usually fills people's voices when they talk about music that has disturbed them in worship. Through music they are dealing with their relationship with God, the center of faith, the reason they have come to church in the first place. (Doran and Troeger 1992, 65)

An oft-encountered attitude is expressed in words something like these: "But when I come to church, I want to sing happy songs." Pastors and musicians who attempt to observe the forty days of Lent are especially likely to hear this refrain. Singing sad songs does not come naturally to everyone. A respected friend of mine is wont to whine about the dirge-like music in the church of which he is a member, claiming that he and his wife were previously involved in a charismatic church in which everything was upbeat. How can we help such people (and their tribe is numerous) take to heart the fact that song is a gift not just for expressing our joys, but also all our grief and sadness?

Do people dislike all sad songs? Or dislike only unfamiliar sad songs? "The Old Rugged Cross" does not lack for friends, yet it can hardly be called a happy song. In a May 2002 survey of a congregation of my acquaintance, favorite hymns included "Abide with Me," "Ivory Palaces" (not in the current hymnal), "Just as I Am," and "Near to the Heart of God." None of these is brimming with joy. One modal (that is, written using one of the medieval scales) spiritual also made the list: "What Wondrous Love is This?"

Of course, there are always the "But we've always done it this way," or "But we've never done it that way," "In the last church we were in . . ." or "That's Catholic, isn't it?" But you have long since learned how to help in these situations, right?

MOVING ON: POSSIBLE GOALS AND TACTICS

~

Browsing in books and articles named in Useful Resources can net you a large variety of suggestions for expanding the music program of your church. And pastors, musicians, and others can profit from their own creative thinking. In the meantime, here are a few possibilities.

Staff-specific Opportunities: The Clergy

The worship service

- Cite hymns as part of the sermon. On occasion, it can benefit both sermon and hymn to point out infelicities or inaccuracies in hymns—like the Magi and the shepherds being present at the same time. How do we relate "we feebly struggle" (in "For All the Saints") with Romans 8:9–17?

- Preach a sermon based on Scripture, but Scripture as seen through the lens of a hymn.

- Incorporate hymns into prayers, and use as responses. Some brave pastors will even break out in song now and then in a sermon. A Met-quality voice is not essential for this, but those whose singing voices are risible are advised not to try it.

- As a very few words before reading Scripture can be of invaluable help to the congregation, so can well-chosen remarks prior to the singing of a hymn. For instance, "This hymn is a prayer to the Holy Spirit." Not to be overly pedantic, but how about a hint as to what the anthem is about, calling attention to the text printed in the bulletin? The musicians may also appreciate this.

- The members of the choir need to know that they are appreciated by clergy and people. The wise pastor will attempt to meet briefly with the choir before every service to demonstrate solidarity in the leading of the worship service, and to lead in prayer.

- Furnish a number of large-print hymnals, and let it be known now and then where they are to be found.

- Encourage the use of congregational song at funerals and memorial services, and insist on it at weddings.

Educational opportunities

- Lead the congregation in an examination of the theology of a hymn or several hymns.

- In addition to expository sermons on the Psalms, offer sessions at Sunday school or in midweek gatherings on the general features of the Psalms and the world of the psalmist.

- Are there teachers of English literature in your congregation who might help the rest understand and appreciate what it is that makes a particular text tick? The sounds of poetry and the cadence are of the poem's essence; the lines can really come alive when read well. Is there someone around who can make that happen? A text-only version of your hymnal (as is the large-print edition) can be useful for looking closely at the language.

- Hymns come out of specific historical situations. Could a history teacher help bring the hymn home to the congregation?

Staff-specific Opportunities: The Musicians

Congregational song

- "What can I do to encourage people to sing?" In most churches, one of the most wonderful things that can happen is for the congregation to find its voice. One enthusiastic, gifted musician spending one hour with staff and people in the sanctuary (or in some acoustically superior space) may be all that is needed. Try singing, a cappella, very slowly and thoughtfully, "How Firm a Foundation" to the tune FOUNDATION. Encourage everyone to listen to other voices, and seek to blend all together. Savor the sound.

- An alternative to the usual kind of choir would be to gather into a group those who especially like to sing; the group could meet once a month to study and rehearse the hymns and any other congregational song that will be used in the following month. On Sunday mornings, these people could sit together in the rear seats, from where their strong singing could reinforce the efforts of the congregation.

- Dispense with the idea of a choir and hire a musician to develop the congregation's song.

- Include at least one congregational song at organ and choral programs. A plus is the needed stretch this gives the audience.

Choral

- In chapter 3 we talked about the choir as a caring community. This is not likely to happen unless someone works at it. An occasional choir party and some time for socializing during one rehearsal a month can help. An annual work-and-play retreat can pay big dividends. The choir director or one of the choristers can do much by showing an active interest in the lives of all the members. Begin each rehearsal with a brief devotional.

- Make a children's choir a high priority. Employing only one person to direct all the choirs in the church can help maintain focus, but this is not always possible/practical. Two rehearsals a week are better than one. Relationships and trust are important. A must for those who work with children's music is the Choristers Guild. The Guild's purpose is to nurture the spiritual growth of children and youth through music. A developmental-level (graded) approach should be followed. Hymns and psalms should be at the center of the children's choir curriculum; the preponderance of them should be lifelong songs, the songs they and their parents and siblings are asked to sing in worship, though some of them may be especially appropriate for children. "We have to sing with our children what is worth singing, what they and we can grow into rather than out of, so that on our deathbeds we will remember what is worth remembering" (Westermeyer 2001a, 43). The service music used by the church should be a part of the curriculum. Teach music from all periods, not just contemporary. Do not sacrifice a natural sweetness of voice for a forced loudness.

- A youth choir has going for it, among other things, the fact that it may help the youth understand that when they have outgrown the children's choir they have not graduated from singing.

- A choir needs an attractive, well-lighted, and ventilated practice room (out of hearing range of the worship space) equipped with a good piano (pianos in the church should be of a type that permits the player, when seated, to see over the top—thus a grand or a studio upright); compartmentalized shelving for the individual choristers' music; sufficient room for the storage of music; a large wall clock facing the director; good acoustics; a secure area where members can leave valuables when they are in the worship service; a budget; and a water fountain near the choir room, preferably at a location the choristers will pass on their way to the choir loft.

- If the choir is to be seen during the worship service, members may need vestments, a place to hang them, and arrangements for cleaning and keeping them in good repair.

- Some singers in the congregation might commit to singing in the choir for a specific season or for a special service.

- Some churches note the anniversaries of choir service by individual members.

- Choirs deserve an annual month-long vacation.

- Establish a men's chorus, determining its role in the life of the congregation, finding a director, recruiting members, and allotting funds for acquiring music.

- Organize a choir for seniors, perhaps in cooperation with other churches.

Instrumental

- The organist can demonstrate the organ to children and adults from time to time.

- An organist has suggested leaving the organ accessible for interested parties to play as a way of stimulating interest in the instrument and discovering talent. Also, it is better for the organ to be played frequently than to be left idle most of the time. Some safeguards may be needed, and of course, any arrangement must be agreeable to the organist.

- Offer a hymn-playing class. Include pianists who have attained a certain level of proficiency, but who do not know the art of leading congregational song from the keyboard.

- Provide good, simplified arrangements of hymns for young piano students.

- Is there unused instrumental talent in the congregation that might occasionally enhance the worship service or some other gathering?

- Weigh the advantages and disadvantages of establishing a hand-bell choir, and proceed accordingly.

Outreach ministry

- Offer noon concerts and hymn-sings, perhaps followed by lunch. Sometimes it is convenient to cooperate with a neighboring church in such an offering.

- The vocal and instrumental choirs may have a ministry awaiting them outside the church—nursing homes, jails, and shut-ins, for instance.

- Working with other organists in the community, the organist can organize a Pipe Organ Encounter to stimulate interest in the organ among youth.

- Organize a local chapter of The Hymn Society in the United States and Canada. Hold monthly interdenominational hymn sings.

- If your congregation maintains a Web site, consider how music can be used in connection with it.

Clergy and Musicians Together

Worship

- Offer an occasional pre-service hymn-sing. Should you offer people the opportunity to sing their favorites? The practice does show respect for the members. It may also reinforce satisfaction with the old and familiar, making people less open to learn new songs. It can also give the impression that what we sing in church is a matter of personal taste—like chocolate-raspberry torte. If the opportunity to request favorites is given, you might require that everyone making a request state why he or she likes the song requested.

- The choir can sing hymn concertatos and hymn anthems from time to time, involving the congregation.

- Even if your church has maintained a choir for one hundred years, do not take its continuance as a given. Rank your musical priorities: How important is a choir in your congregation in relation to congregational song? Do its efforts help the congregation to sing?

Does the music of the choir enhance worship? Does your church have the resources to field a passable choir? Is it in the congregation's interest to engage nonmembers to beef up the choir? To offer scholarships to music majors in area colleges? The question of integrity arises when paid singers do not share the faith of the congregation—especially if they depart the service after singing the anthem.

- Plan and execute a pre-service rehearsal of some of the music the congregation will be asked to sing in the service, making brief, helpful comments.

- Use short musical responses sung by the congregation, such as an "amen" after the benediction/blessing. People can sing Taizé and other simple choruses during communion.

- Use alternate ways of singing songs.

- Singing the Doxology, the *Gloria Patri*, or some other familiar song each week provides a good opportunity to accustom the congregation to singing a cappella. A slight amount of leadership is needed, of course.

- At appropriate times in the service, sing specific, appropriate hymn-stanzas.

- If your service includes a children's time, one of the songs or stanzas sung in the service for that day can be the focus.

- If your seating permits it, for singing a song and for reciting a creed, people on one side can turn ninety degrees to face members across the aisle, who have done likewise. Stanzas can be alternated between the two sides.

- Verify that lighting in every area in the worship space is adequate for reading from the hymnal.

- Give a brief musical welcome to new members, a musical farewell to departing.

- Lessons and Carols services are not just for Advent–Christmas. Plan them for other seasons.

- Plan and lead a hymn-based service of worship.

- Take an acoustical survey of your worship space, and decide what steps might be taken to enliven the sound in it.

Educational opportunities

- Explain the order of the worship service to the congregation, telling why this music and not some other is used in this particular spot.

- A very significant gain could result from exposing both the choir and the rest of the congregation to parts of this book.

- Gather the program staff once a week for an hour to sing through the hymnal, making everyone familiar with its contents, and with the songs for the following Lord's Day.

- Learn new songs, or learn old songs more thoroughly and profoundly, by following a song-of-the-month plan.

- Institute an ongoing program for systematically teaching songs to the children. Teach tunes. Once children know the tune, they can read the words. Children can teach adults songs they have learned.

- Include in your confirmation and new member classes a session on the music in your congregation, telling the members how songs are chosen. Ask new members about their musical tastes and abilities.

- Offer a course aimed at demonstrating the significance of the psalms for worship and ways of singing them.

- Study one song: author, composer, background/occasion of song having been written, theology, images, where in calendar and where in liturgy it fits, and the music.

- Adopt and learn a congregational song, for instance, "Now Thank We All Our God." The congregation will then have something to sing besides the Doxology when it gathers for a meal or on some other occasion.

- Thoughtfully rehearse the song of the month or another song, commenting on it.

- Introduce Wesley's *Directions for Singing*. Any Methodist pastor should have or be able to find a copy of these seven directions for you. They all fit on one page.

- Expose the congregation to the specific heritage of congregational song of your communion.

- The musician can point out the different kinds of tunes found in your hymnal. There may be some people who are candidates for an explanation of how the hymnal is organized, and the significance of the information on a typical page in the hymnal.

Professional opportunities

- Clergy and musicians need updates and inspiration. Does the church provide for them to go to conferences? Both clergy and musicians would benefit from the annual conferences of The Hymn Society in the United States and Canada. For musicians (and often for pastors, also) there are denominational conferences on music and opportunities to participate in master classes.

- Seek help to expand your musical horizons to include other styles of music, to understand that what matters is not whether music be in this or that style, but whether it is well crafted.

- Musicians and clergy can include one another in their professional meetings.

Outreach

- Plan and realize hymn festivals, possibly with one or more other congregations.

- Present an evening featuring twelve to fifteen of the congregation's favorite anthems, including brief comments about the texts and the music. If remembering that many anthems is too much for the congregation, let them name favorite hymns, then seek anthems or hymn concertatos based on those hymns.

Cooperative ministry

- If your funds are limited, you may want to pool your resources with others to secure the time of a musician brought in to work with the congregations, with the keyboardists, and with other musical groups.

- What relevant resources not presently used by your church might be obtained from some agency within your denomination or from other denominations? Consider requesting your denomination to supply certain aids such as recordings of hymns.

- Lead the congregation in supporting the inclusion of singing in the curriculum of schools.

- Encourage colleges to include offerings in choral singing, seminaries to include courses in the musical part of worship, and colleges and conferences to include instruction in teaching congregations to sing.

Some Areas of Endeavor

Communications

- Disseminate information about hymns and other music in bulletins and newsletters.

- Send e-mail letters to musicians to show appreciation for the music of the preceding Sunday's service.

Midweek gatherings

- Midweek gatherings provide the only opportunity in many congregations for the faithful to sing from the church's store of Evening Hymns.

- Some songs lend themselves to liturgical dance or miming. Even people with no experience in dancing can mime Isaac Watts's "I Sing the Mighty Power of God," for instance.

The church library

- Before investing much time and money in the church library, it is well to determine to what extent the library is used or likely to be used.

- Stock CDs of hymns and other church music—for sale or loan.

- Include at least one text on hymnology.

- Invest in books of stories of hymns, both their authors and occasions for writing.

- Include copies of hymnals formerly used by your congregation and collections from other communions.

The home

- Acquire one or more copies of the currently used hymnal for singing and for reading for every family.

- Memorize hymns together. See who can remember the words when you are on an automobile trip.

- Encourage people to gather around their home computers and sing away! A search engine can find several Web sites that give hymn texts and some that even play the tunes.

- A member can host a hymn-sing for a dozen or more people.

The Sunday school

- Sing at least one thoughtfully chosen song every Sunday in every department and class.

- Every three years or so, offer a course in congregational song.

- Lead a class in writing new hymns or hymn stanzas.

- Upgrade the music in your Sunday school. How about the old-fashioned custom of a Sunday school assembly by department or for all those in the school, held before the individual classes begin their study? Adopting for the Sunday school the same hymnal you use in the worship service has much to commend it. Sing songs you will or did sing at the worship service that day. This would also be a good time to make helpful comments about those songs.

All groups that gather

• Encourage every group in the church that gathers, including the governing board, to include the singing of at least one hymn or psalm every time it gathers. Familiar songs can be sung without anyone playing the piano.

– Useful Resources –

Albert Edward Bailey, *The Gospel in Hymns: Backgrounds and Interpretations* (New York: Charles Scribner's Sons, 1950).

John L. Bell, *The Singing Thing: A Case for Congregational Song* (Chicago: GIA Publications, 2000), 93–133, about why people do not sing.

Emily R. Brink, ed., *Songs of Life* (Grand Rapids: CRC Publications, 1994). A children's hymnal with leader's edition.

The Calvin Institute of Christian Worship awards music-related worship renewal grants annually to churches and other institutions for specific undertakings. You may get some helpful ideas for your own project from the list of approved grants. Visit www.calvin.edu/worship. You may even be able to get a grant.

The Choristers Guild, 2834 Kingsley Road, Garland, TX 75041. Children's music.

Harry Eskew and Hugh T. McElrath, *Sing With Understanding: An Introduction to Christian Hymnology,* 2nd ed. (Nashville: Church Street Press, 1995). The authors include a list of one hundred hymns especially appropriate for teaching children and youth.

Marilyn M. González, *Choir Care* (New York: American Guild of Organists, 1993).

C. Michael Hawn, ed., *Stepping Stones: An Ecumenical Children's Choir Curriculum* (Garland, TX: Choristers Guild, 1995, 1996, and 1997), a three-year curriculum based on seven hymns each year, these being hymns that appear most often in mainline denominational hymnals.

Hal H. Hopson, *100+ Ways to Improve Hymnsinging* (Carol Stream, IL: Hope Publishing Company, 2005).

The Hymn, 50.3, July 1999. The entire issue is dedicated to children's music.

The Hymn Society in the United States and Canada. Web site: www.hymnsociety.org.

Austin Lovelace, *Hymn Notes for Church Bulletins* (Chicago: GIA Publications, 1987).

Kenneth W. Osbeck, *101 Hymn Stories* (Grand Rapids: Kregel, 1982). Osbeck gives much attention to gospel songs.

Kenneth W. Osbeck, *101 More Hymn Stories* (Grand Rapids: Kregel, 1985).

Kenneth W. Osbeck, *Amazing Grace: 366 Inspiring Hymn Stories for Daily Devotions* (Grand Rapids: Kregel, 1990).

Alice Parker, *Melodious Accord: Good Singing in Church* (Chicago: Liturgy Training Publications, 1991).

William J. Reynolds and Milburn Price, *A Survey of Christian Hymnody,* 4th ed. (Carol Steam, IL: Hope Publishing Company, 1999).

Carl Schalk, *Praising God in Song: An Introduction to Christian Hymnody for Congregational Study* (St. Louis: Concordia Publishing House, 1993).

James Rawlings Sydnor, *Hymns and Their Uses: A Guide to Improved Congregational Singing* (Carol Stream, IL: AGAPE, 1982).

James Rawlings Sydnor, *Hymns: A Congregational Study* (Carol Stream, IL: AGAPE, 1983). Student's and Teacher's Editions. Recommended for Sunday school classes.

James Rawlings Sydnor, *Introducing a New Hymnal: How to Improve Congregational Singing* (Chicago: GIA Publications, 1989).

John D. Witvliet, "Church Music, Congregational Life, and Theological Education in Harmony: Toward a New Approach for Musical Advocacy," *The American Organist*, December 2006, 76–81.

Alec Wyton, *What We Should Expect from Young People* (New York: American Guild of Organists, n.d.).

CHAPTER
ELEVEN

PLANNING MUSIC FOR THE WORSHIP
SERVICE: WHO, WHEN, FOR WHOM?

~

Having looked in chapter 10 at the overall program of music in the congregation, we turn now to consider planning for the weekly worship services. Music that glorifies God and builds up the church is more likely to happen if planned. Planning does not mean that there is no room for spontaneity and responsiveness to the dynamics of the worship service or that the freedom of the Holy Spirit is restricted. Perhaps it is in the sermon and the spoken prayers that spontaneity can find the most opportunity. Who can best plan the weekly worship service? When is planning done? For what areas of musical endeavor is planning needed? For each area, what needs to be taken into account, and what resources are available? These are our topics for this chapter.

SOME ASSUMPTIONS

~

Even for those whose worship service is given shape by a fixed liturgy, it can be helpful to keep in mind certain principles that are the fruit of our having reflected on worship in general and, in particular, music's role in worship. These principles—convictions, if you will—guide us in the choices we make. They include:

1) Corporate worship is important, more important than anything else the church does.

2) Music, which may occupy from one-third to one-half of the time in worship, is an integral part of worship. Though it may indeed contribute much toward setting the tone for the service, and facilitating the flow of the service, it is not to be considered merely as preparation for something else.

3) While there is no divinely given order of service, God is a God of order, not of disorder (Gen. 1:1–2:4; 1 Cor. 14:33). For us who are made in God's image, the most effective service of worship, all else being equal, will be a service that follows a logical order, a service that flows from one item to the next. Isaiah 6:1–13 gives us a concrete example of flow in a worship service. The service is a whole in which all the parts fit together in a natural order.

4) All present are called to participate actively in the service of worship. Though active participation includes participation that is interior, mental, and emotional, the entire assembly is also called to participate overtly, physically, and congregationally. The chief means of so participating is congregational song.

Keeping Silence

~

How much music must we plan? Must we paper over every crack between the components of the service? Most organists have probably long since heard the old line about the preacher who asked the organist to doodle a bit to fill in a gap in the order of worship, to which the organist replied, "How about you just mumbling a few words?" Liturgical actions do not always need musical accompaniment, and pastors and musicians must resist the compulsion to fill every gap with sound.[1] Any silence observed in the worship service is best directed, coming just before or just after certain parts of the service. Appropriate times include the beginning of the service, just after the spoken confession of sin, the sermon, the offertory, or the Supper. Do not startle people by any abrupt, loud sound at the end of the period of silence.

Who Does the Planning?

~

Before we get into the planning itself, let's think a little about the planners. Who are they? The scene was the reception for the new pastor. My organist-wife, greeting the just-arrived, told him that she looked forward to working with him. The pastor's facial response was a look of mystification. Subsequent experience confirmed the initial diagnosis: For this pastor, whatever worship planning was done did not include the organist.

For every pastor who has left off playing the lone ranger, the questions arise: Who, in addition to me, determines the shape of the worship in the congregation I serve? Who plans worship—overall and the details of all the individual worship services? (Here, of course, we are looking especially at the musical parts of worship.) If the church you serve has any kind of a governing board, then presumably that body has some overall authority regarding worship. The board may include a worship committee and perhaps a sub-committee for music. From such a board or its committees you may expect general oversight of the congregation's worship. Certainly this will be the case when any major changes in the order or contents of the worship service are contemplated. (All changes in worship practice tend to be viewed as major!)

Part of changing worship is being realistic about church politics. Because worship is a congregation's most regular public event and because it is an experience in which meaning and relationships are symbolically enacted, it is a meeting ground for the forces that are at work throughout the church's life. (Doran and Troeger 1992, 138)

Planning for worship should for certain involve the musicians and the pastors—planning together, yet taking into account the specific responsibilities and expertise of both clergy and musicians. Let's begin with the pastors.

The Pastors: What We Would Like to Assume

1) Pastors believe that worship that is worthy and helpful must be planned. They understand that planning good worship not only takes time; it also presupposes knowledge of the subject, and gaining this knowledge requires effort. The same is true in regard to all the other areas of the work to which the clergy is called; any one of them is a candidate for full-time specialization. These competing demands, coupled with the congregation's likely expectations of their pastor, mean that only a very determined person will give worship planning its due.

2) Pastors are committed to the proposition that the best worship requires partnership, both in planning and in execution.

3) They have long since gotten over the idea, if indeed ever afflicted with it, that their goal on Sunday morning is that the people leave the service with the three points of the sermon uppermost in their minds; what matters is that in all parts of the service, people worship God.

4) If not yet fully persuaded of music's powerful potential and of the vital role of music in worship, they are at least working on it.

5) Of all the music in the worship service, pastors are committed to the proposition that no part is as important as the congregation's song.

6) Pastors are resolved that they will no longer continue to be hymnologically challenged; that they will make reading hymns, including some of more recent origin, to be a part of their devotional life; that they will read the stories behind some of the hymns; and that they will commit some hymns to memory.

7) They will begin or continue to mine the riches of the church's song for help in sermon and prayer.

8) Pastors will spend a little time with their hymnal, and perhaps a staff musician, to become better acquainted with the hymnal's structure and contents.

9) They will even seriously consider taking voice lessons—which also can work wonders for the speaking voice—or they will at least be open to any hints the musician may give them. Even people who pass for tone-deaf can very often be helped.

10) Planning for worship is best a collaborative effort, but pastors accept ultimate responsibility for the service. If poor choices are made, they may not seek refuge in saying that the musician did it. The buck stops with the pastor.

The Musicians: Between Reality and Ideals

1) Church musicians are constantly striving to upgrade their general musical skills. Many church organists received most of their musical training on the piano. They probably need (or needed) help in making the transition. Many of those who received solid training on the organ do not understand the very special demands of leading congregational song. Even as many pastors were drawn to the ministry not by love for people, but rather love of theology, many church organists did not fall in love with the instrument because of its usefulness for leading congregational song.

2) Ideally, church musicians are open to learning performance practices that are different from any in which they have been trained.

3) Church musicians should have some understanding of theology and worship, the role of music in worship, and the liturgical tradition of the church they serve. They can bone up on these matters through reading and attending conferences.

4) Church musicians should be as committed as are pastors to the priority of congregational song in the worship service. They should be convinced that their most important function is to lead the song of the congregation. Charles R. Gardner puts it clearly: Church musicians must come to love the sound made by a singing congregation more than any other musical sound (1991, 103). "Church music is music which supports, encourages, and does not get in the way of congregational song" (Ferguson 1993, 32). It may well be the case, as John Ferguson maintains, that however organists see themselves, most worshipers see them above all else as the leaders of their song (1994). But even among those who are fundamentally committed to this proposition, all too many have given up on their congregation ever singing well. Many times resignation to low expectations has come after a long period of attempting to develop a more robust congregational song. Perhaps the pastor and other leaders were not supportive of the efforts. It is just possible that a wrong approach was used. It is possible that even a gifted musician does not know how to develop the song of a congregation, and must yet learn. The first lesson to be learned is that the congregation will never sing well if their leaders do not expect them to do so.

5) Church musicians are in a position to minister to the spiritual life of those musicians who serve under their leadership, not to mention the whole congregation. Ideally, they share the faith of the communion they serve. The favored Roman Catholic term, "pastoral musician," has much to be said for it.

6) Church musicians should have a growing knowledge of the congregation and other members of the staff.

7) Other important qualifications for church musicians are enthusiasm, good communication skills, and the ability to teach new music.

Help from Others?

Is it advantageous to bring members of the congregation into the process of planning the specifics of the worship services? Adopting this course would certainly not be the easiest and quickest way to select music for the service, and it might be seen as involving more time than clergy and musician want to give and more risk than they want to take. The more difficult course, however, has a very great deal going for it. (See Doran and Troeger, and Malefyt and Vanderwell in this chapter's Useful Resources.) Making planning for worship a collaborative effort has the potential for strengthening the church in general, and the music in particular. It can provide opportunities for growth on the part of the members so involved. Pastor and musician can well benefit from the members' input in the meetings. The congregation's sense of ownership of the church's musical program may be enhanced. One very valuable contribution a non-staff person can make is to serve as a channel of communication between congregation and worship staff, supplying feedback from the former to the latter, and enthusiastically communicating to the governing board and congregation the plans and dreams of the worship leaders. A non-staff member of the congregation may be much more effective than a staff person in interpreting worship plans and practices to the congregation. Non-staff persons who serve may well include a member of the church's governing board.

WHEN PLANNING TAKES PLACE

~

The Weekly Meeting

For at least the pastors and musicians, a weekly meeting is basic. In such meetings the service of the previous Lord's Day can be discussed and evaluated, perhaps a recording of it watched or heard. What in the order might be improved? Was anything too long? Did the service flow? The service for the next Sunday will have long since been planned, but details of that service should be reviewed, and any appropriate revisions made.

Periodic Worship Planning for the Long-Term

Every kind of planning is, by definition, done in advance of that for which we plan. Planning for worship should take place well in advance—weeks or months before the services planned. Before every meeting for this purpose, it will be helpful if the pastor first presents the musicians with his or her plans for the upcoming months; the musicians can then begin to merge this data with their own. Some pastors set down at least the basics a year in advance. In any case, it is well to get them down for every service no less than three months in advance. The musicians need to know that far ahead what the pastor has in mind for every Sunday in view—Scripture, theme, emphasis, whether baptism or Lord's Supper will be administered, confirmands received, lay missionaries commissioned, Sunday school officers and teachers recognized, members of the governing board installed, and anything else that might take place. If you are following the church year and a lectionary, possible parameters are already in place. How often are choirs (adult, youth, and children), ensembles, and soloists to be desired? Will any of the worship leaders be on vacation? Knowing as much as possible about what is planned for a given Sunday, the musicians can look through their music for what is most appropriate. If they find nothing, they have time to order and learn or teach new music. Arrangements may have to be made for a vocal soloist or for instrumentalists. What pastors must bear in mind always is that musicians need sufficient lead time. Periodic review of what has been chosen should take place, and revisions made as desired—being certain that all worship leaders are informed without delay of all changes. (May it never happen in your church that the musicians discover on Friday, when they pick up a bulletin for the coming Sunday, that the original choices have been changed—without consulting the musicians. They discover that all their preparation for a specific service was off the mark!) By all means, bear in mind spiritual, social, and intellectual needs of all present at meetings.

PLAN WHAT FOR WHOM?

~

The Congregation

Practical limits of the repertory: Less is more

I have already shown my hand as to which of the areas—congregation, choir, instruments—takes priority: the congregation. In chapter 5, I discussed the potential musical repertory of the congregation. At this juncture, I want to set forth and defend a very particular concept regarding congregational song, namely, the idea of a "core repertory." The committee that prepared the hymnal you are using followed certain criteria as they considered the tens of thousands of English-language hymns in existence. The committee eventually settled on the six hundred or so songs in your collection. Many churches also include in the pew racks hymnal supplements of still more songs. Other and somewhat different collections may be used in Sunday school or in gatherings other than for Sunday morning worship. No one expects a congregation to know everything in its hymnal; the average congregation may feel more or less at home with between 100 and 150 tunes—counting 15 to 20 Christmas tunes. Think of all the treasure people are missing! At the same time, pastors and, perhaps even more so, church musicians, must ever remember that they and the congregation-at-large are not at the same point in this matter; while the congregation is warming up to "God Is Working His Purpose Out" (1894), you have long since become fascinated by "When in Our Music God Is Glorified" (1972).

Only repetition breeds familiarity

The contemporary church in North America tends to be made up of people of diverse traditions. They sing less, both in and out of church, than did their ancestors. How large a hymnic repertory is it realistic to expect for such people? We noted some of the things that may happen when the congregation sings: We worship God, we are moved to worship more fervently, we are built up in faith and duty, we pray and learn better how to pray, we experience our oneness in Christ, and we proclaim a message to others.

That these things happen presupposes that what we are singing is familiar to us, and familiarity is a product of repetition. We may say that there are three things that we can do more or less well only in our own language: swear, pray, and make love. For congregational song to work its full effect, what we are singing has to be ours! Just as the Jews in exile found it difficult to sing the Lord's song in a strange land (Ps. 137), so we find it very hard to sing strange songs—unfamiliar texts and, even more so, unfamiliar tunes. "Where there is congregational singing it is important that familiar melodies should be employed, or at least those which have stood the test of time" (Ralph Vaughan Williams, Preface to the *English Hymnal* of 1906). "Congregational songs have formative and inspirational power only when repeated, repeated, and repeated until familiar. When the song is familiar and beloved, people sing their hearts out" (Wren 2000, 110). "With familiar music, people put down their books and sing their hearts out" (Clark 1994, 28). The biggest mistake, Frank Brownstead tells us, is to attempt to learn too many songs (1991, 90). Congregations will never offer themselves up to God in song, never get "lost in wonder, love, and praise," if what they are asked to sing is not their song. At the very heart of worship is the familiar. It is an instance of "less is more." Even in an age when North Americans sang more, that wise dean of North American hymnologists, Louis F. Benson, said that hymnals had become too encyclopedic, too compendious to breed familiarity with their contents; congregations were being given too much on their plates (1915, 305; 1927, 275–77)—far more than they could digest and make their own. Liturgical music cannot only bear repetition; it requires it. Liturgical music, if it is to have its full effect, must be repeated over and over; its work as the mother of memory continues over a lifetime, over the centuries

(Mark Searle 1991, 11). The late nineteenth-century evangelist Dwight L. Moody also expressed concern about the large number of songs people were being asked to sing.

> We ought to be limited in our range of selection of hymns. . . . I have a profound conviction that the great size of our congregational hymn-books is killing congregational singing. (cited by VanDyke 2006, 149)

Unfortunately, the huge amount of liturgical experimentation in the second half of the twentieth century and since has not fostered this kind of familiarity. Neither has the large volume of new song produced and rapidly disseminated in that period. The late John Wilson, an English music teacher known for having encouraged a number of the hymnists who contributed to the Hymn Explosion of the second half of the twentieth century, did himself speak of an overproduction of new hymns in the period (Leaver 2006, 21). Breadth has been bought at the expense of depth. Martin Luther's words from the sixteenth century remain a challenge for the church in the twenty-first: In choosing music for the service, care must be taken "lest the people should either be bored by too much repetition of the same or confused by too many changes. . . " (*Luther's Works* 53:38).

Selecting a core repertory

The congregation's familiarity with the song it is asked to sing is crucially important. This is what leads me to argue here that the selection of hymns for your congregation to sing needs to be guided by, among other considerations, the principle of the core repertory.

> The rhythms of the church year and the liturgy itself call for a core of music that does not change constantly, but is integral to the patterns of worship. . . . Planning music for worship calls for careful attention to the people's memory. It is important that a congregation's repertoire include music of lasting value and durability so that it can bear repeated use and remain vital in the life of the congregation. (Evangelical Lutheran Church 2001, 30)

The congregation's target repertory should be a delimited body of songs that the church has determined to make its own through repeated use. (See Nuechterlein 1978, 122.)

No one can supply you with a list of titles that should be in your core repertory, a hymnological analogy to the "Great Books" list; this is a do-it-yourself project, requiring much time and thought. Some very valuable help, however, is readily accessible. If your congregation could have only one hundred or so hymns and psalms in its collection, which ones would you choose? Which invite you to sing them? Which are moving? Which songs are memorable? Which will bear singing again and again? Which songs will serve your people from cradle to grave? Which are called for by the church's faith, calendar, and rites? Which hymns have by the simple fact that they have already been around for a long time proven their durability? This should be understood and kept in mind: Our concern is not that songs from outside the core repertory should not be sung. Rather, it is that the songs in the core repertory are sung, and sung enough to impress them on the hearts of the people. "New hymns are also essential to the lifelong work of faith formation. As new songs are introduced in worship, God's Spirit continues to open and shape lives" (Evangelical Lutheran Church 2001, 30).

A guiding principle: At the core of your core should be the classic devotional hymn—hymns of adoration, thanksgiving, praise, confession, lament, and petition. Forget about any felt need for hymns that will clench this or that point of the sermon—homiletical hymns, hymns about this or that issue. Issues can be addressed in sermons (to a certain extent) and classrooms, but for congregational song, major in the generic. At the core of your core, you will want not didactic songs but doxological.

I've made reference to a list of basic (ecumenical) hymns, and listed several criteria for choosing a hymnal.[2] Such lists can give guidance in arriving at your own core repertory. You do want your repertory to reflect the whole church, not just a particular tradition or period. At some point you will want to inventory your congregation's current store of hymns. It is possible that what your congregation has sung over the course of time has been noted—in the church musician's hymnal or elsewhere, as in each Sunday's worship bulletin. You will surely find a number that are already known that are also included in your proposed core repertory. Are some tunes used for more than one text? A tune's familiarity helps the congregation concentrate on the text.

In the same vein, you may want to consider, in introducing new texts to the congregation, the use of tunes already known. A familiar tune will be more likely to make your people want to sing than would an unfamiliar one.

Making the core repertory familiar

The worship planners should next devise and implement a plan for teaching unfamiliar hymns in the core repertory to the congregation. Following the basic pedagogical principle that a good teacher begins where the pupils are, you will, in the spirit of 1 Corinthians 14:26, when selecting hymns and psalms for the worship service, give special consideration to songs already known. Particularly in helping our congregations to stretch their range of musical styles, we must take great care; we must not be perceived as imposing our personal tastes on others. If we have chosen well-crafted tunes in establishing our core repertory, we can know that they will, with repetition, likely grow on the congregation, even if they were questioned or resisted at first. Good tunes bear repetition.

A specific step toward making the congregation's songs familiar to them is suggested by Benson, who asks, how much Scripture would people know if the only Bibles were those in the pew racks and pulpits? How can we expect people to know the hymns in a book found only in the pew racks? The church must get the hymnal back into the hands of the people. ". . . it is only the precedent [to the worship service] appropriation of the hymn's message by each individual heart that makes its congregational singing worthwhile" (1927, 228). The congregation's musical homework, its personal assimilation of the church's song, not only makes corporate musical worship worthwhile; it at the same time nourishes the congregation's life in the wider world—over the sink, behind the steering wheel, and behind the desk. A recurring concern of writers in the early church, in the sixteenth-century Reformation, and since has been that the songs of the congregation are to be sung not only in the service of worship, but in all of daily life. There is a special concern that young people sing not lascivious, worldly songs that conduce to debauchery, but those of the faith; the complete song repertory of both young and old alike is to be hymns and psalms. Strangely enough, in North American society today, this concern may well be realized, for the only time most people sing anything at all is in church! But to what songs do people listen outside of church? That many pay no attention to some of the lyrics is cause for gratitude. But there is still the music!

If we do not need the music, we may prefer a text-only edition for the hymnal we have at home. A thoughtful reading of the text is much easier if we are reading from a text-only hymnal. Most large-print editions of hymnals are printed in this fashion.

The service music

There is much to be said for all service music to be sung not by the choir alone, but by the whole congregation—part of its core repertory. Sung every Sunday, the *Gloria Patri*, the Doxology, and other service music affords us, if not always the most exciting, then the most robust congregational singing most of us are likely to hear. Since it is quite familiar, this music may also be sung thoughtlessly at a tempo that is too fast; discipline is required. It may be time for your congregation to give the tunes they have long used for these two items a rest, and sing alternative tunes.

Spoken prayers and affirmations are appropriately followed by a spoken (by the congregation) "Amen." The pastor's call to worship and benediction/blessing (both are grace-filled formulas; neither one is a prayer) do not need to be followed or preceded by choral or congregational versions of the same. Catholics are provided chant settings.

Choirs, Vocal Soloists, and Instrumentalists

There is a vast and ever-expanding quantity of music available for the choir. It is of great variety as to style, complexity, and what resources it requires. Catalogs have been prepared that list, in biblical order and according to particular days in the church calendar, many anthems and vocal solos that are available at the time of a catalog's publication. Just as music for organ has tended in recent years to incorporate hymn tunes, contemporary choral music for the church is very often hymn-based, making use of both texts and tunes of hymns. Hymn-based anthems not only may serve to strengthen the song of the congregation indirectly, but also are more likely to have an immediate appeal to the people. The popular form, hymn concertato, involves not only the choir and instruments, but the congregation as well.

In planning for the long term, a balance should be sought between the old and familiar and the new and unfamiliar. There are anthems of high quality that bear repetition over the course of time. As these anthems become familiar and accumulate associations, they will become more effective. The congregation will find them increasingly accessible. People in the pews will recognize them as "our song." Remember that choristers can be challenged not only by being asked to sing music they have never seen, but also by being expected to sing that which is familiar to them—to more nearly attain perfection than they did the previous time they sang the piece.

Production of quality music for children's choirs has grown rapidly since the end of World War II. Materials are not lacking! At every week's rehearsal, the children should practice the songs that the congregation is to sing in the following Sunday's worship.

The role of instrumentalists in the worship service is twofold. The first is to support all song not sung a cappella, the most important being the congregation's, but also that of choir, choral ensemble, or vocal soloist. Only instruments capable of producing considerable volume will serve for leading the song of the congregation. The second is to provide appropriate solo or ensemble instrumental music. A wealth of instrumental music is available. The number of high-quality instrumental variations on hymn tunes available continues to multiply. As noted in chapter 7, a number of instruments can be used to give variety and freshness to the music of the service, and can prevent the congregation from settling into an expectation of the same thing every week. There is much music for organ with other instruments. Are there instrumentalists in your congregation who might be grateful for the opportunity to use their gifts in this way?

Of perennial concern to the keyboardist, along with the issues of compensation and clergy-musician conflict, are questions about the prelude and postlude. (Music for a prelude or postlude is often called a "voluntary." The term, of British origin, may get us out of the semantic difficulty of "prelude" and "postlude," but probably does not say much to most people.) Most often the question is, "How can we get people to stop talking and start listening to the music I have prepared for them?"

Responses to the keyboardists' plaints have been varied: Encourage people to do their greetings and farewells in a location outside the worship space; begin the service before the prelude; end the service after the postlude; discontinue the use of prelude and/or postlude; discourage talking during the prelude, but expect people to talk during the postlude.

The use of a prelude is defended as a means of creating a mood, setting the tone for worship, and helping to make the transition from other activities to worship. Lionel Dakers opines that the organ prelude can do for Protestants what incense may do for Roman Catholics: "Carry us over the 'threshold' into worship" (1997, 124). A postlude can provide a festive ambience while the people are departing.

Questions concerning the prelude and the postlude should be evaluated in terms of their place in the service. The very names, prelude and postlude—meaning "to play before" and "to play after"—indicate that these two items are liturgical orphans. They come before and after the service. They accompany no rites. An attempt to smuggle the prelude and the postlude into the liturgy may be made by renaming them "Music to Begin Worship" and "Music to Conclude Worship." The service, however, begins with the pastor's greeting or a call to worship (Catholic Mass begins with an antiphon, most usually a hymn) and ends with the pastor's benediction/blessing. No music before the former or after the latter is part of the worship service. The church has neither mandate nor authority to compel people to listen to organ music outside the service. Seeking to put the question in perspective, the organist John Ferguson reminds us that at the center of our concern here is not the prelude or the postlude; these are no more than "nice but unimportant frills in comparison to the primary obligation of organ and organist to sing with and lead the people's song" (1993, 32).

– Useful Resources –

The Choristers Guild: 2834 W. Kingsley Road, Garland, TX 75041. Web site: http://www.choristersguild.org/index3.html. Music for children.

Thomas Day, *Why Catholics Can't Sing: The Culture of Catholicism and the Triumph of Bad Taste* (New York: Crossroads, 1991). Day also argues for a core repertory of congregational song to which other selections can in the course of time be added.

Noni Espina, *Vocal Solos for Christian Churches,* 3rd ed. (Metuchen, NJ: Scarecrow Press, 1984).

Marion J. Hatchett, *A Guide to the Practice of Church Music* (New York: The Church Hymnal Corporation, 1989).

Carl Halter and Carl Schalk, eds., *A Handbook of Church Music* (St. Louis: Concordia Publishing House, 1978).

Hal Hopson, *The Creative Church Musician Series* (Carol Stream, IL: Hope Publishing Company), includes *The Creative Use of Choirs in Worship*; *The Creative Use of the Organ in Worship*; *The Creative Use of Descants in Worship*; *The Creative Use of Instruments in Worship*; *The Creative Use of Handbells in Worship*; *More Creative Ways to Use The Choir, Handbells, and Other Instruments in Worship*.

Donald P. Hustad, *Jubilate II: Church Music in Worship and Renewal* (Carol Stream, IL: Hope Publishing Co., 1993). Pages 512-33: "Music for Soloists and Small Ensemble."

James H. Laster, *Catalogue of Choral Music Arranged in Biblical Order* (Lanham, MD: Scarecrow Press, 1996). Supplement, 2002.

James H. Laster and Diana Reed Strommen, *Catalogue of Vocal Solos and Duets Arranged in Biblical Order* (Lanham, MD: Rowman and Littlefield Publishers, 2003).

James H. Laster, *Catalogue of Music for Organ and Instruments* (Lanham, MD: Scarecrow Press, 2005).

Austin Lovelace and William C. Rice, *Music and Worship in the Church* (Nashville: Abingdon Press, 1960). Pages 139–46: "The Soloist," including list of suggested repertory.

Norma deWaal Malefyt and Howard Vanderwell, *Designing Worship Together: Models and Strategies for Worship Planning* (Herndon, VA: The Alban Institute, 2005). How pastor and musician may collaborate in planning worship.

James McCray, *Church Choir Director's Guide to Success* (Santa Barbara: Santa Barbara Music Publishing, 1997).

Carlos R. Messerli, "The Music of the Choir," in Halter and Schalk, 127-71.

N. Lee Orr, *The Church Music Handbook: For Pastors and Musicians* (Nashville: Abingdon, 1991).

Carl Schalk, *First Person Singular: Reflections on Worship, Liturgy, and Children* (St. Louis: Morningstar, 1998).

Leslie Spelman and Jayson Rod Engquist, *Organ Plus,* 4th ed. (New York: AGO, 1999). A list of almost 1,500 pieces for organ with instruments.

CHAPTER TWELVE

CHOOSING THE MUSIC FOR THE WORSHIP SERVICE

~

Fixed-liturgy churches normally celebrate the Lord's Supper every Lord's Day. Their service may well include at least an entrance hymn, an offertory hymn, a communion hymn, and a post-communion or recessional hymn, in addition to appropriate service music. The psalm for the day is likely sung, being led by a cantor. What follows in this chapter, though relevant for the Lord's Day service in all churches, has in view particularly the needs of the free-liturgy church. In this church, it is often the songs—their content and placement—that more than anything else give shape to the liturgy.

CHOOSING THE SONGS OF THE CONGREGATION

~

How Many Songs?

If any of your members are present at every Sunday morning service for a year, and your service normally includes three psalms or hymns, they will have sung only 156 songs, some of them repeats—in a whole year! Surely three songs per Sunday morning is not too much. In chapter 2 we discussed

the wonderful things that can happen when the congregation sings; surely
you do not want to deprive your people of such blessing. Remember, anyone
in your congregation who sings anywhere but in church is highly exceptional.
If in the hour or more allotted for the service you simply have not the time
to sing three songs, it is just possible that the clergy is making too many
announcements, or even preaching beyond the attention span of the people.
An early twentieth-century edition of my denomination's *Directory for
Worship* gave this caution to preachers:

> As one primary design of public ordinances is to pay social acts of homage to
> the most high God, ministers ought to be careful not to make their sermons
> so long as to interfere with or exclude *the more important duties of prayer and
> praise* [italics mine].

In some services, it is not the pastor's wordiness, but other forms of
music that preempt the congregation's song. In a recent Maundy Thursday
service in which I worshiped, the men's chorus sang twice, the bell choir
played twice, and a male vocalist sang once; all we in the congregation got
to sing were three stanzas of "Were You There?"

Any Psalm for the Day Is Already Chosen

The psalms of the Old Testament constitute the universal and oldest
genre of congregational song for both synagogue and church. In many traditions, a psalm, the whole or in part, is a given in every Sunday morning
service. If this is not your practice, you may want to consider it.

Those churches that follow a lectionary will likely sing or read a psalm
in every Sunday morning worship service. You must decide whether to read
the prescribed psalm or sing it. The fact that the psalms are songs makes it
especially fitting that they be sung. Maybe, apart from the psalm for the
day, you have your quota of songs you would like to sing on a particular
Sunday. This may lead you to opt for reading the psalm rather than singing
it. Whether you sing the psalm depends, of course, on whether you have it, or
at least the part of it you want to use, in your collection of songs, and whether
its tune is one you want to use. Also, Isaac Watts's counsel still merits consideration today: Psalms that present theological or ethical difficulties are better

read as the Word of God than sung as the congregation's prayer. The Revised Common Lectionary, in the choice of its readings, has omitted about two-thirds of the potentially difficult passages in Psalms.

The pedagogical demand of singing a new psalm every Sunday may be reduced by using one appropriate psalm or psalm-portion for an entire season. This would also mean a gain in familiarity and depth of understanding with respect to the one psalm sung. A lectionary's four different readings every Sunday does run the risk of pedagogical overload. Worshipers are also supposed to relate these readings to those of the preceding Sunday! If an able and willing cantor is available, then without difficulty a different psalm can be sung responsorially every Lord's Day if desired, since the congregation's part is short and easy to sing. Though the music involved is simple, the cantor should practice it until it comes effortlessly. Pastoral concerns demand that we be sensitive to any in the congregation who are unaccustomed to cantoring in their worship service. A gradual introduction in an informal setting may be advisable, perhaps first at a midweek gathering. Choir and congregation may also sing familiar metrical psalm settings antiphonally.

Making the Choices

Coherence

In choosing the songs for a particular Sunday, situations vary, but generally speaking there is much to be said for pastors, in consultation with the musicians, making the choice of any song chosen for its coherence with the sermon or Scripture. One such song is enough for a service. Let the other songs be generic praise, thanksgiving, or petition, chosen by musician or pastor, each in consultation with the other. Though the song choices are made by pastor or musician, comments on the choices from other members of the planning committee should be sought; they may prove to be very helpful.

We may call another kind of coherence pastoral or contextual coherence. Are there overarching concerns currently in the air? Tragedies of community, national, or international scope that have resulted in fear and despair? Gloom in the congregation brought about by a tragic death or a looming schism? Racial strife that has erupted in the community? Unusual motives for rejoicing and giving thanks? What songs in your hymnal can be helpful to your people in such situations? What are people in a given situation likely to hear in a particular song? What are they likely to appropriate for their very own?

As noted in chapter 1, the mutual interaction of text and tune on one another inclines us to conceive of a hymn as neither text nor tune alone, but the product of the reciprocal interaction of text and tune on one another. This means that in planning worship, we must give attention not to the text in isolation, but to how that text will be experienced as sung to the tune with which it is paired.

Even some of the highly seasonal hymns, such as those sung at Christmas, are more appropriately sung at certain points in the service than at others. The rites of baptism and the Lord's Supper have their own hymns. Some Supper hymns focus on the cross, others on the resurrection life or some other aspect of the Gospel, some on Christ, others on Christ's body—the church—among which you may choose according to your particular emphasis. If your congregation's celebration of the Lord's Supper has tended to be somewhat funereal, a bit more solemn than you judge it should be, you may be able to open the windows to let in a little more joy by choosing hymns with that in mind. Any songs before, during, and after the Supper may well move from the more meditative to the more exuberant, from crucifixion to resurrection.

Reception into membership, confirmation, ordination, and installation of officers, and other rites have their own hymns. Coherence with whatever local tradition there is with respect to repertory (including your established core repertory), its extent and its favorites, should be taken into account. Keep a record of every song's use.

If you are following a hymn-of-the-month program, this will also influence the choice of hymns on every Sunday in the month. Many Lutherans follow a schedule that assigns a different hymn for every Sunday; its text relates to the Scripture or theme for the day, and it is sung just after the sermon.

Ease of singing

While our choices are not limited to songs that are easy to sing, it is well to have some idea as to the relative difficulty of what we are asking of the congregation when we ask them to sing a given song. Some tunes are easier for a congregation to sing than others. The tune RATHBUN, to which we may sing "In the Cross of Christ I Glory," is not an easy tune. But if a congregation knows a song, it does not matter if it is difficult. It may be helpful to know, however, what kinds of unfamiliar tunes the congregation will find easier to sing. In addition to points made earlier, the following may be noted as helps in selecting easier tunes:

1) Choose folk-tunes or folk-like tunes, such as the ones we use for "Good Christian Friends, Rejoice," "Go, Tell it on the Mountain," and "Come, Thou Fount of Every Blessing".

2) Employ the short, traditional, four-square tunes that are widely used (ST. MAGNUS, for example, used with "The Head that Once Was Crowned with Thorns").

3) Songs that are complete on one page or on facing pages, and whose entrances are straightforward, are not likely to cause the congregation uncertainty as to when to begin singing, as may be the case with regard to the tunes for "I Danced in the Morning," "Here I Am, Lord," and "Down to Earth, as a Dove."

4) Even those who do not read music very well find it easier to sing when text and tune are together as a unit, not on different pages.

Some limitations

1) No choice should be made without regard for the other songs chosen.

2) No choice should be made without regard for the song's specific place in the liturgy. How will that song relate to what is to come before it, and to what is to come after?[1]

3) Never ask people to sing more than one unfamiliar or difficult tune per service. Ideally, helpful preparation will have been made for even that one (keyboardist playing the tune or choir singing a stanza earlier in the service, for instance). It is also a

good idea to consider how many unfamiliar or difficult songs we are asking people to sing over the course of time.

> Hymns are the folk-song of the church militant . . . the people's music. If a hymn cannot be sung by the congregation present, it has become for that occasion not a hymn but a choir-anthem or even an organ solo. (Routley 1953, 3)

4) Ideally, neither the opening nor the closing song should involve an unfamiliar tune.

5) Never use the same tune for more than one text in a service.

6) Whatever the season, choose no more than one somber song per service.

7) Normally, use the same style of tune no more than once in a service—ST. ANNE and CHESHIRE, for instance.

8) Normally, use no more than one minor-key or modal tune per service—PICARDY and WONDROUS LOVE, for instance.

9) Before settling on any song, check to see how often it has been used in the preceding weeks, and how long it has been since the congregation last sang it.

At the beginning of the service

What better way to come into God's presence than with singing?

> Make a joyful noise to the Lord, all ye lands.
> Serve the Lord with gladness:
> Come before his presence with singing.
>
> **(Ps. 100:1–2, KJV)**

The focus should be not on us, or any other part of creation, but on God. Singing "Just As I Am" is no way to begin worshiping God. Our first song is the forward edge of the worship service. It, among other things, serves to move us from the time and space of daily life into the time and space of worship. The first song can make a major contribution toward establishing the tone of the service. Other than that it be centered on God and familiar to the congregation, what should characterize the congregation's first song in the worship service?

1) Having come into God's presence, our first song should be one of praise or thanksgiving, a prayer for God's presence and blessing.

2) Other options for the congregation's first song include those songs found under rubrics such as "Morning," "Opening," "Sunday/Sabbath," or "Resurrection of Christ."

3) In recent years concern has been expressed across denominational lines for the significance of the very gathering of the congregation for worship. The gathering of the congregation is itself a rite that is part of the liturgy. The intent of this self-conscious act of gathering is to form all those present into a community that is aware of its corporate nature, and one that is ready to worship. Some newer hymnals include hymns specifically written for gathering. There is nothing more efficient in making a congregation aware of its gatheredness, however, and the reason for being gathered, than engaging in congregational song itself. Is an explicit reference to being gathered really necessary?

> Music unites—it is an important aspect of communal worship, of being congregation. Singing together is the quickest way to unite a gathering of individuals, no matter how large or small, into one corporate worshiping body, the body of Christ. (Notebaart and Sedio 1998, 4)

4) If the first song is used for a processional, it must of course be appropriate for such use and should be familiar. Many songs work less well as processional hymns.

5) The congregation that likely has not sung since last week will find a hymn of medium pitch easier to sing.

In the middle of the service

The middle song should be chosen and placed in the order of service so as to move the service forward. It may be the one song you seek to relate particularly to the emphasis of the service. It may be the one unfamiliar song. If sung in connection with the offering, it may be a song of stewardship or commitment. The middle song is most often best a quiet song, one that may be more contemplative. The middle of the service is normally no place for "A Mighty Fortress Is Our God"—the choice in a service in which I recently participated. Unless it is time for the people to stand, let them remain seated for this song; this can result in a more meditative reading of the text.

At the end of the service

Some view the last song in the service as one of response. Often for this place a song of commitment is chosen. Songs whose theme is service or witness are also appropriate. Your hymnal may include a category called "Closing Hymns," under which you may find songs such as "Lord, Dismiss Us with Thy Blessing." You may desire the last song to reiterate the theme of the day's message, or at least to share the same tone. If the last song is to serve as a recessional, remember that some songs work better than others for this purpose.

Hymn stanzas

Individual stanzas of hymns and psalms can be used very effectively at appropriate places in the order of service—after the Assurance of Pardon, for instance. Single, appropriate stanzas can be sung between divisions in a sermon. The texts should be printed in the bulletin if not projected. Familiar tunes requiring minimal introductions should be used. The people should, in most cases, remain seated.

Groups of stanzas

Occasionally, you may find it helpful to sing part of a hymn at one point in the service and part at another, for instance, two stanzas before the sermon, and two after it. Choices should be made thoughtfully.

Alternative practices

Other than the use of an individual stanza at certain points in the service, should all stanzas of a song be sung? North American hymnals currently tend to do the shortening of hymns for us; the result tends to be hymns whose length usually does not overtax unaccustomed singers. It also may save confusion if all the stanzas are sung in the order in which they are printed. If, however, you choose to reduce still further the number of stanzas to be sung, do it thoughtfully, respecting the sense and continuity of the hymn. On a hymn as long as "All Creatures of Our God and King" (six stanzas in my hymnal), stanzas may be sung alternately by men, women, and choir. One stanza may be given to the organ alone. It is commonly noted that, after groups have taken turns singing, when all once again sing together the singing is more robust than normal. All present should be encouraged to read along even on those stanzas when they are not singing. All such choices should be made and understood by clergy and musicians before the service, and made clear to the congregation—by notes in the bulletin to which you call attention just before singing the hymn. The rubrics "Men" and "Women" may be more helpful than, for instance, "Low Voices" and "High Voices."

THE MUSIC EXCLUSIVELY OF THE CHOIR, VOCAL ENSEMBLE AND SOLOIST, AND INSTRUMENTALISTS

~

Music for the Choir and Vocal Ensemble and Soloist

It is hoped that our choice of vocal music for the choir, vocal ensemble, and vocal soloist will not be dictated simply by what the musicians happen to have ready at the time. Especially is this scenario likely to happen in the case of the vocal soloist. Our choices of choral anthem and vocal solo should be guided by these criteria: theological soundness of the text, the church calendar/emphasis of the particular service, location of the song in the liturgy, well-craftedness of the music, aesthetic appropriateness for the particular congregation, and the capability of the musicians. Only texts in the English language should be used in the worship of English-speaking congregations. If another language is used, a translation should be provided.

Finding and preparing liturgically appropriate choral music for every service is a challenge, even in a church with above-average resources. Finding such music for the vocal soloist is even more difficult. Even as it should not be required that every hymn in a service be related to the theme of the day, so there is plenty of room for generic praise and thanksgiving in choosing music for the choir and vocal soloists. A psalm or other biblical passage chanted in unison or unison-octave is an alternative for the choir's anthem; this practice would strengthen the congregation's familiarity with and appreciation for chant. Routley suggests that instead of "constantly singing irrelevant or indifferent anthems," a choir might enter into partnership with the congregation and sing the psalms antiphonally (1967, 86). Such a suggestion should have considerable attraction for a musician whose choir is below par.

One anthem in a service is sufficient. If your church lacks the resources, even one may be too many. The distribution of the Lord's Supper provides opportunity for the anthem, a vocal solo, or an instrumental piece; the clergy to speak appropriate words; all to sing from the hymnal; the instrumentalists to play hymns or hymn arrangements; or all to keep silence.

The offertory is often the most convenient place in the order of worship for an anthem by a choir, a vocal solo, or an instrumental piece. (Any vocal music at this time does involve the congregation, especially the ushers, in a certain amount of less-than-ideal multitasking.) The reception of the offering may well be the part of the service that is the most difficult to make worshipful. In some parts of the church, the people, at the appointed time in the service, go forward with their offering. Which is more helpful during the offertory: music or silence? Anyone engaged in making music will be unable to participate in offering his or her gifts of money.

Any vocal solo should normally be sung in place of the anthem, not in addition to it. It probably happens most often that an individual is asked to sing a solo precisely because the choir is not going to have anything ready to sing by the date in question! Maybe the choir is on vacation that month. Or perhaps the invited soloist is going to be in town that Sunday, home from the Santa Fe Opera for a few days. The temptation may be to think in terms of special music, rather than to see the vocal solo just as all other music in the service—as an integral part of the total worship service. Ideally, the church's staff is involved in not only the invitation to the soloist, but also in consulting with him or her in the choice of what is to be sung. What shall we do with the older, romantic, potboiler solo pieces like "Open the Gates of the Temple" and "The Holy City"? Both present Scripture, and their associative power for seniors cannot be denied. And art music? How about virtuosic pieces such as arias from Handel? The worship service is not a concert. A hymn or psalm set to a simple folk tune sung by one voice can be moving and meaningful. Depending on the music sung, a solo may be unaccompanied, or accompanied by keyboard, guitar, harp, or autoharp, for instance.

Music for the Instrumentalists

The keyboardist may well find maximum opportunity to exercise freedom and creativity in choosing and playing music for the offertory, for accompanying the distribution at the Lord's Supper, and for the prelude and postlude, if these are used; no one, not even the pastor, is likely to dictate what is to be played on these occasions! Of course, all such music must be of appropriate length—in the case of music used to accompany rites, not extending very long after the rite is completed. Especially in choosing music for the offertory and the Lord's Supper should it be kept in mind that the role of music is not to dominate, but to serve. In recent years a wealth of quality hymn tune-based keyboard music has become available, and its use at these points in the service is widespread. This music brings text associations with it. Congregations find it much more accessible than most of the classic organ repertory, and it can reinforce the congregation's hymn tune repertory. Many worshipers are likely to enjoy it. When a prelude is based on the tune of a hymn that is subsequently to be sung, it can help prepare the people for singing that hymn. A hymn tune-based postlude can reinforce the experience of singing a hymn in the service.

When the instrumentalist's role is that of supporting song, the instrumentalist's planning has to do with deciding how this support can best be given. Thoughtful planning of the introductions to the hymns can be of great benefit. Instrumental music that reinforces the particular songs sung by the congregation in each service should be given careful consideration. The challenge is to discipline oneself to search out, obtain, and rehearse in good time what is most fitting for each service.

~

Musicians should think themselves into each service, given the data they have. What kind of music will be most fitting and most helpful in reinforcing the theme of the particular service?

– Useful Resources –

Virgil C. Funk, ed., *The Singing Assembly* (Washington: The Pastoral Press, 1991), being No. 6 in "Pastoral Music in Practice."

William S. Smith, *Hymnsearch: Indexes for The Presbyterian Hymnal*, 3rd ed. (Jackson, MS: Self, 2007). A detailed book of indexes for this 1990 hymnal, but its 440 pages are of some value for use with various collections.

Marilyn Kay Stulken, "Easy Service Music," a monthly feature in *The American Organist*. Suggestions for songs of the congregation, an anthem, prelude, and postlude for every Sunday in the lectionary-based service. Date of issue allows about six to ten weeks lead-time prior to service.

Joan Welles, *Soloists' Guide to Selecting Sacred Solos* (Indianapolis: PGP Publishing, 1985).

John D. Witvliet, *So You've Been Asked to Sing a Solo* (Grand Rapids: CRC Publications, 1996).

CHAPTER THIRTEEN

HELPING THE PEOPLE WORSHIP

~

W hen you have chosen the congregation's songs, you are not through; in addition to thoughtfully choosing the songs, think through how the congregation might respond to each choice. Will they need extra help because the tune is not familiar? Are the entrances to any of the songs tricky? Might the printed format of any songs cause confusion? Four (or more) stanzas of "All Creatures of Our God and King" can be a real sprint for out-of-shape or older people who have not sung since last Sunday! How can pastor and musicians help them sing each song in a helpful way? What can you do to make the service as user-friendly as possible?

THE CHURCH BULLETIN

~

Our concern here is mainly with the primary intended function of the bulletin, that is, to help people get through the service. Like the service itself, the name of the game here is not education, but worship. It may be hoped that having in their hands a visual overview of the service's elements and sequence will indeed foster understanding and appreciation of what we do in worship and why, and why this now and that later. But the bulletin's principal reason for being is to assist people in getting through a particular service together, with a minimum of trepidation and confusion. Whatever beyond this basic information we want to communicate to the congregation can best be given on pages other than those on which the order of service is displayed.

As for the treatment of musical items in the bulletin, here are some suggestions:

1) If you do designate each hymn with a rubric like "Hymn of Praise," or "Hymn of Intercession," or "Hymn of Commitment," then be certain that the hymns at those places do indeed correspond to the rubrics; if not, it is better not to use such rubrics. If the hymn in question really is a prayer, why not so label it in the bulletin? Thus, for instance:

   *Sung Prayer: "Lord Jesus, Think on Me"   Hymn 321

2) To assist the worshipers to keep together throughout the service, what are needed in connection with a hymn are only the title or first line and the number in your hymnal. Other basic facts about the hymn are given on the page in the hymnal. If you are omitting a stanza, or singing the hymn in some partic-ular way, that, of course, also needs to be indicated. Also, call attention to the matter from the pulpit or choir loft.

3) If singing only one stanza of a hymn, it may be advisable to print the text in the bulletin, referencing any copyright data to some other part of the bulletin by means of a superscript number.

4) You may prefer to use the words "Praise God, from Whom All Blessings Flow," and "Glory Be to the Father" rather than "The Doxology" and the *Gloria Patri*. You may want to print these short texts in the bulletin.

5) In labeling hymn-based service music, it may be more helpful to the congregants if the title of the hymn is used rather than the name of the tune.

6) Periods of directed silence need to be indicated in the bulletin.

7) It is potentially helpful to print in the bulletin the text of all songs not sung by the congregation. Even in the case of a trained singer with good diction and adequate volume, intelligibility in a large space is often problematic; the soloist should not be insulted if the text of the song is printed in the bulletin. Both the author and the composer should receive attribution. Including the name of the author identifies him or her for the worshiper, gives the author his or her due, and demonstrates the value the church places on the word. Dates may also be given. Music under copyright must also be attributed; this, too, can be done with minimal clutter to the bulletin by reference numbering in small type to the information on another page.

8) The music of the choir and soloists should not be called or thought of as special music. The terms "Anthem," "Solo," "Quartet," etc. should be used.

9) Texts taken from the Bible should be indicated by name of book, chapter, and verse.

10) An asterisk or some other sign can be used to indicate at what junctures people are to stand.

11) Names of the church's music staff (not just the clergy) should appear in every bulletin; names of soloists or ensemble members should be printed in the bulletin for that day. All of this information should be given on some page other than those on which the order of service appears.

12) A quantity of large-print bulletins may be printed to accommodate the visually impaired.

In some churches, hymn boards still are in use, and may be helpful. Placed for all to see, they indicate the numbers in the hymnbook of the hymns and psalms to be sung in a particular service. They must be kept up to date—or left quite blank.

Remember that your bulletin must be clear to those not normally in your service, so be careful what you assume your congregation may know on any given Sunday. You may want to experiment with more than one format to determine which most clearly displays the information. Is there someone handy who knows graphic design and layout?

Be sure at least one person other than the one who typed the bulletin proofreads it before it goes to press. Confer with the originals—the Bible passages, the songs of the congregation, and all other music. Are there errors? Is there any room for misunderstanding? A capable person not on the church's staff may well be the best candidate for this weekly chore.

CONGREGATIONAL SONG: A SONG LEADER?

~

Centuries' worth of congregational singing has established the principle that the congregation must have leadership for its singing. Whose responsibility is this? The answer for many is a song leader. Alice Parker makes a strong case for using an unaccompanied song leader rather than a musical instrument for teaching songs (1991, 78–89). Normally, in teaching new music, a song leader will line-out, one line at a time, one stanza of the song being taught. I strongly recommend that you use some other time than the Sunday morning worship hour to teach new music— other than indirectly, through the use of hymn-based organ and choral music, for instance. What Parker sets forth is also applicable to the leading of more familiar music in the worship service. The two kinds of leading may be compared thus:

Instrument
- Instrumental sound
- Delay in hearing sound

Song leader
- Human voice that is to be imitated
- Immediate sight of song leader
- Facial expressions, movements, and gestures
- Words

"If they [song leaders] do nothing more than stand, facing the people, singing with heart and voice, face and body, they are giving a visual image of how each individual should participate." Ideally, they can do yet more to help the people sing (Parker 1991, 82). An effective song leader need not be a professional, but should possess a true, even if untrained, voice. He or she should have not only musical ability, but also be a person people will trust to lead them through unfamiliar territory. The overall tone of the worship service must be maintained. Electronic amplification is best forgone.

For many, however, the use of a song leader would mean a break from a tradition of at least a certain age. Some consider (wrongly, I believe) the use of a song leader to be undignified, unnecessary, or even a distraction. To an unaccustomed congregation, a song leader may be threatening. It is far easier to remain indifferent to the leading provided by an instrument than to that which is incarnate in the song leader who makes it clear that he or she expects something from us. A capable song leader is certainly to be preferred over a keyboardist who does not play musically.

~

What follows has to do with the specific responsibilities of the several individuals or groups that lead in the worship service. It will be helpful if clergy and musicians all read not only what is expected of them particularly, but of all leaders. Clergy may want to ask musicians to demonstrate this or that point.

THE KEYBOARDIST

~

Keyboardists Can Make It or Break It

"Few congregations are able to transcend any lack in the skills of the instrumentalist" (Hatchett 1989, 30). Keyboardists have it within their power to make or break congregational song. Leading the assembly's song from the keyboard is an art, one unknown even to some otherwise very competent players. My wife has a degree in church music, with a major in organ; notwithstanding, she was not prepared by her academic training to lead the congregation's song from the organ. Skillful leading of the congregation's song by the keyboardist is not simply a matter of the once-and-for-all acquisition of useful techniques, but requires diligent, ongoing effort. "Thoughtful hymn preparation is a lot of work, but, I maintain, FAR more important than that which many organists spend most of their preparations doing—the POP (prelude, offertory, postlude)" (Cherwien 1997, 44).

What May Be Expected from the Keyboardist

Unless there is a song leader, leading the congregation's song generally falls to the keyboardist. In such instances, the organist's or pianist's role, it must be understood, is not to accompany (too passive a term), but to *lead*.[1] Against this backdrop, here are some specifics:

1) A keyboardist's introduction to a song will, through articulation and appropriate registration (if playing an organ), inspire confidence on the part of the congregation. To introduce a song, the keyboardist will play the whole song, if it is only two lines long or unfamiliar; in any case, he or she will play enough for the people to find the song and to get into a comfortable standing position. The tempo followed in the introduction will be that followed throughout the whole song. The keyboardist will retard only at the end of the last stanza, and gradually. On familiar songs, a keyboardist can greatly enhance the experience of congregational song by playing a thoughtfully planned free introduction, rather than simply playing what is printed in the hymnal. Much published music to assist the keyboardist in this endeavor is available.

2) In playing the stanzas of a song, these items are crucial:

   A. Phrasing (keeping step with the words of the text, allowing for taking a breath between phrases and between stanzas).

B. Tempo (steady, fast enough that people can sing a whole phrase or thought on one breath). Tempo that is appropriate for the text of the song, the occasion, the mood of the people present, the music being played, the congregation's familiarity with the song, the size of the assembly, and for the size and acoustics of the space can be a delicate matter. Any consideration of tempo should involve knowledge, wisdom, humility, and charity. Playing at an uneven tempo can be even more disastrous than playing too fast or too slow.

C. Volume (sufficient that people can hear the instrument, not so much that they cannot hear themselves; the keyboardist should also be able to hear the people). In most situations, an organ has the potential to overpower the congregation. This probably happens more than many organists will admit.[2] Unfortunately, whereas the sound of the organ is "developed" in traveling from its source to the congregation, the sounds made by the people tend to be absorbed by other people before they have any opportunity to develop. Depending on circumstances, it may be difficult for the organist to judge the volume of the instrument relative to that of the congregation. The organist may play too loudly because someone, maybe a whole chorus of people, encouraged him or her to turn it up! The thing about an organ that impresses many people the most is the instrument's power, its ability to make a lot of sound. After all, it is a big instrument! When the organ is not played at least *forte*, people may complain that the organist is not getting out of the organ all that could and should be gotten. Never mind whether they can hear themselves singing above the organ. So, organist, play louder! We want to hear that thing! Education may be called for in this situation.

3) On unfamiliar tunes, the keyboardist can assist the congregation by doubling or soloing out the melody.

4) Varying the harmonization, as satisfying as that can be, for the sake of the musically challenged should be done only in connection with familiar tunes, and then with restraint.

5) On familiar tunes, on some stanza after the first, the congregation can experience an enhanced sense of communion of the saints if the keyboardist, after beginning the stanza, gradually ceases to play until the beginning of the next stanza. The choir should be told beforehand that this may happen, and should help the congregation maintain the tempo. In the opinion of some (Farlee 1998, 53), unaccompanied singing works best with lyrical or folk tunes (NETTLETON, for instance) and majestic tunes (EIN' FESTE BURG and some Welsh tunes, for instance).

6) Transposing up should be done with restraint, and not require the congregation to sustain for any length of time any note higher than D.

7) Playing a phrase or two between two stanzas, especially on those songs that are likely to tax the congregation's endurance (all four stanzas of "A Mighty Fortress Is Our God," for instance), can furnish a very-much-appreciated break for catching a breath. Such an interlude can also help shift gears in the transition between two contrasting moods expressed in one song. The playing should signal, of course, that something different is about to happen.

8) An organ of any size offers the keyboardist the opportunity to exercise almost unlimited creativity and variety in the central task of leading the congregation's song—far more than a great many organists even dream of. It is important, however, that the organist be constantly monitoring the response of the congregation to make certain it is positive.

9) It is strongly recommended that the keyboardist not play during spoken prayers. The practice is quite unnecessary and is distracting, easily resulting in decreased intelligibility. It is demeaning both for prayer and for music. It also makes it difficult for the keyboardist to pray—or to prepare for the next musical item.

10) Skillful keyboardists may segue from one musical item to another, as from the offertory to the Doxology, by modulation. If this cannot be done tastefully, however, without theatricality that calls attention to itself, then simply breaking between the two items is recommended.

None of these matters is to be left undecided until the hour of service, but thoughtfully rehearsed well in advance. Helps for improving the keyboardist's skills in leading congregational song are mentioned in the Useful Resources for this chapter.

THE CHOIR'S SUPPORT OF THE SONG
OF THE CONGREGATION

~

1) Following the worship service one Sunday morning, I asked one of the choir members what he thought of the tune used for the second hymn, DONNE SECOURS. He replied that by the second stanza he had "gotten the hang of it." This from one of those whose central, specific role in the service is to help the congregation sing! Choir members should understand that nothing the choir does is more important than its support of the congregation's song. Even if all the choir members are able to sight-read any hymn in the book, the choir, like the keyboardist, will have rehearsed the songs of the congregation before the service, becoming familiar with not only the tune, and perhaps other voice parts, but also the text and general theme of every song to

be sung. If they are to support the congregation's song, they must own that song. (Ideally, choristers will also appreciate the value for themselves of an in-depth acquaintance with the church's song.) "Too many choir directors neglect or ignore the hymns[,] assuming that they will take care of themselves or that they are not worth the same care and effort as the choral pieces" (Mark Sedio 1998, 20). Amen!

2) On familiar songs, parts may be sung on all inside stanzas of music harmonized for part-singing. (Bass and alto singers may prejudice their lower pitch registers by singing the melody first.)

3) Unison singing may be helpful for the congregation, especially on unfamiliar tunes.

4) Some tunes lend themselves to alternation between choir (or solo voice) and congregation, and some are written with that in mind. This simplifies the congregation's responsibility. See, for instance, SALVE FESTA DIES, CHEREPONI, GLORIA, and THUMA MINA. Be certain to explain this to the congregation before beginning to sing.

5) Introducing an unfamiliar tune is another reason for alternation. Let the choir sing the first stanza, all sing the second, the choir on the third, and all on the fourth, for instance.

6) Descant will be used with restraint, and always only after rehearsal by the choir.

7) If the choir is seen by the congregation, posture, body language, and facial expression have significant potential for enhancing or diminishing the message sent to the assembly, with respect to both anthem and congregational song.

What Is to Be Expected of the Clergy

~

Pastors may be more important for the congregation's song than they might wish. Here follow some things they may wish to bear in mind:

1) Modeling the congregation's song is not the place for winging it. During the week prior to the service, ideally, pastors have immersed themselves in the songs the congregation will be asked to sing. They have made the songs deeply theirs by analyzing their content and their mood, meditating on them, and praying them. They have reflected on their place in the service—how they relate to what comes before and what follows.

2) It is not necessary, and may even be counterproductive, to ask the people to sing and to announce the song numbers if the bulletin indicates as much. Also, as has been pointed out, the worship service is first of all about worship, not education; hymnological lectures have no place in the service. Even so, a few well-chosen words spoken preceding a song can make all the difference between the congregation getting and not getting the song's message. For instance, "We see in this hymn the paradox of a God who is altogether beyond anything we might imagine, and at the same time as close as the air we breathe." Or, "This hymn came out of a church that was living under the cruelest kind of tyranny." Or, "The author of this wonderful hymn of thanksgiving had experienced great loss." The congregation's experience of singing a song very rich in imagination may also be enhanced by a few words spoken just prior to the singing. How many in the congregation are likely to relate the words of "People, look east" to the future coming of the Lord? How do people process the words "Rock of ages, cleft for me"? Or "Here I raise my Ebenezer"? Of course we do not want to treat the images of poetry and history in too pedestrian a way! Sometimes, a reference to tempo can be helpful:

"This song is a very thoughtful prayer, so we shall sing it somewhat slowly so that we shall have time to immerse ourselves in it." Brief remarks by the pastor or musician can help. Their remarks can also help by underlining the importance of congregational song; they help make it clear that it is not only the sermon that matters to the pastor, not only the anthem that matters to the musicians. Normally, any such comments should be planned, and all the worship leaders should be aware that they will be made.

3) Pastors are the head worship leaders, and one of their responsibilities is to get the people on their feet in plenty of time for them to be ready to sing—and to gesture for their taking their seats when it is time.

4) Like it or not, the worship leader models singing for the entire congregation—well or badly. As model, he or she is enthusiastic about singing, looks up and holds the hymnal accordingly, has feet slightly spread and planted firmly on the floor, breathes deeply, is not multitasking but wholeheartedly, single-mindedly engaged. Looking the congregation in the face, singing clergy have a splendid opportunity to witness to their faith.

5) Pastors should sing heartily, but try not to bellow, and should not sing into a microphone, especially if they are singing anything other than the melody.

Projection?

~

Many congregations are now projecting on a large screen or screens the lyrics to be sung by the congregation. Some also project the points of the sermon and announcements. Is this something for you? Here are some considerations favoring and some in objection to such practice. (I am indebted largely to Anne Burnette Hook for the material that follows that is not in brackets.)

Advantages of Projection

1) It forces the people to look up instead of down, and focuses all members of the congregation on one point in front of them. This results in improved singing and also frees the hands for any movement desired to be made in worship.

2) It enables you easily to use lyrics not in your hymnal. [But keep in mind the goal of a familiar core repertory.]

3) Projected lyrics can be more easily read as the poetry they are, and the projected format can be less confusing and easier to read than the text as printed in the hymnal. Each line of text should be formatted complete, as one line.

4) It may be easier to project in some rooms in the church than to transport hymnals between those rooms and where they are normally kept.

And I add two more:

5) Projection may be more appealing to youth than are hymnals.

6) With respect to music sung by a choir or soloist, people are more likely to read a projected text than one printed in the bulletin.

Disadvantages of Projection

1) People seated in the rear may find it difficult to read the lyrics.

2) Areas at the front and rear of the worship space may not be adequate for projection.

3) Most often, only the text is projected; some would miss the music. [If the tune is unfamiliar, many would miss the music! My observation is that this happens all too frequently.]

4) Worship leaders up front, including any choirs, need to know the lyrics from memory or have their own copies, so that they will not have to turn their backs on the congregation.

5) Projection requires equipment and someone knowledgeable in its use.

And I have several additional points:

6) Projecting the text alone contributes to the diminishment of people's ability to read music.

7) Worshipers can consult the text only while it is being projected, not before or after, both of which can sometimes be desirable.

8) A large screen up front definitely creates an aesthetic and liturgical challenge in many settings.

If You Project

Hook lists these considerations for those contemplating the projection of lyrics for the worshiping congregation:

1) Make sure you have a legal right to project the lyrics [and music] you want to use.

2) Is your space suitable? Do you have, or can you acquire, adequate equipment?

3) Is there someone who can make any needed transparencies and attend to other matters involved?

4) White text on a dark background is usually easier to read than the reverse. [The general illumination of the room is a factor.]

5) The projectionist must practice beforehand. Goofs can be very disruptive to worship.

6) Hymnals may be available for those who prefer to sing from them.

7) Provide copies of the lyrics to all the worship leaders.

HELPING THE CONGREGATION RESPOND

~

Clap your hands, all you peoples;
shout to God with loud songs of joy.

(Ps. 47:1 NRSV)

Could anything like that ever happen in your church? Should it? One ache I have in my pastor's heart is caused by the fact that we desire so much to *move* our people, and then, when we just might have by God's grace succeeded, we leave them in the lurch with all the movement bottled up inside. It is not unlike shaking a bottle of carbonated beverage with the cap still on the bottle. We want to stir the people's passions with ringing words and soul-touching music. We are ever so grateful for congregational song, which may give us our best shot at doing that. But what if the Spirit moves the people through the heavenly music of the choir? Or by the melt-the-hardest-heart singing of the children's choir? Do we not think more highly of our flock than just to leave them there with their emotions all bottled up? Should we expect the people to hold it all in until the next hymn furnishes an opportunity for them to express themselves?

A possible outlet is applause. Clapping the hands in the worship service is a venerable custom among God's people; there are references to the practice in the early church. In many churches today in North America, applause is a normal part of worship. I have witnessed applause in the most staid congregations who might, in a meeting of the governing board, never admit they approved the custom; one Sunday, though, the choir's black gospel version of "Amazing Grace" got to them in such a way that they had to do something. For many churchgoers today, applause in the worship service is, for one reason or another, questionable, if not considered downright inappropriate. I question the validity of one argument put forth against the custom, namely, that applause is appropriate only in response to performance for a human audience, and that what worship leaders do is of an altogether different order, that is, worship offered to God. Perhaps no one claims that this fact rules out every kind of response on the part of the congregation. On the contrary, all would agree that a response is to be desired. But what kind of response is suitable? Are all external expressions of a heartfelt response to be ruled out? Is applause ruled out simply because of its associations with performance? Is applause too closely associated with spectatorship? The debate continues. Dean McIntyre (2003), rather than try to give an answer, refers us to fifteen Web sites dealing with the question. For sure, if applause is an honored custom in a congregation, it should by no means be reserved for the children's efforts. Or is there nothing else in a service to move people?

To combat the notion that the children's song is performance, rather than leading in worship, have the children sing at times when the congregation is least likely to applaud—giving the call to worship, for instance. Or prepare one of the children to ask the congregation to join them in prayer as they sing.

Is a spoken or shouted "amen" an agreeable alternative or supplement to applause? Pastors may be in a position to free their people from those inhibitions that make them repress their legitimate urge to respond vocally or physically to the stimuli of worship. Such freedom is a double-edged means of grace: salutary for the worshipers, and affirming for their leaders. Yes, an acid test of the worship service is whether it results in lives lived in faith and grateful obedience (Rom. 12:1–2). But this no more makes superfluous a spontaneous response within the service of worship than such a life excludes the worship service of the gathered community. To the praise offered by some within the assembly, it is only appropriate that the other members of the assembly respond in kind—that is, audibly (Ezra 3:11; 1 Cor. 14:16; Rev. 4:8–11. Seek out the references to "amen" in a concordance to the Bible.). Spontaneous response will not wait until church is out, or even until it is time to sing the next song! In some situations, a note in the bulletin may indicate the appropriateness of an "amen." The worship leader may come to the aid of a congregation that has been moved—by saying, "And all the people of God said ————."

∽

WHEN YOU LEAVE

∽

One day you will leave your present pastorate or position of church musician. The steeple will still be standing. Also, the fruits of your labors in the development of a more musical church will remain and long continue to bless the congregation. You would hate to see any of it come to an end with, or soon after, your departure. All things being equal, if you have done your work well, the congregation you leave will expect the musical program of the church to continue. Ideally, your successors will be made aware early on (in case it had gone unnoticed) that in terms of music, the congregation they have come to serve is not run-of-the-mill, and that they will be expected to continue the work, building on past accomplishments.

∽

Be zealous [to build up the body],
be ardent in spirit,
[in this way] serving the Lord.
(Rom. 12:11, author's translation)

– Useful Resources –

The American Guild of Organists offers the following:

John Ferguson, *A Mini-Course in Creative Hymn Playing*, cassette or CD.

Paul Manz, *Practicum on Service Playing and Improvisation*, CD.

Sue Mitchell-Wallace, *The Art and Craft of Playing Hymns*, DVD.

Margot Ann Woolard, *A Mini-Course in Hymn Playing*, cassette or CD.

David M. Cherwien, *Let the People Sing: A Keyboardist's Creative and Practical Guide to Engaging God's People in Meaningful Song* (St. Louis: Concordia Publishing House, 1997).

Robert Buckley Farlee, ed., *Leading the Church's Song* (Minneapolis: Augsburg Fortress, 1998).

David Heller, *A Manual on Hymn Playing: A Handbook for Organists* (Chicago: GIA Publications, 1992).

Robert Hovda, *Strong, Loving, and Wise: Presiding in Liturgy* (Collegeville, MN: Liturgical Press, 1980). Oriented to the Roman Catholic Mass.

Joy E. Lawrence and John A. Ferguson, *A Musician's Guide to Church Music* (New York: Pilgrim Press, 1981).

Austin C. Lovelace, *The Organist and Hymn Playing* (Carol Stream, IL: Hope Publishing Company, 1981).

EPILOGUE

~

Early on, we noted how pivotal events in the history of Israel and the history of the church have been accompanied by fresh outpourings of song. Two very important movements related to the creation of song were not named: The Oxford-Cambridge Movement that began in the 1830s in the Anglican Church, and the much broader worship renewal movement that began in the larger Western church, both Roman Catholic and Protestant, in the 1960s. These two movements, like the sixteenth-century Reformation, sought historical correctness; both sought renewal of the church—including the church's worship. Like the Reformation, both the Oxford-Cambridge Movement and the worship renewal movement resulted in the production of a prodigious amount of congregational song. The Hymn Explosion that began in the context of the twentieth-century effort to renew the church's worship shows no signs of slackening, continuing to produce a far larger number of new texts and tunes each year than most people might ever imagine. Some of the newer songs are in more recently published hymnals; others are in collections, awaiting their turn to be incorporated, their originators and publishers hope, into hymnals yet to be produced. For instance, the Winter 2006 issue of *The Hymn* lists about 120 "author and composer collections" currently available from The Hymn Society.

The two movements also share characteristics that distinguish them from the Reformation and other movements noted. Both may be termed "top-down." Whereas the Reformation, the awakenings, and the great nineteenth-century missionary movement and revivals quickly became people's movements, the motivating zeal in both the Oxford-Cambridge

Movement and the twentieth-century worship renewal movement was fueled not by the hearts of the people, but by the enthusiasm of professionals. The result has been that of supply exceeding demand.

Congregational song does not always translate into congregational singing. Some of the congregations impacted by the Oxford-Cambridge Movement did sing. In others, the newly upgraded choirs did most of the singing. Today, approaching a half century after the beginnings of the Hymn Explosion, what is the state of congregational singing in that part of the church in North America that we might expect to be most affected by this more recent movement? Has the song of the assembly become more vital? Overall, it surely has within the Roman Catholic communion, even though many of the church's priests and musicians have been less than enthusiastic about the democratization of the Mass. After all, when the starting point was so near zero, almost any singing done by the assembly would be an increase. Hearty singing by the assembly can certainly be heard in gatherings that feature CCM, and in the services of conservative congregations that tend to major in familiar gospel hymnody. But has the volume been turned up in those Protestant communions that have lived through forty or so years of the worship renewal movement?

This book is in no small part another "how-to" manual; followed conscientiously, it will bring results. By implementing some of the ideas set forth, you can certainly achieve a heartier level of song on the part of your congregation. Before congregational singing becomes a genuine people's movement, however, before it achieves the level associated with the notable movements of the past, there must be deep stirrings on the part of the people, there must be passion. For a song to catch on, take off, and fly, there must be a people waiting for it. Recent, unpopular wars have inspired protest songs sung by celebrities. In contrast with other conflicts in our history, however, they have not moved the masses to seek songs to sing, nor have they moved composers and authors to produce songs that have served impassioned masses. In contrast, the very simple "We Shall Overcome" caught on like prairie fire, not only because it is so simple, but because there was a civil rights movement, there was a people waiting for it, a people with a cause, a people whose hopes and determination carried the song into a nation's streets. With respect to congregational song, it is out there—a huge amount of it. But where are the people waiting for it? It is not enough to have the tools; there must also be the impulse. What will move congregations to engage enthusiastically in song? In the last analysis, great congregational song cannot be made to happen. Like all good gifts from God, the song of the congregation is at the mercy of the Holy Spirit. Recognition of this truth should be enough to make pastors and church musicians humble for a long time. And prayerful.

> Come Thou Fount of every blessing,
>   Tune my heart to sing Thy grace.
> Streams of mercy, never ceasing,
>   Call for songs of loudest praise.
> Teach me some melodious sonnet,
>   Sung by flaming tongues above;
> Praise the mount! I'm fixed upon it,
>   Mount of God's unchanging love!
>
> (Robert Robinson, 1758)

Jesus, Thy Boundless Love to Me — 366

ST. CATHERINE 8.8.8.8.8.8

Paul Gerhardt, 1653
Trans. John Wesley, c. 1739; alt.

Henri Frederick Hemy, 1864
Alt. James George Walton, 1874

1. Je - sus, Thy bound - less love to me No thought can reach, no tongue de - clare; O knit my thank - ful heart to Thee, And reign with - out a ri - val there! Thine whol - ly, Thine a - lone, I'd live, My - self to Thee en - tire - ly give.

2. O grant that noth - ing in my soul May dwell, but Thy pure love a - lone; O may Thy love pos - sess me whole, My joy, my trea - sure, and my crown! All cold - ness from my heart re - move; May ev - ery act, word, thought be love.

3. O Love, how gra - cious is Thy way! All fear be - fore Thy pres - ence flies; Care, an - guish, sor - row melt a - way, Wher - e'er Thy heal - ing beams a - rise. O Je - sus, noth - ing may I see, Noth - ing de - sire, or seek, but Thee.

APPENDIX
What Is On a Page in the Hymnal?

"Jesus, Thy Boundless Love to Me"

Strophes/Stanzas and Verses

You quite possibly recognize the nineteenth-century hymn appearing on the page facing this one. Like all congregational hymns, this one is what we call strophic, that is, the text is divided into strophes—units of uniform structure and length. Instead of singing the whole hymn with one tune that takes us from the beginning to the end of the complete text (through-composed), we sing one strophe and then return to the beginning of the one tune to sing the second strophe, and so on until we have finished singing the last strophe. In other words, we sing the text in installments, each succeeding strophe of the text being sung to the one tune. Obviously, recycling the one short tune in this way is much easier for a congregation than singing one longer tune that would take us to the end of the text. For a congregation, the music has to be relatively simple.

A more common synonym for strophe is the word "stanza." Thus this hymn as given here comprises three strophes or stanzas. In common parlance, the word "verse" is also used to mean the same thing. Technically, however, a verse is one line of poetry. Our hymn, then, consists of three stanzas or strophes, each one of these comprising six verses or lines.

Running Heads

There are no less than ten data expressed on the page. Are you able to understand all the words and numbers you see? The uppermost rubric is "LIFE IN CHRIST." It is what is termed a "running head," indicating to us the general theme expressed by the text of the hymn. Is "Life in Christ" the way you would classify this hymn? How might you more precisely describe the theme of this hymn? Before and after this hymn you will find other hymns in this hymnal classified under the same rubric or running head. The running heads reappear in an index of your hymnal—the one called "topical," or some similar name, and perhaps also in a table of contents. When you are looking for a hymn on a particular subject—trust, for instance—you can get help by looking for that word in the topical index, and perhaps the table of contents.

Title of Hymn and Number

The next line gives us the name or title of the hymn, "Jesus, Thy Boundless Love to Me."

- Most often the title is the first phrase of the words of the hymn, as in this case.
- Some hymns, however, have a title that is not from the first line, but from some association or use the hymn has had, for instance, "The Battle Hymn of the Republic."
- Some hymns are known by two titles, one being the first line of the text, the other being the first line of a refrain, for instance: "Come We That Love the Lord," and "We're Marching to Zion." In this case, the refrain was added subsequently to the original hymn. This is often the case with gospel songs (which most often have refrains), for instance: "When We Walk with the Lord"="Trust and Obey," or "Dying with Jesus"="Moment by Moment."
- The title "How Great Thou Art" derives from its appearance at the end of the fourth stanza, and its four-fold use in the middle and end of the refrain.

On the same line on the page is the number 366, indicating not the page number, but the number of this hymn—the 366th song in the hymnal. Some hymnals give both the number of the hymn and the page number; this is unnecessary and sometimes leads to confusion. To locate a particular hymn in your hymnal, you will probably look in your hymnal's "Index of First Lines."

Tune Name

Line three from the top gives us the name of the tune, ST. CATHERINE, and also 8.8.8.8.8.8—the hymn's meter. Saint Catherine was the virtuous, fourth-century Alexandrian martyr who resisted the adulterous advances of Emperor Maxentius. Hymn tune names derive from a variety of sources: the name of the composer, the composer's birthplace, a particular street, or a church.[1] Hymn tunes from Germany are often the first words of the original text, thus: WER NUR DEN LIEBEN GOTT, the tune for the English translation of that hymn, "If Thou but Trust in God to Guide Thee." Most often the names are written as here, in large and small capital letters. Sometimes the first letters in the parts of the name are in larger type. Occasionally we may forget the first line of a hymn, but remember the name of the tune associated with it; by using the index of tunes in the hymnal we can find the hymn. The provenance and significance of many older tune names can be found in Robert Guy McCutchan, *Hymn Tune Names: Their Sources and Significance* (New York and Nashville: Abingdon Press, 1957). A facsimile edition from 1976 may be available from Scholarly Press, St. Clair Shores, Michigan. Your hymnal probably has all its tunes indexed in its tune index.

Meter

The numbers 8.8.8.8.8.8 indicate the meter of this hymn, that is, the number of syllables per line of text, in this case the eight syllables from "Jesus" to "me," inclusive, thus not quite all of the first line as printed in this hymnal. You can verify this by counting the syllables on your fingers. In this hymnal, the dots that follow all but the last 8 serve only to tell us that we are looking at six 8s, rather than the six-digit 888,888. (Yes, *six* 8s, not four. To conserve space, the six lines are compressed into four. If the text were printed without the music, it would be printed in six lines.) The same thing is accomplished in some hymnals by leaving spaces between the numbers, thus, 8 8 8 8 8 8. In a few hymnals, dots are employed in an even more sophisticated way, to indicate rhyming patterns. The lines of most hymns have six, seven, or eight syllables. "Mine Eyes Have Seen the Glory of the Coming of the Lord" has how many? You have to use your fingers and your toes to count this one: 14! What is the meter of "Amazing Grace"? Its meter is 8 6 8 6, also known as Common Meter (or Ballad Meter, since this meter has commonly served for ballads), abbreviated CM. The term Short Meter (SM) is applied to a four-line hymn that has six syllables in lines one, two, and four, and eight syllables in line three, thus: 6 6 8 6. Long Meter (LM) translates into 8 8 8 8. My mnemonic device for keeping this much of things straight is to remember "BAJ," standing for the hymns "*B*lest Be the Tie that Binds" (SM), "*A*mazing Grace" (CM), and "*J*esus Shall Reign Where'er the Sun" (LM). Hymns that are twice as long as these three meters are termed respectively, Short Meter Double (thus SMD), Common Meter Double (CMD), and Long Meter Double (LMD). In the metrical index of your hymnal you can find a number of other meters, including "irregular," for texts whose number of syllables is unlike that of any other text in a given collection. A hymn text can be used only with tunes that have the same meter.

Author's Name

Dropping down to the fourth line on our page, we see on the left the name Paul Gerhardt. This tells us that he was the author of this text. (The original German text comprised sixteen nine-line stanzas!) This Lutheran gave us some of our most wonderful hymns, and his warm, deep evangelical piety greatly influenced the Wesley brothers. The date 1653 is the year in which Gerhardt wrote the hymn.

Hymnals vary from one another in the way in which they arrange the data on the page. When the names of the author and the composer appear at the top of the page, you can usually count on the author's name being on the left side, and the composer's name being on the right. Newer hymnals tend to put most of the data at the bottom of the page, sometimes all on one side, sometimes divided between the two sides. Many newer hymnals will label the names as author and composer, respectively. When the name of the author is unknown, you may find the word "anonymous" (anon.) or some other designation. In some cases we are not sure of the author, but the text has been attributed to this or that person; this may be indicated by the abbreviation "attrib." Sometimes all we know about the origin of a text is the name of the collection in which it is first found, and that name is given, for instance: *The United States Sacred Harmony*, 1799. The same customs prevail with respect to composers about whom we are uncertain.

Your hymnal is probably supplied with an index of authors, translators, and sources.

Translator's Name

Just under Gerhardt's name is that of the translator of the hymn from German into English: John Wesley. The translation was made c. 1739, that is, circa 1739. Often we do not know the precise year in which a text or tune was written, in which case the dates of the author's or composer's birth and death may be given. The abbreviation "alt." tells us that some wording in Wesley's translation has at some point been altered to read as we have it before us in this hymnal. Alteration of older hymns has been so commonplace that some hymnals do not bother to indicate that it has taken place. (John Wesley even altered some hymns of his brother Charles!) In many cases, we are uncertain as to what the original, unaltered text was.

Rhyme Scheme

This datum is not given on the page. When you analyze the text of the hymn for rhyme scheme, do you come up with ABABCC? Do you find the same scheme in every stanza? Is every rhyme perfect?

Composer's Name

On the right side of the fourth line is given the name of the composer of the tune, Henri Frederick Hemy, a nineteenth-century English organist. The tune was not written for this or any other hymn, but to carry the text, "Sweet Saint Catherine, Maid Most Pure" (hence the name of the tune), which was part of a collection assembled by Hemy, *Crown of Jesus Music*, Part II, published in 1864. In some instances, the composer is unknown to us, but we do know the collection in which the tune first appeared; in this case, that name may be given in lieu of a composer's name.

Name of Adapter of Tune

But the story of this tune is a little more complicated. Though the tune ends quite satisfactorily eight measures before the end, James George Walton lengthened the tune in 1874 by adding the last eight measures of music; he published the lengthened tune as part of a collection. Subsequently, the text of Gerhardt-Wesley was married to the tune to give us what we have on this page. Can you think of another text set to this tune?

If your hymnal contains this hymn, you can probably find the names of both Hemy and Walton in one of your hymnal's indexes, the index of composers, arrangers, and sources.

Copyright

Something else you do not see on this page is any reference to copyright. Text and music in this case are, because of their age, in the public domain. They belong to everyone. If the text of the hymn had recently been altered, or if the tune had been given a new harmonization, these might well be protected yet by copyright law, but such was, we may judge, not the case here.

A third item not shown on this page, but often found in hymnals is a Scripture reference. The fact that so many hymns have drawn so heavily on Scripture for their inspiration, concepts, images, and even particular language, is transparent. When this is the case in a given hymn, the particular passage of Scripture underlying the hymn may be noted on the page. There is probably an index ("Index of Scriptural Allusions") in your hymnal to help in this regard also—even if the pages of the hymnal do not themselves indicate such allusions. A hymn's relation to Scripture is often the most helpful datum of all.

We can gather lots of information about a hymn from the page in the hymnal and from other resources. What kind of information will be most helpful to pastors and musicians in their shared ministry? What will be most helpful to the congregation?

NOTES

Chapter 1

1. The sixteenth century also witnessed within the Roman Catholic Church great creativity and reforms (simplification) in the music of the Mass; Palestrina was commendably zealous for the intelligibility of the text. He and his contemporaries in Italy and in Spain produced glorious music. The role of the masses in worship, however, continued to be a largely passive one.

2. Was David's organization of music in the temple, as related by the Chronicler (1 Chr. 25), to be understood as merely an adaptation of the previously given law of the Lord regarding the work of the Levites? See Zimmerli 1978, 114–15.

3. The harsh polemic of rabbis and church fathers against musical instruments (associated with pagan practices) and female voices (sensual and associated with pagan practices) does not surface until relatively late, and had in view, moreover, not the worship service, but other areas of society. As late as 1903, Pope Pius X would ban women from choirs. Had this rule been followed, there would have been no choirs in most North American parishes! Males were also scarce in many Protestant choirs.

4. But hymns could be sung outside worship! At least a couple of hymns from Zwingli's hand are sung in church today. One is a prayer for the church, which may be translated as "Lord, now hold the wagon yourself," found in a contemporary collection in the seafaring Netherlands as "Lord, steer the ship yourself."

5. Nazi anti-Semitism and the related deprecation of the Old Testament are well known. That and the following statement together seem to confirm the claim put forth in this paragraph. "As late as 1938, Foreign Office representatives—servants of the Nazi state—could still regard performance of a text of the Old Testament as an appropriate example of German culture so long as it came in a musical form, set by one of the most famous German musical composers" (Bergen 2002, 141). Closer at hand, we have only to note the times in program notes and church bulletins when attribution is given for the composer, but not the poet.

6. The term "keyboardist" is sometimes used to indicate specifically the player of an electronic keyboard. The term is used throughout this book to indicate, as well, both organists and pianists.

7. The Hebrew people seemed, in contrast to the Greeks, to prefer vocal music over instrumental. The rabbis pronounced that whereas slaves could play instruments, only Levites could sing. Only vocal music, words set to music, could convey ideas. A perusal of a concordance to the Bible will show how terribly important was the role of the voice and the word, both the divine and the human, in the relation between God and Israel.

8. " . . . the creation of beauty is not the purpose of worship . . . , though beauty may be of considerable value in worship. Much music with pretty minimal aesthetic qualities nevertheless functions as a satisfactory vehicle for some individuals to express their worship. One cannot criticize a church service by the same standards one would apply to a concert. Many who have been educated to know what is 'good' church music for sophisticated people fail to recognize that they should also learn what is 'good for-ness' in terms of people and circumstances when music is used" (White 1980, 99).

9. A false and unhelpful distinction is commonly made between "liturgical" worship and "nonliturgical" worship. It should be understood, however, that *all Christian worship is liturgical*. The word "liturgy" comes from words meaning "work" and "people." The word is most often understood in the Western church to mean "work of the people." (Worship is also the work of God!) Thus all worship in which people participate may be termed liturgical. To worship is to participate in the liturgy. For "liturgical" and "nonliturgical," I propose that we substitute "fixed liturgy" and "free liturgy." Thus churches, as to their worship, are either fixed-liturgy churches or free-liturgy churches.

10. See also Wilson-Dickson 1992, 244, on "What is Excellence?"

Chapter 2

1. Even as the happy father of the parable, so in the prophet's vision of the great future, the Lord God rejoices over Jerusalem in song (Zeph. 3:17). The Midrash on Leviticus 11:9 pictures God leading the righteous in a dance at the last day.

2. Do not the proponents of multicultural worship pose a serious challenge to this principle? There is no denying that such efforts might well bring about growth in self-denial and a wholesome other-directedness on the part of its practitioners. The fact of bringing disparity into unity, moreover, can itself be cause for doxology. Such an effort is likely, however, to exact a heavy toll on the doxological. "Experimental worship" sounds like an oxymoron. A brief treatment of some of the problems of multicultural worship is given by Westermeyer 2005, 288–91. On the inevitable adaptation of the gospel to culture, see Plantinga and Rozeboom 2003, 63–64.

3. On the limitations of hymns for "doing theology," see Wren 2000, 350–52.

4. The reference here is to singing outside the worship service, when youth might have been tempted

to sing love tunes and carnal songs. In church, the congregation sang only the melody.

5. English translation of Aulén's work: *Christus Victor: An Historical Study of the Three Main Types of the Idea of the Atonement*, trans. A. G. Herber (New York: Macmillan, 1977). Hymns cited include "A Mighty Fortress" and "Christ Jesus Lay in Death's Strong Bands."

6. If we cannot find, in the church's vast repertory, songs about a particular item in our theology, two possibilities present themselves: 1) That item is not authentic theology and has no relevance for our faith; or 2) There exists a lacuna in the church's song repertory. It is this latter that is the case in connection with one of the fundamental articles of the church's faith: the resurrection of the body. No amount of searching, especially in hymnals currently in use, will turn up even half a handful. (See Smith 1996.) Why this scarcity of songs about something so fundamental? Is the hope of the future resurrection not something to sing about? Have preachers failed to proclaim this part of the Good News in an authentic way?

Sometimes it is in a particular hymnal, not in the vast repository of the whole church, that songs about a particular article of faith are hard to find. The church does not lack, for instance, songs about another item in the creed, "the life everlasting"— under whatever metaphors are used to present the topic. In my denomination's current hymnal, however, there is no song devoted in its entirety to the subject. (See Smith 1997.)

7. Though congregational singing is not in view, the singing in Luke 1–2 is intergenerational. Elizabeth, Zechariah, Simeon, and Anna are all getting on in age, Mary is a youngster.

8. It is a somewhat curious thing that some communions today that do not allow women to teach men do allow all to be taught by women hymnists, singing from hymnals prepared by committees that included women!

9. That the psalmist is quite conscious of the fact that his songs to God are intended to be heard also by his fellow-worshipers may often be assumed; in a number of cases, it is made explicit that he intends his song to God to benefit the congregation, those with him in the house of God, his brethren (Pss. 22:22; 40:9; 66; 68:25–26). Rather than hiding or holding back the burden of his song, he tells it forth, so that others may respond appropriately (Ps. 40:3). By means of his sung testimony to benefits received, the psalmist benefits others. Praise contains a "forensic" element, always occuring "in a group," in which we tell others what God has done for us (Westermann 1981, 27, 30, 78).

10. On several indirect benefits that accompany worship, see Hull 2002, 16.

11. Alas, our terminology for what we call the worship service leaves something to be desired. The word "liturgy," as remarked in chapter 1, means "work of *the people*." As just noted, however, worship is also the work *of God*. The word "liturgy," moreover, though used several times in the New Testament, is never used there to refer to what *we* mean by the word: the worship service. The New Testament refers to this service, rather, as a "gathering together" (Matt. 18:20; 1 Cor. 14:23, 26; Heb. 10:25; Jas. 2:2). This term does not indicate anything about corporate worship other than that it is something that takes place when we are gathered together. The contexts of all the passages just cited do relate the gathering to salutary things that may transpire in them. Merely going to church may well be a means of grace.

Chapter 3

1. It is especially James W. McKinnon who has published fundamental criticism of "the old orthodoxy" in this matter. Among other things, McKinnon understands the synagogue to have been initially not a place of worship, but a venue for judicial and penal activities. McKinnon also assigns the development of psalmody in both synagogue and church to a date several centuries into the Christian era, and believes that psalmody developed in both institutions independently of one another. The discussion continues.

2. However we understand 1 Corinthians 14:33–35, 1 Corinthians 11:2–16 makes it clear that women in the church in Corinth were free to pray and prophesy in the worship service. Perhaps the solo singing referred to in 1 Corinthians 14:15, 26 was in the vein of what the psalmist speaks of in Psalms 22:22, 25; 35:18; 40:10—a kind of personal testimony to some favor received from the Lord.

3. Baptists began to come on the scene in the early seventeenth century. Just as they opposed the use in the worship service of any set formulas such as the Lord's Prayer and creeds, also, and for the same reason, they resisted the practice of singing in the assembly—until the latter part of that century.

4. Here is a summary of what I found in the fifteen sources I consulted on the question:

A. With the exception of a few smaller communions, the church in North America makes room for both congregational song and choir.

B. Two sources explicitly state that the only indispensable song is that of the congregation.

C. Two other sources express a concern that a choir threatens the song of the congregation.

D. Four sources speak of a choir enriching or enhancing the worship experience. Does this involve aesthetic experience? Presumably, the choir in view is one that is musically satisfying—at least for these advocates; perhaps their congregations would settle for less.

E. Four sources explicitly, and one implicitly, indicate that leading, supporting, and enhancing the song of the congregation is the most important role of a choir.

F. Two sources indicate that a choir may pray for or on behalf of the congregation.

G. Two sources explicitly deny that a choir sings on behalf of the congregation.

5. This way of putting it is to be preferred to saying that a choir is to lead the congregation's song. 1) There can be only one leader; 2) There seems to be universal agreement that this should be the organist or pianist, or, if there be one, the cantor or song leader; 3) This means that a choir's leadership of the congregation's song is not original, but derivative. The choir may be said to lead the congregation's song only in the sense that it reinforces the (original) leadership of the song leader or organist/pianist. Compare: " . . . the prime responsibility of the choirs is the leadership of congregational singing" (Sydnor 1982, 107; likewise, Young 1995, 38).

6. Paul Westermeyer lists eight "Further Threats to the People's Song" (2005, 265–69). In the same work, see also pages 394–95.

7. Paul Westermeyer gave the same title to a book he published in 2005, only without the exclamation point.

Chapter 4

1. The author of the hymn, Frances Ridley Havergal, testified that she had indeed experienced the blessedness of true consecration. Thus she could in good conscience sing her lines.

2. You will not find in your hymnal the names of many whose names also appear in your college anthology of English literature. George Herbert, John Milton, William Cowper, Christina Rossetti, Gilbert Keith Chesterton, Oliver Wendell Holmes, and John Greenleaf Whittier may be among the exceptions. Some whose names appear in both places did not write hymns as such, but poems that came to be used as hymns.

3. A few of us, regrettably, know a meaning given the name by slang, which further muddies the waters.

4. In Wren's 1989 hymn, "Bring Many Names," found in this hymnal, for instance, God is spoken of as "Strong mother God," "Warm father God," "Old, aching God," "Young, growing God," and "Great, living God."

5. Margo G. Houts points to an irony in the contemporary debate about language: "Often, churches embracing more contemporary forms of worship . . . have retained traditional forms of language. . . . Those for whom language is an issue—especially mainline and liberationist seminary professors and denominational staff—have had minimal involvement in, and consequently minimal impact upon, the Contemporary Worship scene. The ironic result is that 'contemporary' worship often reflects 'traditional' language, while more 'contemporary language' flourishes mostly in 'traditional' worship" (in Plantinga and Rozeboom 2003, 37).

6. It is possible for a musician to compose a folk-like tune, a tune that sounds like it was not composed by any one individual, but that rather just emerged from the populace. See, for instance, the tune SOUTHCOTE, by Sydney Carter, who is also the author of the hymn "I Danced in the Morning." Composers, of course, can hardly escape being influenced by the tunes, including folk, they hear in their respective cultures. (See Routley 1981, 133.) Among composed tunes, the influence of folk is much more readily heard in the (for many, instantly and enduringly appealing) tunes of gospel hymnody than in tunes such as ST. BRIDE and ST. ANNE.

7. Some qualification must be made here with respect to the identity of the hearer. The foundational music of white, Anglo-Saxon Protestant churches has "Northwest Europe and North America" stamped all over it. North Americans of other traditions may have differing expectations as to what church music should sound like. The larger picture is changing rapidly, of course.

8. What truth resides in the oft-made assertion that Luther freely plundered popular music to find tunes for hymns? What Luther did is much more complicated than that. Carl Schalk identifies five sources of the tunes used by Luther and his colleagues: 1) Gregorian chant; 2) The pre-Reformation German folk hymns called *Leisen*; 3) *Cantios*, Latin songs that were religious but not used in the Mass; 4) Secular tunes; and 5) Newly composed hymn tunes (in Stulken 1981, 19–22). The reformer inveighed in no uncertain terms against the misuse of music for carnal purposes; he must have performed at least minor surgery on the popular tunes he used. Calvin expressly favored a distinctive music for Christian worship, and he ensured its composition and use. In the 1930s, as noted above, folk tunes did begin to proliferate in hymnals published in North America, but these tunes had by then long been out of circulation in the world outside the church. Recent Roman Catholic pronouncements on music fit for the liturgy make interesting reading. While they profess openness to modern music, Gregorian chant still has a special place, and is the norm by which all other music is evaluated (John Paul II 2003, No. 7).

9. Linda J. Clark's survey asked the question (of worshipers in general): "Which of the following statements comes the closest to your view of the kind of music to be used in worship?" Forty-seven percent responded that any kind of music is appropriate as long as the congregation can use it to praise God; twenty-four percent responded that since music in worship is an offering to God, only the best is appropriate (1994, 31).

10. I am indebted for some of the above to Doran and Troeger 1992.

Chapter 5

1. The word "Psalter" is not always used in the same sense. In this book, it refers to the collected psalms of the Old Testament, separated physically from the rest of the Bible, intended for singing in corporate worship.

2. Already by the Middle Ages, the church had taken a step in this direction by appending a Trinitarian Doxology to every psalm and hymn sung. At least some of the psalms themselves, as we have them today in the Old Testament, seem to be the result of re-contextualizing. The songs given us in Luke 1 and 2 and in Revelation may also be cited as examples of re-contextualizing earlier biblical language. All of this may be seen as a part of the larger appropriation of ancient Israel's scriptures by the New Testament writers.

3. It has to be granted that reformed singers of the psalms did themselves place a Christological interpretation on the psalms they were singing; they did in their minds what Watts set down on paper.

4. For instance, Matt. 11:25–30; Acts 4:24–30; Eph. 5:14 (cp. Rom. 13:11–12); Phil. 2:6–11; Col. 1:12–20; 1 Tim. 1:15; 3:16; 2 Tim. 1:9–10; 2:11–13; Tit. 2:13–14; 3:4–7; 1 Pet. 1:3–5, 17–21; 2:4–8, 21–25; 3:18–20; Rev. 5:8–14; 19:6–8.

5. In Psalm 29, for example, the personal, covenant name, "LORD" (*Yahweh*), appears eighteen times, clearly distinguishing the God of Israel from the nature gods of their neighbors. In one metrical setting from 1972, it appears not at all. What is indicated to be Psalm 30 may be only Psalm 30:4–12.

6. The first phrase of ST. ANNE is also found elsewhere, including works of Bach and Handel. Note how this tune moves by small steps up and down—"saw-edge"-like.

7. Regarding the possible noncorrespondence between some hymns and the biblical texts that inspired them, see Smith 1999.

8. The debt the English-speaking, North American church owes to the church in England for its song, even today, was illustrated at the service for the late Gerald R. Ford in the National Cathedral on January 2, 2007. The two Psalms (Watts's 90th and Baker's 23rd), the two hymns ("Eternal Father, Strong to Save," and "For All the Saints"), and the four tunes were all from the hands of Englishmen. Of course, that service was under Episcopal direction, and the Episcopal Church is, more than any other American communion, oriented to England. Also, all four texts and three of the four tunes were pre-twentieth century in origin.

9. A personal testimony of the singers, coupled with an appeal to any hearers to receive the Gospel, is by no means a nineteenth-century North American discovery. See, for instance, "Jesus Sinners Will Receive," from the German original of Erdmann Neumeister (1671–1756), a number of invitational hymns by Charles Wesley, and "Come to Calvary's Holy Mountain" by James Montgomery (1771–1854). John Mason Neale's nineteenth-century paraphrase, "Art Thou Weary, Art Thou Languid?" was inspired by an ancient Greek hymn.

10. Divisions among denominations in the United States accelerated following the American Civil War. At one end of the spectrum was the "more respectable," elitist position; at the other was a more populist faith (Noll 2006, 62). This spread is reflected today in the incidence of four representative authors or composers of gospel hymns in the hymnals published between 1978 and 1991 by five denominations.

	Bradbury	Crosby	Mote	Scriven
Episc. '85	1	0	0	0
Luth. '78	3	0	1	1
Presby. '90	4	2	1	1
Meth. '89	7	7	1	1
Bapt. '91	8	17	1	1

It must be borne in mind, of course, that the choices of songs for inclusion were made by committees, not by rank-and-file members.

Some collections that included gospel songs gathered them together in the rear of the hymnal under a rubric such as "Songs for Evangelistic Services," "Songs for Informal Occasions," or "Songs for Social Worship."

11. Thomas A. Dorsey was not the Tommy Dorsey of mid-twentieth century Big Band fame!

12. Precisely what constitutes global song has been difficult to pin down. Westermeyer, in categorizing hymn tunes according to geographico-historical criteria, does not use the term "global song" (though he does take note of it in passing). Under "Folk Tunes and Folk Influences" (2005, 325–54), he does, however, include some tunes, composed as well as folk, recent as well as older, that are cited by some writers as global songs. Mainline hymnals have, of

course, for generations included texts and tunes that, though from North America or Europe, may be said to have derived from those circumstances that are said to define global song—"an experience of Christians beyond our immediate world view" (Hawn 2000, 28). The ancient Celtic "Be Thou My Vision" with its "High King of Heaven" certainly comes from such a milieu. And the even more ancient pre-Christian, Hebrew psalms! In any case, all the songs I have seen classified as "Global" have in common these features: All (at least their words, if not the tunes, which may be traditional) originated during my lifetime; their original language was most often not English; all derive from Asia, Latin America, or Africa. The ubiquitous "Kum ba Yah" (originally "Come by Here") is not global song. Both text and tune were created by a seventeen-year-old Oregonian named Marvin Frey in 1936.

13. See Smith 2002, also Chapter 11 concerning the size of the congregation's repertory of song.

14. For this classification I am, to some extent, indebted to Eskew and McElrath 1995.

15. Four of my own communion's twentieth-century hymnals reveal how a part of this communion's distinctive heritage of tunes that had been lost has been progressively recovered and recycled. The hymnals of 1901 and 1927 each used a Geneva Psalm tune (OLD HUNDREDTH) once; that of 1955 included thirteen instances; that of 1990, twenty-two. A similar increase can be seen in the number of plainsong tunes used.

16. We may be reluctant to admit it, but many churchgoers put a higher premium on socializing than on putting on their thinking caps. That may be why many churchgoers prefer Sunday school over worship service, and why some college graduates want their Sunday school curriculum to be written for the ninth grade. It is also likely the reason why many people prefer to be a long-term member of a non-rotating Sunday school class rather than of a class organized around some particular issue for a defined term.

17. "The laborer is deserving of payment" is a principle enunciated no less than four times in the New Testament. (See also 1 Cor. 9:5–14.) For those who feel the need of proof-texts, Paul Wohlgemuth cites Lev. 19:11, 13; Prov. 3:27; and Matt. 5:16 in this connection (1981, 31–33). The fundamental commandment to love our neighbors certainly means that we should not steal from them what they have labored to produce. "Neighbor" in this case includes the publishers and any others who have labored to make the fruits of intellectual labor available to us. A second motive for obeying the law is concern for your own conscience. A third reason for observance of copyright law is your desire to set a

good example for others, not least those who look to you for leadership. A fourth motive is your desire to avoid public embarrassment. If you still need a motive for compliance, know that noncompliance has resulted in legal trials and heavy fines for more than one church. Returning to higher moral ground, we may say that the copyright principle is a way of society paying its indebtedness to the artists and publishers for their enrichment of its corporate life.

18. Three such companies are Christian Copyright Licensing, International (CCLI), www.ccli.com; OneLicense.net,www.onelicense.net; and LicenSing online.org, www.licensingonline.org.

Chapter 6

1. Shown at http://www.ministryandmedia.com/CCMchart/default.htm.

2. The Roman Catholic Frank C. Senn makes a strong case for the evangelistic potential of the Mass—in conjunction with a catechetical program. In this way inquirers are gradually incorporated into Christ and his body, the church. (I see no reason why CCM cannot serve in this context.) Others question whether this approach really works. They also point out that the apostles evangelized wherever there were people, including a variety of public places—not just places of worship. Indeed, down through the centuries, evangelists have proclaimed the Good News wherever they could find an audience. At least as early as the Wesley brothers in eighteenth-century England, a kind of niche music was employed in the evangelists' gatherings—the evangelical hymn, in large measure the Wesleys' own creation. In the Great Awakenings on the eighteenth- and early nineteenth-century American frontier, the niche music was the camp meeting song. The urban evangelists Moody and Sankey and their successors, including Billy Graham, all used niche music: gospel songs. In many of these cases, the ecclesiastical establishment tended not to be amused. (Undeniably, there was considerably more theological content in much of the music just mentioned than there is in much of CCM.) Whatever we may think of adapting our music to the tastes and capabilities of a target population, no one can say that the practice is without pedigree. If such niche music is so used, however, to introduce people to the faith, then what next, music-wise? Are they to continue on this restricted diet, or will they be introduced to a more varied fare? You doubtless know of the influence of gospel songs in the church, so often sung for not the best of reasons, to the neglect of other, readily available options.

Robin Knowles Wallace raises a question in connection with the use of CCM in seeker services:

The language of CCM tends to be the language of intimacy, not the language of those who are seeking or just beginning a relation with God (2004, 27–28).

3. On the other hand, according to Hull, CCM worship may not flow, at least from start to finish. Hull refers to a common CCM worship practice of a bipartite service. The first part, the praise part, may be carefully planned to flow; one song leads seamlessly to the next. Between this part of the service and the other part, the sermon, however, there is no flow, but only a disconnect (2004, 20). At least there is "no necessary thematic link." CCM proponents, however, may well claim there does exist a link, one more important, stronger, than the thematic—an emotional one—since the aim of the praise part of the service is affective, preparing the worshipers for the message to follow.

4. A. It is well to remember, though, that there are also traditional hymns in which the motive for praising God is not God's mighty acts, but the divine attributes ("Holy, Holy, Holy," "Immortal, Invisible, God Only Wise," "Ye Servants of God, Your Master Proclaim," for instance). Perhaps there are even more traditional hymns that give no reasons whatever for the praise that is expressed or enjoined ("Ye Watchers and Ye Holy Ones," "Holy God, We Praise Your Name," for instance. See also Rev. 4:8 and 5:13.).

B. Also, we should not erect too high a fence between what God does in history and, based upon the record of such activity, a confession of what God is like. See Exodus 34:6–7 and Psalms 29 and 117; none of these passages has reference to any one, specific act of God in time. We can hold on to both the mighty acts of God of biblical theology and the divine attributes of systematic theology—as does Psalm 150:2. See Claus Westermann's "declarative praise" for God's specific deeds in history, and "descriptive praise" for God's actions and being as a whole (1981, 22–23). Believers may often be moved by a welling up of a kind of generic gratitude; it would be asking too much to require them to produce a rationale for their praise.

C. It is important to look at the service as a whole and the context in which particular songs are used, not just the parts in isolation.

5. A very ample connotation of the word "praise" can at least claim some notable precedents. Not only did the ancient rabbis refer to the whole book of Psalms as "Songs of Praise," any number of modern collections uses the word in an equally broad way.

6. In seeking to arrive at the place of lament in the weekly Lord's Day Service, among the considerations that need to be borne in mind are:

A. Claus Westermann raises the question of whether the absence of lament in Western Christendom is based not on the New Testament, but, in part, on Greek thought—Stoicism (1981, 264–65, 273–75). Yet Westermann tells us that even within ancient Israel, the lament underwent a history. "The prevailing prayer in post-exilic Israel arose out of praise (thanksgiving) and petition . . . the lament remained silent" (1981, 213).

B. The New Testament was written and the church was born *after* the passion and the resurrection, *after* the righteousness of God had been revealed (Rom. 3:21)! Life in the "last days" is lived in the light of an assurance and a hope that radically transcend the prospects enjoyed by the psalmist (Heb. 13:14). Many New Testament passages relate suffering to present joy and future blessedness.

C. Of those passages in the New Testament which refer or may refer to song, and whose burden is known, all or almost all have unequivocally to do with thanksgiving, praise, and cheerfulness. (Does Acts. 4:24–30 refer to song?) May we infer that the vehicle for any lament is *spoken* prayer?

D. According to Peter Sellars, the absence of [sung] lament extends to the wider world of modern Western classical music. This absence is owing to the extermination of Gypsy and Jew in the death camps of Europe (Eichler 2006). Is it possible that a congregation's resistance to sung lament is a kind of faith-informed intuition that sung lament is foreign to the worship of the church? What *does* explain the striking differences among cultures, families, and individuals with respect to responses to suffering and death? May we not say that currently the *tune* AMAZING GRACE serves many people in North America as an all-purpose lament, a dirge to be sung in the face of personal and communal disaster and loss, the tune iteself carrying the emotional freight?

E. Certainly there are many Christian hymns that originated as responses to a preceding lament (at least in the basic form, "Why?"), whether expressed or suppressed. Instances include "When Peace, Like a River" (response to tragedy experienced by an individual), and "Now Thank We All Our God" (response to prolonged, communal suffering). *The Psalter Hymnal* (1987), under "Laments," lists thirty-four items. Of these, thirty-three are metrical psalms! The thirty-fourth is "A Congregational Lament," adaptable for varying circumstances, and set to GENEVAN 51.

F. The Lord's Day Service for most contemporary North American Christians is *the* service, and must include all that the congregation does in its corporate worship. It is to be, above all else, a service of praise and thanksgiving. Where in this service is the most appropriate place for lament? John D. Wivliet locates lament in two places: in connection with the confession of sin and the *Kyrie*; and in the prayer of intercession, in which we pray in solidarity with those who suffer. Advent and Lent offer opportunity for increased emphasis on lament (2003, 39–63). Laments for choir, solo voice, and instruments are available.

7. CCM's rediscovery of hymns is also noted by Margaret Leask (2004, 13), Terry W. York (2004, 30–33), and Peter W. Rehwaldt (2004, 6). Old hymns, not new ones, set to new arrangements and instrumentation, have been recorded in both Great Britain and North America. Again, the music (some complete with vocal "scoops"), tends to be by solo or group performers, not by congregations. On a more positive note, newspapers in both the United States and Canada, in March of 2006, took note of the initiation, in a couple of well-known megachurches, of congregational hymn singing—complete with hymnals.

8. Some of the same concerns surface in connection with some pietistic hymns and some gospel songs.

9. "It is fruitless to search for a single musical style, or even any blend of musical styles, that can assist all Christians with true worship. The followers of Jesus are a far too diverse group of people—which is exactly as it should be. We need, rather, to welcome any worship music that helps churches produce disciples of Jesus Christ. We need to welcome the experimental creativity that is always searching out new ways of singing the Gospel, and banish the fear that grips us when familiar music passes away. For this kind of change is the mark of a living church—the church of a living God, who restlessly ranges back and forth across the face of the earth seeking out any who would respond to his voice" (Hamilton 1999, 34–35).

10. Having expressed his reservations about the praise chorus, Kenneth R. Hull offers suggestions for including it "as one among many styles used in Sunday worship": 1) Use in liturgically appropriate ways within a strong liturgical structure; 2) Use at one point in the service, and not at very beginning nor at very end; 3) Minimize aspects that are more

performance- than congregation-oriented; 4) Avoid creating expectation that praise choruses are a weekly feature of worship (2004, 22).

Chapter 7

1. Smith 1962, 42–54. Though they mine the Old Testament for formulating an understanding of the church's worship, writers on Christian worship, excepting some in the CCM movement, do not usually look to the Hebrew Scriptures for practical norms.

2. See James W. McKinnon, *The Church Fathers and Musical Instruments* (1965 doct. diss., Columbia University, pub. as book in 1976); by same author, "The Exclusion of Musical Instruments from the Ancient Synagogue," in the author's *The Temple, The Church Fathers and Early Western Chant* (Brookfield, VT: Ashgate, 1998), 77–87. McKinnon's research overturns the views of a number of influential scholars of the twentieth century with regard to both Jewish and early Christian sources on the subject.

3. It is left to nearer instances of ecclesiastical authority to determine the application of the terms "suitable" and "fitting." Note that here only an accompanying role of instruments is in view—though other documents make it plain that instruments may also have a solo role at certain points in the Mass.

4. In late 2006, however, the largest non-instrumental Church of Christ in the United States, the thirteen-thousand-member Richland Hills Church in the Fort Worth, Texas area, broke ranks, opting to initiate a service that would include instruments—on Saturdays.

5. A distinctive and now long-discarded way to lead the congregation's singing without instrument or choir arose in sixteenth-century England, where a man would sing a line or so of the psalm, to be followed by the congregation's singing the same line. The British Parliament gave official sanction to the practice in the *Westminster Directory* of 1644. Called "lining out," this practice was brought to New England, where it survived until the rise of the singing schools made it obsolete. You may, however, on occasion witness lining out being used today to teach a new tune.

6. One of the most frequent problems with an organ is what is called a "cipher"—a note will sound when it is not played. Your organist may be able to solve this and other minor problems. One organ with which I am acquainted seems to be especially favored by ladybugs for their final resting place, sometimes resulting in a cipher. Dust, bats, wasps, and spiders are also fond of the organ.

7. Similar concerns about the organ's role in the church's worship were spelled out at more length

in nineteenth-century Anglicanism by some in the high-church (Cambridge-) Oxford Movement (Westermeyer 1998, 274).

8. Understandably, this development has not been welcomed by pipe organ builders nor by organists generally. The beleaguered Associated Pipe Organ Builders of America has insisted with irrefutable logic that a pipe organ has to have pipes to be a pipe organ! An advertisement of the association in the April 2004 issue of *The American Organist* proclaimed "Your Pipe Organ is a Permanent Witness to Your Faith." A full page in the same journal for September 2005 proclaimed these words from the association: "Butter Doesn't Taste Like Margarine!" And "It's not about fooling your ears. It's about thrilling your soul." In 1997, however, the association adopted a position paper sanctioning the use of electronics for the very large thirty-two-foot pedal stops, extensions, percussion effects, and MIDI—if these are added to a genuine pipe organ. Such devices would only be seen as ancillary, and not substitutes for the sound of real pipes! The American Guild of Organists has been caught between not wanting to offend the builders and advocates of pipe organs on the one hand, and the manufacturers and advocates of the electronic organ on the other, and has taken a cautious approach.

9. We may be inclined to wonder if the same people might have used the same arguments against the substitution in the nineteenth century of the electric blower for the men who had supplied muscle power to the organ bellows. We are here, however, talking about something quite different.

10. An organ is itself hardly a living and breathing entity. (See the apostle's "lifeless instruments that produce sound," in 1 Cor. 14:7.) According to the predictions of some who should be in the know, the next challenge to the presence of living and breathing worship leaders in the assembly will be iPods held by all present. Already a multisite church near my home has begun beaming the one sermon from the "mother church" to various sites; all music, however, originates live on each site.

Chapter 8

1. Musicians, from players in string quartets to Sacred Harp singers to large symphony orchestras, arrange themselves as closely as they can to this ideal. Joseph Gelineau tells us that to celebrate the liturgy, to sing together, we must look at one another welcomingly (in Funk 1991, 62).

2. Occasionally we find the choir's place in the front, but the choristers visible only when standing (a leftover from a time when a paid quartet from outside the congregation provided the choral music?). No choir should be consigned to such a place.

3. The optimum duration of reverberation in most churches should range from 1.5 to 3.5 seconds. The ears, common sense, and comparisons with worship spaces considered to have good acoustics can be trusted to make the final judgment.

Reverberation (desirable) is sometimes confused with echo (undesirable). At room temperature, and at normal atmospheric pressure, sound will travel in air at approximately 1,125 feet per second. Our brain will retain the memory of a sound for up to one-tenth of a second, long enough thus for a sound to travel about 112 feet. This means that for a sound to leave us and be reflected back to us within the one-tenth of a second we can retain that sound in our mind, the reflecting surface cannot be more than 56 (half of 112) feet from us. The result is reverberation. When sound has to travel farther than 56 feet before it is reflected back to us, we perceive an interval between making the sound and hearing that sound reflected back to us—as an echo. This is because our mind retains a sound for only one-tenth of a second, and more than one-tenth of a second is required for sound to travel more than 112 feet. Reverberation results in one continuous sound, whereas echo is perceived as a sound split into two or more parts by an interval or intervals in which the sound is not heard at all. More than one distant reflecting surface will result in multiple echoes. In practice, of course, there is not just one reflecting surface, but many, at varying distances from the sound source and with varying reflection coefficients. Even using the most sophisticated equipment and design to get things acoustically right, it seems that what in the last analysis matters is how it sounds.

4. My observation is that Episcopal and Roman Catholic worship spaces use carpet more sparingly than do many other communions. Both *The Church for Common Prayer, A Statement on Worship Space for the Episcopal Church,* and *Environment and Art in Catholic Worship* recommend against carpeting. (Exchanging being seated for kneeling and more frequent standing in Episcopal and Roman Catholic services may lessen the amount of thought given to any discomfort involved in sitting on unpadded pews or chairs.) *Principles for Worship* of the Evangelical Lutheran Church in America also recommends limiting the use of carpet and other absorbent materials. Challenge your members, if they travel to Europe, to see if they can find a church with carpeted floors and upholstered seating.

5. Whereas the choir and the organ project their sound into the space of the whole room, most of the sound made by the congregation is projected into the sound-absorbing backs of the people in the next

row forward. For that reason the people may hear the organ and choir sounds as relatively reverberant in their midst, while the sounds of their own singing travel no farther than the next row. The distance between the organ or choir or preacher and the sound-absorbent cushion on the seat is most often great enough to allow the sounds they produce to develop, to bounce off one or more reflective surfaces. In unfortunate contrast, however, the distance between the singers in the congregation and the nearest cushions, carpets, and the backs of fellow worshipers is quite short, so the sound of congregational song is absorbed before it has a chance to develop. Regrettably, the organist in this situation is often blamed for playing too loudly; we can hear the organ loud and clear, but not hear the congregation singing. Of course, it is possible that the organist is in any case using too much volume or the wrong registration.

6. It has to be admitted that some worship spaces that do contain a certain amount of carpet and cushions have so very much in their acoustical favor otherwise that the end result is above-average acoustically.

7. It is not my intention to oppose Holtkamp's views regarding the importance of a stable humidity level, but it does seem to be widely agreed upon that excessive dryness can damage wood—causing it to split—and that excessive moisture is conducive to mold.

Chapter 9

1. One full-time church musician tallied up his on-the-job time this way: choirs (two voice, one handbell), 39.1 percent; organ practice, 32.3 percent; administration, 20.2 percent; Sunday worship services, 4 percent; music-in-the-park series, 1.4 percent; wedding and memorial services, 1.4 percent (*The American Organist*, May 1993, 14).

2. On the importance and the scarcity of regular spiritual discipline and opportunity for corporate worship in the lives of the church's leaders, see Doran and Troeger 1992, 44–45.

3. Any shortage of organists, however, seems to be confined to certain localities. The number of people majoring in organ studies at any one time may not be a helpful statistic, moreover, in connection with the church's needs; of all the church organists I know, only a fraction enjoyed academic studies on the instrument.

4. Martin Luther would refuse ordination to any man who could not sing ("Table Talk," No. 794). Candidates for the priesthood in Eastern Orthodoxy may find their vocation in question if they cannot sing.

Chapter 11

1. It was precisely in the context of instructions about music in the Mass that the late Pope John Paul II recommended "the experience of silence." For such a people as we are today, the prophet's "shush" may be one of the most salutary sounds we hear, a word for us to keep silence—for a change (Hab. 2:20). A time of disciplined, corporate silence can be just as honoring to God and helpful to God's people as any word we may say or music we may make. Even in heaven, the most appropriate response may be to keep silent (Rev. 8:1).

2. Paul Westermeyer provides a list of foundational tunes and texts keyed to the days and seasons in one year of the church calendar, based on the contents of the fourteen hymnals he surveyed, his aim being to provide "a modest common ecumenical memory bank" (2005, 399–426).

Chapter 12

1. Remembering that the congregation's song is prayer (see chapter 2, under "When We Sing We Pray"), C. Michael Hawn frames the question of a song's suitability at a given place in the service in terms of its function as prayer: How does that prayer fit at a given point in the service? (in Plantinga and Rozeboom 2003, 148–49).

Chapter 13

1. John Ferguson points out, however, that "leading" the congregation's song (in congregations that sing) can be quite subtle: "Sometimes one must lead: presenting a new tune, or revitalizing an old one. Sometimes one must follow, or, better, accompany: singing's going well, so no need to be too powerful; just support and subtly encourage the congregation in its singing. Sometimes one must get out of the way: some songs beg to be sung unaccompanied, either in harmony or in a stirring, strong unison" (in Plantinga and Rozenboom 2003, 119).

2. Here is the opinion of one veteran church musician: " . . . organists usually overplay at all times in all places and in all types of music— anthem, hymn, response—a characterization that organists deeply resent, resentment that may be expressed through increasing the volume even more" (Young 1995, 33).

Appendix

1. Some of the prefatory words in the biblical psalms may be tune names, for instance: *Muth-lab'ben* at the head of Psalm 9, in which case it is indicated that the psalm is to be sung to the tune known by that name, the name meaning "the death of the son."

SOURCE LIST

Adhikari, Hrishikesh Das. 1989. *The American Organist* (September): 16, 18.

Applegate, Celia and Pamela Potter, eds. 2002. *Music and German National Identity.* Chicago: University of Chicago Press.

Beach, Waldo. 1987. "With Spirit and Understanding." *The Hymn* 38.4 (October): 26–30.

Bell, John L. 2000. *The Singing Thing: A Case for Congregational Song.* Chicago: GIA Publications, 121–29 about acoustics and disposition in space.

Benson, Louis F. 1915. *The English Hymn: Its Development and Use.* Philadelphia: The Presbyterian Board of Publication.

———. 1956. *The Hymnody of the Christian Church.* Richmond: John Knox Press, reprint of 1927 edition.

Bergen, Doris L. 2002. "Hosanna or 'Hilf, O Herr Uns': National Identity, the German Christian Movement, and the 'Dejudaization' of Sacred Music in the Third Reich." In Applegate and Potter 2002, 140–54.

Brownstead, Frank. 1991. "On Your Mark! Get Set! Ten Steps." In Funk 1991, 87–91.

Byars, Ronald P. 2002. *The Future of Protestant Worship: Beyond the Worship Wars.* Louisville: Westminster John Knox.

Carvey, Michael. 1999. "Liturgical Music in the Postmodern Age." *The Hymn* 50.1 (January): 15–23.

Cherwien, David. 1997. *Let the People Sing! A Keyboardist's Guide to Engaging God's People in Meaningful Congregational Song.* St. Louis: Concordia Press. Suggestions for both piano and organ, as well as unaccompanied song. Attention given to both traditional and nontraditional styles.

Clark, Linda J. 1994. *Music in Churches: Nourishing Your Congregation's Musical Life.* New York: Alban Institute. Clark took a "bottom-up" approach to church music, canvassing pastors and people in the pews and choir lofts. Her survey included twenty-four United Methodist and Episcopal congregations in the Northeast of the United States.

Coffin, Henry Sloane. 1946. *The Public Worship of God: A Source Book for Leaders of Services.* Philadelphia: Westminster Press, 115–21.

Collins, Patrick W. 1992. "Liturgy as an Art Form." *The American Organist* (February): 42, 44.

Dakers, Lionel. "The Contemporary Scene, 1976–96." In Routley 1997.

Dawn, Marva J. 1995. *Reaching Out Without Dumbing Down: A Theology of Worship for the Turn-of-the-Century Culture.* Grand Rapids: William B. Eerdmans Publishing Company.

Delling, Gerhard. 1952. *Der Gottesdienst im Neuen Testament.* Göttingen: Vandenhoeck and Ruprecht.

Doran, Carol and Thomas H. Troeger. 1986. "Choosing a Hymnal: An Act of Ministry on Behalf of the Whole Church." *The Hymn* 37.2 (April): 23–24.

———. 1992. *Trouble at the Table: Gathering the Tribes for Worship.* Nashville: Abingdon Press. On the clergy-musician relationship, see chapter 2 of this book, written by a professor of preaching and a musician who have for several years collaborated in the area of worship, especially pages 78–83.

Driscoll, Michael S. 2005. "Musical Mystagogy: Catechizing Through the Sacred Arts." In Kroeker 2005, 27–44.

Eichler, Jeremy. 2006. In the *New York Times* (January 22): Arts and Leisure, Sec. 2, p. 29.

Engquist, Jayson Rod. 1998. "Using Instruments in Worship." In *Music in Worship*, occasional newsletter of Selah Publishing Company. http://www.selahpub.com/MusicInWorship/WorshipUsingInstruments.html.

Eskew, Harry and Hugh T. McElrath. 1995. *Sing with Understanding: An Introduction to Christian Hymnody*, 2nd ed. Nashville: Church Street Press.

Evangelical Lutheran Church in America. 2001. *Principles for Worship.* This 167-page position paper is very much worth consulting. Available at http://www.elca.org/worship/renewing_worship/principles_for_worship/index.html and also in print, from Augsburg Fortress Press.

Fackre, Gabriel. 1999. "Christian Teaching and Inclusive Language Hymnody." *The Hymn* 50.2 (April): 26–32.

Farlee, Robert Buckley, ed. 1998. *Leading the Church's Song.* Minneapolis: Augsburg Fortress. The nuts and bolts of leading congregational song, whether traditional or otherwise, by either a song leader or a keyboardist. Puts in a good word for unaccompanied, unison singing.

Farley, Edward. 1998. "A Missing Presence." *Christian Century* (March 18–25): 276–77.

Ferguson, John. 1993. "The Organist as Church Musician." *The American Organist* (December): 32–34.

———. 1994. "The Church Organist and Hymn Playing." *The American Organist* (January): 82–83.

————. 2001. "A Conversation with Walter Holtkamp Jr." *The American Organist* (February): 56–58.

————. 2003. "Hospitable Leadership of Songs for Worship." In Plantinga and Rozeboom 2003, 117–19.

Fleisher, Dennis. 1990. "Acoustics for Congregational Song." *The Hymn* 41.3 (July): 7–10.

Foley, Edward. 2001. "Yielding the Spotlight or Sharing the Center? Musician as Prayer Leader." *The American Organist* (January): 95–100.

Foote, Henry Wilder. 1940. *Three Centuries of American Hymnody*. Cambridge: Harvard University Press.

Funk, Virgil C., ed. 1991. *The Singing Assembly*. Washington: The Pastoral Press. No. 6 in Pastoral Music in Practice.

Gardner, Charles R. 1991. "Ten Commandments for Those Who Love the Sound of a Singing Congregation." In Funk 1991, 101–6.

Gelineau, Joseph. 1991. "Balancing Performance and Participation." In Funk 1991, 61–64.

Glaeser, Mark and Richard Webb. 1988. "Contemporary." In Farlee 1998, 82–95. Glaeser and Webb deal helpfully, succinctly, and almost exclusively with the musical aspects of CCM, touching on instrumentation, performance practice, and recruitment of musicians.

González, Marilyn M. 1997a. "If You Can't Beat 'em, Lead 'em." *The American Organist* (April): 37–39.

————. 1997b. "Our Heritage as Church Musicians." *The American Organist* (May): 38–41.

Halter, Carl and Carl Schalk. 1978a. *A Handbook of Church Music*. St. Louis: Concordia Publishing House.

————. 1978b. "Music in Lutheran Worship: An Affirmation." In Halter and Schalk 1978, 13–25.

Hamilton, Michael S. 1999. "The Triumph of the Praise Songs." *Christianity Today* (July 12): 34–35.

————. 2001. "A Generation Changes North American Hymnody." *The Hymn* 52.3 (July): 11–21. Hamilton delineates the origin and characteristics of CCM, and contrasts two different approaches to the renewal of the church's worship, that of the "revolutionaries" (the proponents of CCM), and that of the more conservative "reformers," who came forth with new hymns in the traditional mold.

Hatchett, Marion. 1989. *A Guide to the Practice of Church Music*. New York: The Church Hymnal Corporation. This is a revised edition of the author's *A Manual for Clergy and Church Musicians* (1981). Practical checklists, principles, and concrete suggestions. Episcopal orientation.

Hawn, C. Michael. 1997. "Gather into One: Praying and Singing Globally." In paper presented at Carson-Newman College.

————. 2000. "From Center to Spectrum: Singing with the Faithful of Every Time." *The Hymn* 51.1 (January): 28–35. About Global Song.

————. 2003. "Sung Prayer." In Plantinga and Rozeboom 2003, 147–49.

Henry, Patrick. 1997. "Singing the Faith Together." *Christian Century* (May 21–28): 500.

Hook, Anne Burnette, "To Project or Not to Project: Hymn Lyrics and Worship." The United Methodist Church. http://www.gbod .org/worship/default_body.asp?act=reader& amp;item_id=1790.

Houts, Margo. 2003. "Contemporary Worship, Contemporary Language?" In Plantinga and Rozeboom 2003, 36–46.

Huizenga, Trudi Huisman. 1990. "The One-Voice Choir." *Reformed Worship* (March): 12–15.

Hull, Kenneth R. 2002. "Text, Music, and Meaning in Congregational Song." *The Hymn* 53.1 (January): 14–25.

————. 2004. "The Challenge of the Praise Chorus." *The Hymn* 55.3 (July): 15–23.

John Paul II. 2003. "Chirograph for the Centenary of the Motu Proprio 'Tra le Sollecitudini' ['Among the Concerns'] on Sacred Music." http://www.vatican.va/holy_father/john_paul _ii/letters/2003/index.htm. This instructive document gives Pope John Paul II's updating of the 1903 motu proprio from the hand of Pope Pius X. The 1903 document gave instruction on sacred music. The approach of Pope John Paul II was a very guarded openness to what is new and different.

Kretzmann, Adelbert Raphael. 1978. "The Pastor and the Church Musician." In Halter and Schalk 1978a, 217–31.

Kroeker, Charlotte, ed. 2005. *Music in Christian Worship: At the Service of the Liturgy*. Collegeville, MN: Liturgical Press.

Kropf, Marlene and Kenneth Nafziger. 2001. *Singing: A Mennonite Voice*. Scottdale, PA: Herald Press.

Leask, Margaret. 2004. "Contemporary Christian Music: Religious Song in an Electronic Era." *The Hymn* 55.3 (July): 7–14.

Leaver, Robin A. 1985. "The Theological Character of Music in Worship." In Young 1985, 47–64.

———. 2006. "John Wilson: 'Our Generation's Most Devoted Encourager of Fine Hymnody'." *The Hymn* 57.4 (Autumn): 20–24.

Lovelace, Austin. 1982. *The Anatomy of Hymnody.* Chicago: G. I. A. Publications. Reprint of 1965 edition by Abingdon Press.

Mardirosian, Haig. 1984. "Art Music and Modern Liturgy." *The American Organist* (April): 210–14.

Marini, Stephen A. 2003. *Sacred Song in America: Religion, Music, and Popular Culture.* Urbana-Chicago: University of Illinois Press.

McIntyre, Dean, et al. "Worship Issues for the 21st Century." Worship Web site of the United Methodist Church. www.gbod.org/worship/default.asp?act=reader&item_id=12473&loc_id=929,1056.

McIntyre, Dean. "Is Applause Appropriate in Worship?" The United Methodist Church. http://www.gbod.org/worship/default.asp?act=reader&item_id=8884&loc_id=9,38.

McNaspy, C. J. 1991. "Helping Your Congregation to Participate." In Funk 1991, 73–77.

Mouw, Richard J. and Mark A. Noll, eds. 2004. *Wonderful Words of Life: Hymns in American Protestant History and Theology.* Grand Rapids: Wm. B. Eerdmans Publishing Company.

Munro, Don. 1997a. "Music and the Electronic Medium, Part I: An Overview of MIDI." *The American Organist* (August): 35–37.

——— 1997b. "Part II: An Overview of Sequencers." *The American Organist* (September): 36, 38;

——— 1997c. "Part III: Using Synthesizers in Worship." *The American Organist* (October): 32, 34.

Noll, Mark A. 2004. "'All Hail the Power of Jesus' Name': The Defining Role of Hymns in Early Evangelicalism." In Mouw and Noll 2004, 3–16.

Noll, Mark A. 2006. "Significant Variations on a Significant Theme." In Noll and Blumhofer 2006, 43–73.

Noll, Mark A. and Edith L. Blumhofer, eds. 2006. *Sing Them Over Again to Me: Hymns and Hymnbooks in America.* Tuscaloosa: University of Alabama.

Notebaart, James and Mark Sedio. 1998. "Introduction." In Farlee 1998, 2–9.

Nuechterlein, Louis G. 1978. "The Music of the Congregation." In Halter and Schalk 1978a, 106–26.

Old, Hughes Oliphant. 1995. *Leading in Prayer: A Workbook for Worship.* Grand Rapids: Wm. B. Eerdmans Publishing Company.

N. Lee Orr. 1991. *The Church Music Handbook: For Pastors and Musicians.* Nashville: Abingdon.

Parker, Alice. 1991. *Melodious Accord: Good Singing in Church.* Chicago: Liturgy Training Publications.

Piunno, John C. 2004. "New Guidance on Sacred Music." *The American Organist* (July): 52–53.

Plantinga, Cornelius Jr. and Sue A. Rozeboom. 2003. *Discerning the Spirits: A Guide to Thinking about Christian Worship Today.* Grand Rapids: Wm. B. Eerdmans Publishing Company.

Randel, Don Michael, ed. 2003. *The Harvard Dictionary of Music*, 4th ed. Cambridge: Harvard University Press.

Redman, Robb. 2003. "The Commercial Connection." In Plantinga and Rozeboom 2003, 75–80.

Reformed Church in America. 2005. *The Theology and Place of Music in Worship.* Available at http:/www2.rca.org/worship/music.html.

Rehwaldt, Peter W. 2004. "CCM on the WWW." *The Hymn* 55.3 (July): 5, 6. Among several addresses, the article mentions Indelible Grace Music, http://www.igracemusic.com, where a free collection of 143 well-known hymns arranged for contemporary instruments may be found.

Routley, Erik. 1953. *Hymns and Human Life.* New York: Philosophical Library.

———. 1967. *Music Leadership in the Church: A Conversation Chiefly with My American Friends.* Nashville: Abingdon Press.

———. 1981. *The Music of Christian Hymns.* Chicago: GIA Publications.

———, ed. 1985. *Rejoice in the Lord: A Hymn Companion to the Scriptures.* Grand Rapids: Wm. B. Eerdmans Publishing Company.

———. 1997. *A Short History of English Church Music.* Carol Stream, IL: Hope Publishing Company.

Saliers, Don E. 1995. "Worship, Music and Technology: Identity, Integrity, and Pastoral Relevance." *The American Organist* (August): 30–32.

Schalk, Carl. 1981. "German Hymnody." In Stulken 1981, 19–33.

———. 1983. "Resounding Praise." *Christian Century* (March 23–30): 269–271.

Schilling, S. Paul. 1981. "Do the Words Matter?" *The Hymn* 32.3 (July): 134–38.

Schultz-Widmar, Russell. 1985. "The Hymn Renaissance in the United States." In Young 1985, 191–216.

Searle, Mark. 1991. "Assembly: Remembering into the Future." In Funk 1991, 3–15.

Sedio, Mark. 1998. "Techniques for Leading." In Farlee 1998, 10–25.

Senn, Frank C. 1987. "The Dialogue Between Liturgy and Music." *The Hymn* 38.2 (April): 25–29.

———. 1993. *The Witness of the Worshiping Community: Liturgy and the Practice of Evangelism.* New York: Paulist Press.

Shade, Neil Thompson. 2002. *Acoustical Planning Concepts for Worship House Sanctuaries.* Ruxton, MD: ADC Press. Brochure is available from 7509 L'Hirondelle Club Road, Ruxton, MD 21204-6418.

Silsbee, Robert H. 2003. "Acoustics." In Randel 2003, 7–13.

Smith, William S. 1962. *Musical Aspects of the New Testament.* Amsterdam: W. Ten Have, 42–54, on question of the use of musical instruments in early Christian worship.

———. 1996. "Resurrection Hymns: Feast? Or Famine?" *The Hymn* 47.3 (July): 21–26.

———. 1997. "In the Sweet By and By: Hymns about the Future." *The Hymn* 48.4 (October): 16–21.

———. 1999. "From Scripture to Congregational Song." *The Hymn* 50.2 (April): 12–16.

———. 2002. "Global Hymnody from a Pastor's Point of View." *The Hymn* 53.3 (July): 15–17.

Stovall, Frank. 1976. *Singing a Solo.* Nashville: Convention Press.

Stulken, Marilyn Kay. 1981. *Hymnal Companion to the Lutheran Book of Worship.* Philadelphia: Fortress Press.

Sydnor, James Rawlings. 1982. *Hymns and Their Uses: A Guide to Improved Congregational Singing.* Carol Stream, IL: AGAPE.

Sykes, Cheri. 1998. "Christian Contemporary Music: Another Performance Practice." *The American Organist* (January): 40–42.

Thornburg, John D. 1996. "Saved by Singing: Hymns as a Means of Grace." *The Hymn* 47.2 (April): 5–10.

Truitt, Gordon. 1991. "How Can We Keep Them Singing?" In Funk 1991, 93–98.

VanDyke, Mary Louise. 2006. "Indices: More Than Meets the I." In Noll and Blumhofer 2006, 122–51.

The Vatican. *Constitution on the Sacred Liturgy, or Sacrosanctum Concilium* (1963) of the Roman Catholic Church. http://www.vatican.va/archive/hist_councils/ii_vatican_council/documents/vat_ii_const_19631204_sacrosanctum-concilium_en.htm.

Wallace, Robin Knowles. 2004. "Praise and Worship Music: Looking at Language." *The Hymn* 55.3 (July): 24–28. An analysis of the language of forty-seven praise and worship songs.

———. 2006. "Interview with Dr. Donald Hustad, F.H.S." *The Hymn* 57.2 (Spring): 12–14.

Webb, Richard. 1998. "Contemporary." In Farlee 1998, 82–95.

Westermann, Claus. 1981. *Praise and Lament in the Psalms.* Trans. Keith R. Crim and Richard N. Soulen. Atlanta: John Knox Press.

Westermeyer, Paul. 1988. *The Church Musician.* San Francisco: Harper and Row Publishers.

———. 1998. *Te Deum: The Church and Music.* Minneapolis: Fortress Press.

———. 2001a. *The Heart of the Matter: Church Music as Praise, Prayer, Proclamation, Story and Gift.* Chicago: GIA Publications.

———. 2001b. "Vocation: A Homily and Three Reflections." *The American Organist* (December): 73.

———. 2005. *Let the People Sing: Hymn Tunes in Perspective.* Chicago: GIA Publications.

White, James F. 1980. *Introduction to Christian Worship.* Nashville: Abingdon Press. (Rev. ed. 1990).

———. 1997. *Christian Worship in North America: A Retrospective: 1955–1995.* Collegeville, MN: The Liturgical Press.

Wilson-Dickson, Andrew. 1992. *The Story of Christian Music.* Oxford: Lion Publishing.

Witvliet, John D. 2003. *Worship Seeking Understanding: Windows into Christian Practice.* Grand Rapids: Baker.

———. 2005. "The Virtue of Liturgical Discernment." In Kroeker 2005, 83–97.

Wohlgemuth, Paul W. 1981. "Church Musician: the Great Offender." *Choral Journal* 21.5 (January): 31-33.

———. 1985. "Church-Music Education in American Protestant Seminaries." In Young 1985, 89–95.

Wolterstorff, Nicholas P. 2005. "Thinking About Church Music." In Kroeker 2005, 3–16.

Wren, Brian. 2000. *Praying Twice: The Music and Words of Congregational Song.* Louisville: Westminster John Knox Press. 230–35, 243–52. On the revision of hymn lyrics, see pp. 297–348. Wren gives seventeen "Principles for Lyric Alteration," and details suggestions for alterations of four well-known hymns.

Wuthnow, Robert. 1998. *After Heaven: Spirituality in America Since the 1950s*. Berkeley and Los Angeles: University of California Press.

———. 2003. *All in Sync: How Music and Art are Revitalizing American Religion*. Berkeley: University of California Press.

York, Terry W. 2004. "Add One Hymn: Recipe for CCM and 'Modern Worship' Congregational Song." *The Hymn* 55.3 (July): 29–33.

Young, Carlton R., ex. ed. 1985. *Duty and Delight: Routley Remembered*. Carol Stream, IL: Hope Publishing Company.

———. 1995. *My Great Redeemer's Praise: An Introduction to Christian Hymns*. Akron: OSL Publications.

Zimmerli, Walther. 1978. *Old Testament Theology in Outline*. Trans. David E. Green. Atlanta: John Knox Press.

∼

ONLINE RESOURCES

Additional information on topics such as:

- Choosing the Best Hymnal for Your Church
- Will a Hymn Preach?
- A Hymn-based Service of Worship
- One Hymnfest
- A Miscellany of Relevant Quotations
- Colossians 3:16–17 and Ephesians 5:18–20
- Music for Weddings and Death Rites
- Hierarchical/Political Language in Songs
- Battle Language in Songs
- Should the Name of the Game Be Sound?

may be found on the Web at http://www.drewgle.com/JoyfulNoise/

INDEX